تحفة الأطفال

CHILDREN'S BEQUEST

The Principles of Tajweed

based upon the text of
Sulaymān al-Jamzūrī

Dr. Abu Zayd
Obaidullah Anwar Choudry

First Edition 2010 / Second Edition January 2011 / Third edition October 2014 / Fourth edition February 2021

ISBN 978-1-7338374-4-6

Published by:
Quran Literacy Press
1320 Hamilton St
Somerset, NJ 08873

quranliteracypress@gmail.com / quranliteracy.org

Cover design by Salsabil Graphics

Seal design by Nushva
www.nushva.com

إِنَّ مَنْ عَمِلَ بِالقُرْآنِ فَكَأَنَّهُ يَقْرَؤُهُ دَائِمًا وَ إِنْ لَمْ يَقْرَأْهُ

وَ مَنْ لَمْ يَعْمَلْ بِالقُرْآنِ فَكَأَنَّهُ لَمْ يَقْرَأْهُ وَ إِنْ قَرَأَهُ دَائِمًا

Those who live by the Qur’ān are as if they are reciting it constantly though they may not be doing so, while those who do not live by the Qur’ān are as if they never recite it though they may be reciting it constantly.

– Muslim Scholars

[from *‘Awn al-Ma‘būd* the commentary on *Sunan Abī Dāwūd*]

Contents

Contents 4

TRANSLITERATION KEY 7

Foreword by Shaykh Yasir Qadhi 8

Author's Preface 9

Acknowledgements 13

Ijāzah [License] 15

Some Isnāds of the Author 18

THE TEXT OF TUḤFATUL AṬFĀL 23

INTRODUCTION TO TAJWEED 34

- THE QUR'ĀN ON ITS RECITATION 35
- THE PROPHETIC PRACTICE OF QUR'ĀNIC RECITATION 37
- THE MEANING OF TAJWEED 39
- THE RULING ON TAJWEED 41

THE RULES OF ISTI'ĀDHA AND BASMALAH 45

- THE ISTI'ĀDHAH 46
- WHAT IS THE SPIRITUAL SIGNIFICANCE OF THESE SUPPLICATIONS? 47
- THE BASMALAH 48
- WAYS OF BEGINNING WITH ISTI'ĀDHAH AND BASMALAH 50
- EXCEPTIONS 52
- JOINING BETWEEN TWO CHAPTERS 53
- JOINING SŪRAH AL-ANFĀL AND AL-TAWBAH 54

THE TEXT OF TUḤFATUL AṬFĀL WITH COMMENTARY 56

Addendum: Ḥisāb al-Jumal 71

Chapter ONE: THE RULES OF NŪN AND NUNNATION 72

- DEFINITIONS 73
- RULE ONE: MANIFESTATION [IẒHĀR] 77
- RULE TWO: MERGING [IDGHĀM] 80
- COMPLETE VERSUS DEFICIENT MERGING 84
- RULE THREE: CONVERSION [IQLĀB] 86
- RULE FOUR: CONCEALMENT [IKHFĀ'] 89

Chapter TWO: RULES OF THE DOUBLED NŪN AND MEEM 92

Chapter THREE: RULES OF MEEM SĀKIN 94

Rule One: Labial Concealment [Ikhfā' Shafawī] 95
Rule Two: Merging [Idghām Mithlayn Ṣaghīr] 97
Rule Three: Labial Manifestation [Iẓhār Shafawī] 99

Chapter FOUR: RULES OF LĀM 101

Part One: The Lām of the Definite Article 102
Manifestation of Lām [Iẓhār] 103
Merging of Lām [Idghām] 106
Part Two: Other Types of Lām 107
Part Three: The Lām of the Grand Word [ALLĀH] 111

Chapter FIVE: THE MAKHĀRIJ (POINTS OF ARTICULATION) 113

4. The Lips 121
5. The Nasal Cavity 121

Chapter SIX: THE ṢIFĀT(ATTRIBUTES OF THE LETTERS) 122

The Paired Attributes 125
3. Elevation versus Depression 128
The Unpaired Attributes 131
Heaviness versus Lightness 137

CHAPTER SEVEN: THE RULES OF RĀ 140

The Heavy Rā 143
The Light Rā 147
Exceptions 148

Chapter EIGHT: THE RULES OF ASSIMILATION 150

Mithlayn 152
Idghām Mithlayn Ṣaghīr 153
Idghām Mithlayn Kabīr 154
Mutaqāribayn 157
Idghām Mutaqāribayn Ṣaghīr 158
Mutaqāribayn Kabīr 161
Mutajānisayn 162
Mutabā'idayn 166

Chapter NINE: THE RULES OF ELONGATION [MADD] 169

The Meaning of Madd 170
The Basic Madd 172
Madd Līn 174
Other Types That Follow the Basic Madd Rule 176
1. Five Disjointed Letters 176
2. Madd 'Iwaḍ [The Substitute Madd] 177
3. Madd al-Ṣilah al-Ṣughrā [The Lesser Connecting Madd] 177
The Secondary or Derived Madd 181

MADD LĀZIM 182
PERMISSIBLE MADD 186
MADD BADAL 189
MADD MUTTAṢIL [ATTACHED MADD] 190
MADD MUNFAṢIL [SEPARATED MADD] 191
MADD AL-ṢILAH AL-KUBRĀ [THE GREATER CONNECTING MADD] 195
COMBINATION OF MADDS 195

APPENDIX ONE: MISTAKES IN TAJWEED 198

Appendix TWO: THE VIRTUE OF TAJWEED 202

Appendix THREE: THE BROKEN CHAINS OF TUḤFAT AL-AṬFĀL 231

BIBLIOGRAPHY 238

TRANSLITERATION KEY

f	ف	r	ر	’	ء
q	ق	z	ز	ā	ا
k	ك	s	س	b	ب
l	ل	sh	ش	t	ت
m	م	ṣ	ص	th	ث
n	ن	ḍ	ض	j	ج
h	ه	ṭ	ط	ḥ	ح
w, ū, u	و	ẓ	ظ	kh	خ
y, i, ī	ي	‘	ع	d	د
		gh	غ	dh	ذ

The difficulties that accompany working with two languages simultaneously are quite obvious to all multilinguals. There are, for instance, certain letters unique to the Arabic language that do not have full equivalents in English. We have, therefore, attempted to use the above commonly used transliteration scheme throughout this work. We have also attempted to preserve some of the original vernacular related to this highly technical topic, choosing to capitalize some terms such as *Tajweed* and including the original terms in the various chapters in transliterated Arabic alongside their English meanings.

Foreword by Shaykh Yasir Qadhi

All praise is due to Allah, who revealed His Word to us to take us from the darkness of our desires to the light of worship, and to guide us from the crooked ways of this life to the wide, straight expanses of the Hereafter.

The Qur'ān is the greatest proof of the truth of our religion, and the primary miracle of our Prophet. Of its clearest miracles is the effect that it has on those who listen to it. It is for this reason that our scholars have always emphasized the importance of understanding the proper manner for reciting the Qur'ān: the science of Tajweed.

The *Tuḥfat al-Aṭfāl* of al-Jamzūrī has achieved universal fame as being one of the most widely-read and memorized poems on the science of Tajweed. It was one of the first poems that I myself read when I began studying this sacred science. It is indeed a noble effort to translate and explain this poem into English.

When Dr. Abu Zayd informed me of his desire to translate this work, many years ago, I was greatly excited. Abu Zayd is a model student of Islamic studies, and one whom all of his teachers are proud of. He has exemplified the dedication, characteristics, manners and skills of a student of the Sacred Sciences. He is a full-time doctor, a memorizer of the Qur'ān, and a full-time ṭālib al-'ilm. Combining deen and dunya, he is a shining example to the future generation of Muslims in North America.

His translation of the *Tuḥfat al-Aṭfāl* is but one indication of his skills. The masterful choice of wordings and the poetic license displayed, which remains faithful to the Arabic intent while producing an English rhyme, is a feat of genius. It is obvious that Dr. Abu Zayd has spent a tremendous amount of time contemplating the best translations for each and every couplet, and then explaining them in simple, lucid English. This work has raised the bar for translations of this genre, and I must admit that, after Dr. Abu Zayd's efforts, I myself would be hesitant to try to match him in this field!

I pray that Allah accept this work from our author, and blesses him with many more works to come. Ameen!

Yasir Qadhi

New Haven, CT
May 13 2010

Author's Preface

Without a doubt, the study of Allah's Magnificent Book ranks in the noblest of human endeavors. After all, is there anything else in the world more moving, more spiritually uplifting than reciting this Splendid Book with its proper code of recitation, with meticulous observation of its rules of enunciation and articulation, initiation and duration, pausing and stopping? The one who does so flawlessly—with careful attention to its minutest details—recites the Book in the same manner as it was revealed to the Holy Prophet himself. This methodology of recitation is referred to as the science of Tajweed and occupies a foremost position among the Islamic sciences.

But alas, Tajweed has largely become a relic among lay Muslims. There are the unfortunate few who are heedless of it and never even bother to recite the Qur'ān at all. Others take time to recite it but do so atrociously, with little regard for its proper method—notwithstanding their sincere intentions. And then there are others who have learned some of the Tajweed rules and deem that sufficient. Though often hailed as experts by the common people, they recite with mistakes discernible only to the real masters. And then there is the catastrophe of entire institutions, seminaries and regions of the world where generations of imāms, reciters and memorizers of the Qur'ān are continually being trained incorrectly, with the same errors being ingrained into student after student.

What happened to us? Once a nation that arose from the Qur'ān and was truly shaped by it, today most of its members cannot even recognize its verses nor recite them properly. Few indeed are those who have achieved some level of mastery over the art of its recitation. The Blessed Prophet of Allah instructed us that Allah prescribes perfection (*iḥsān*) as a methodology in all our affairs, and what matter is more noble and worthy than the recitation of His Sacred Scripture?

In my personal journey as a student of Islam, Tajweed has held a particular allure and I soon found myself utterly endeared to it. Perhaps it had to do with the fact that my first interest in Islam as a young boy was kindled by the discovery of recorded recitations of the Qur'ān and the feeling of absolute captivation experienced from their melody and rhythm. Or perhaps it was the realization that the only tangible connection we have as human beings with the Divine—in the rough and tumble of life—is the Noble Qur'ān and its recitation and study. I have been fortunate to observe from personal experience that whenever I found myself at low points in my life, the Noble Qur'ān was right there in front of me, to rescue me and sustain me to better times. I have found that whenever there came a period of time upon me where I was neglectful or far away from this Book, Allah promptly created circumstances that humbled me and brought me back to it in blissful reunion. A personal relationship with the Qur'ān is indeed the greatest treasure human beings can possess.

There are many important lessons in the path to Tajweed for students of knowledge. Foremost among them is the need for great resolve and determination. If one is really serious about any task or endeavor, especially with respect to knowledge, he or she *will* find the ways and means to achieve that in any circumstance. Too many of our colleagues are afflicted with what I term the *Overseas Syndrome*. *I want to go overseas to learn Arabic* is an all-too familiar statement that echoes in our communities today. Unfortunately, these statements often become excuses to procrastinate and put off serious study. The tragedy is that this journey never materializes for the majority of people. And in this illusion—that knowledge is to be found elsewhere, as in other countries—they remain for the rest of their lives.

Another lesson is to utilize every opportunity at our disposal, never belittling any of them. Whether it is the local halaqah of Young Muslims in your area, the lectures in your masjid from your local or guest imāms, or the regional and national conferences available in your country, the benefits found in these gatherings cannot be quantified in tangible terms, and are often realized too little, too late.

Over the course of my studies in Tajweed, I became acutely aware of the need for more resources in the English medium for more serious students. Many of the existing works in English were either cumbersome or difficult to understand, or inadequate from the perspective of language and organization. This work is a small, humble contribution toward this end.

In my study with various teachers, one particular text kept surfacing. It is a classical poetic treatise that has been used for centuries in great centers of learning throughout the Muslim world—*Tuḥfat al-Aṭfāl* by Sulaymān al-Jamzūrī. Surely this is a method that has withstood the test of time. It continues to be the most utilized text by teachers of Tajweed in the world today. I decided to translate it into English and use it as a base for a coherent and comprehensive compilation of Tajweed rules.

The *Tuḥfah* is a condensed treatise on the rules of Tajweed written in verse form, with a rhyme and meter designed to facilitate its easy memorization. Indeed, the popular appeal and widespread use it has enjoyed since its publication is testimony to its foremost standing among resources of learning Tajweed.

Interestingly, the title of the work (which means *the Children's Bequest*) reflects an important but abandoned characteristic of Muslim civilization—the proper raising and cultivation of our children in Islam (*tarbiyah*). In other words, literary works such as the *Tuḥfah* were not considered authoritative references for scholars, but rather, essential and basic learning for children and beginners, as its title suggests. More advanced sciences were learned later on, building upon a base of these elementary texts. In today's day and age, unfortunately, we find few adults who can grasp even the basic principles in these introductory works.

PHOTO 1: A stone slate upon which students in traditional Muslim countries hand-write verses of the Qurʾān while memorizing them. This slab was gifted to the author by Naima Ben Yaich, director of the Ummul Mumineen Aisha Institute in Tangiers, Morocco.

In my translation of this text, I have tried my best to render it in a form similar to the original text itself, in poetic verse form with rhyme and meter. To facilitate that I was forced to exercise, on occasion, the liberty of departing from the original in some aspects of wording and order. Nevertheless, I have tried my best to remain as faithful to the original as such a process allowed. I have benefited immensely from the edition of this poem translated into Urdu by Shaykh Iẓhār Aḥmad Thānwī and published by the Qiraa'at Academy of Lahore, Pakistan.

Much like the Tajweed classes I teach, I have designed this work to function on two levels—one for those interested in following the text of the *Tuḥfah*, and second, for those who are only interested in the rules of Tajweed without necessarily referring to that text. Those who are not interested in the *Tuḥfah* may feel free to skip that text in the beginning of each chapter, and this would not detract from their study of the rules of Tajweed in any way.

My primary aim in this work has been to facilitate comprehension of the rules and principles of Tajweed for English-speaking audiences. To that end, I have attempted to render the work in plain and simple English. I have also abandoned in many cases traditional definitions—which tend to be highly technical and cumbersome, especially when translated directly into English—in favor of more functional definitions of various Tajweed terms. I hope this does not offend some of our colleagues who are oriented to a more conventional and formal teaching of our tradition, but this is being done in the sincere interest of conveying the teachings to a contemporary audience that is less and less familiar with Arabic and Islamic tradition. In addition, certain supplementary material—related either to finer grammatical points, phonetic/acoustic issues that have to do with the sounds of the letters, or other miscellaneous matters—has been separated from the main body and placed in boxes with appropriate titles.

Ultimately, I have attempted to gather the rules of Tajweed into one comprehensive and organized work in order to serve as a basic textbook for the teaching of Tajweed for students at all levels. It should also be noted that these are the rules of Tajweed according to the Ḥafṣ reading of the Qur'ān which is predominant throughout the world today.

I have no qualms to admit that I have benefited immensely from other English works in the field of Tajweed, such as the early classic of Dr. Syed Kalimullah Husaini—*Easy Tajweed,* and the more recent 3-volume work of the esteemed sister Kareema Carol Czerepinski—*Tajweed Rules of the Qur'an.* This text is a humble addition to the genre and not a replacement for these excellent works.

In this project I have also benefited immensely from my own Tajweed students. They have provided for me constant inspiration and energy, and this work has been written for them. I also appreciate the support, encouragement and criticism of all my family and friends. In the end, if there is any good or benefit in this work, it is solely from Allah and all shortcomings are solely mine.

Abu Zayd

Qur'ān Literacy Institute

May 2010

Acknowledgements

The one who doesn't show gratitude to his fellow men can never truly be grateful to Allah. After Allah's grace, mercy and support, I am indebted to countless individuals in making this project a reality. Some of them deserve even more credit than I. It is impossible to name them all, and yet some attempt—however imperfect—must nonetheless be made.

Credit goes first and foremost to my parents who, after providing for all our basic amenities, instilled in us the acute awareness that devotion to Allah and working for His way of life was the most important matter in our lives. I must acknowledge as well my wife and children who were forced to endure the many years of effort that went into this work and took precious time away from them.

Following that, acknowledgement is owed to the many teachers and shuyūkh who have honored me with the opportunity to learn and benefit from them, both formally and informally. These include the late Shaykh Al-Faheem Jobe, the dynamic and energetic West African scholar from Umm al-Qura University—my first formal teacher in Islamic studies—who inspired me to a lifelong pursuit of knowledge. He passed away in a tragic car accident on May 30, 1997, leaving behind a generation of grieving students and colleagues he had touched and inspired across the greater New York region—may Allah continue adding to his list of deeds and have mercy on his soul.

I would also acknowledge all of my teachers in the field of Tajweed: Shaykh Abu Es-haq Sa'd Hassanin, from whom I received my first Ijāzah; Shaykh Usama Hasan of the Islamic Center of Jersey City, with whom I read the Ten Readings over a period of a decade; Shaykh Rashid al-Jazā'irī, with whom I studied and read the Warsh Reading over a few years; "The Voice of Alexandria" Shaykh Walīd Āṭif, with whom I studied the text of the Tuḥfah in quite some detail; our former Imām Shaykh Waleed Idrees Meneese, an ocean of knowledge and a hidden treasure in the United States, who has served as a constant inspiration over the years; my friend Shaykh Ramadan Elsabbagh, with whom I spent many loving years before both of us got married; the popular Egyptian reciter Shaykh Muḥammad Jibreel, who first ignited the flame, many years ago in his annual visits to our community; and finally Shaykh Muḥammad Rafat Imām, with whom I read the Ten Readings of Ṣughrā and Kubrā as well as the various texts of Tajweed and the Shādh (Irregular) Readings.

I also acknowledge the popular Indian jurist-scholar and author Maulānā Muḥammad Yūsuf Iṣlāḥī, who has been the official scholar of our family since my childhood and is a man who has spent the better part of the last century singularly devoted to guiding people to the Book of Allah. This work is, in a way, one fruit of his passion and efforts.

I also invoke Allah's mercy for all my other teachers and guides—too many to name here.

I could not end without also acknowledging the advice of Dr. Hatem Elhadj, Dean of Mishkah University, who has been a personal mentor and inspiration, and a true model of balancing Islamic studies with the medical profession.

And may Allah reward all those who helped me with this work, including my friend and fellow student of the Qur'ān, Saleem Bendaud, who was quite diligent in recording the lessons of Shaykh Walīd Āṭif and quite gracious enough to provide them to me for review, providing the early stimulus for this project. I also thank my friend Dr. Uzair Sarmast who diligently provided many valuable resources that aided me, a "Man of Few Words" who shall remain nameless for lending me his poetical skills, my brother-in-law Hāfidh Usman Khan and Dr. Umer Akbar for helping me review the manuscript and providing very valuable critical comments, and my friend and neighbor Yaseen Younus for his support, encouragement and endless hours of technical assistance. Also, Shaykh Yasir Birjas was gracious enough to review the entire book and provide valuable comments on nearly every section. Finally, the wonderful cover was designed by my sister-in-law Nadia Ansari of Salsabil Graphics, with my 6-month-old nephew Ismail cheering her on the background.

This humble work is a culmination of the sincerity and efforts of all of these great individuals, and true credit is theirs much more than it is mine.

Ijāzah [License]

Praise be to Allah, the Most Merciful, the Most Beneficent. We praise Him, seek His help and forgiveness and turn to Him in repentance. We seek Allah's protection from the evils of our souls and from our bad deeds. Whoever Allah guides can never be misguided and whoever He allows to be misguided can never be guided. I testify that there is no God but Allah, with Whom there is no associate. I testify that Muhammad is His servant and Messenger. May Allah bless him, his family, his Companions, and all those who will follow them until the Day of Resurrection.

It was an honor and blessing for me, with my humble knowledge, to review this book of Tajweed written by my student Dr. Obaidullah Choudry. It is indeed a glad tiding for me as well as for the entire Muslim ummah that we now have a comprehensive English-language text on the science of Tajweed, containing such in-depth knowledge and information as to adequately teach any beginner and add to the knowledge of any expert. This text is based upon a translation of the celebrated Arabic text *Tuḥfatul-Aṭfāl wal Ghilmān* by Sulaymān al-Jamzūrī.

Tajweed is a discipline that requires practice and rehearsal to accompany its rules and principles. Such practice should be garnered and learned from an individual excelling in the makhārij (points of articulation), attributes, and the particular sounds of each letter alone and in combination with other letters. The rules of Tajweed themselves as well as their application in reading the Noble Qur'ān is an art learned from the Blessed Prophet through a chain of narration.

I have found this book sufficient for whoever seeks the knowledge of Tajweed, the art of reading the Qur'ān correctly. It includes in its pages authenticated information from its original sources and presents that to its readers in an easy-to-follow and simple format. This comes as no surprise to me, since Dr. Obaidullah is a pioneering medical doctor (*Māshā'Allah*) who, from his career, has gained essential skills in life, such as punctuality, the concern for accuracy, and an impeccable way of delivering information to those who lack knowledge and those who seek it in its higher forms. Furthermore, his profession and the associated limitation of his time did not stop him from seeking Islamic knowledge and becoming an excellent reader of the Qur'ān. It was the greatest of privileges for me to be among his teachers in Tajweed and other aspects of Islamic knowledge. He has recited to me the entire Qur'ān through the Ḥafṣ narration earning an Ijāzah (scholarly license to teach) from me in that mode of recitation through four chains of narration. He has also memorized and recited the text of the *Tuḥfatul-Aṭfāl* to me, and I have granted him authorization to teach it to others, as I was authorized by my teacher the noble Shaykh Abdul Basit Hashim, may Allah preserve him, through a continuous chain that extends to Shaykh al-Meehī, the teacher of al-Jamzūrī.

Again, as a humble servant of the Qur'ān I recommend this book for individuals and institutions to adopt as a curriculum for the art of reading the Qur'ān.

May Allah accept all of our humble works and meager good deeds and grant whoever reads this book or teaches it forgiveness and Paradise. I conclude with the saying of the Prophet: *The best amongst you is the one who has learned the Qur'ān and teaches it to others.*

Abo Es-Haq Saad Hassanin, Ph.D.
May Allah forgive him and his family
Garland, TX
24th of Jumāda al-Ūlā 1430 / 19th of May 2009

المجيز بما فيه
خويدم القرءان الكريم والسنة النبوية الشريفة
أبو إسحاق
سعد الدين بن محمد كمال رزيقه حسنين
عضو اللجنة التأسيسية لجمعية قراء أمريكا
وعضو نقابة القراء بجمهورية مصر العربية
غفر الله له ولوالديه ومشايخه وأهله وأولاده والمسلمين أجمعين

المُجيزُ بما فيه
سعد الدين بن محمد كمال بن رزيقة
بن حسنين الشافعي السكندري

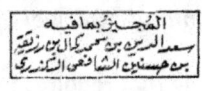

بسم الله الرحمن الرحيم

DAR EL QURAN WAL HADEETH
Knowledge & Personal Development for All.

دار القرءان الكريم والقراءات والحديث النبوي الشريف ريتشاردسون تكساس

إجازة في متن تحفة الأطفال للإمام الجمزوري رحمه الله تعالى

الحمد لله الذي علم القرءان ، خلق الإنسان ، علمه البيان ، والصلاة والسلام على عبده ورسوله سيدنا محمد سيد الأكوان ؛ القائل "خيركم من تعلم القرءان وعلمه " وعلى آله وصحبه ومن تبعه بإحسان إلى يوم الدين . وبعد :

فلقد قرأ عليَّ الدكتور / **عبيد الله أنور شودري** تحفة الأطفال للشيخ سليمان الجمزوري رحمه الله تعالى وطلب مني أن أجيزه بها بالسند المتصل إلى صاحبها رحمه الله تعالى ولما آنست منه الضبط والإتقان ووثقت من أهليته في قراءتها وحفظ معانيها أجزته بها بأن يقرأها ويُقرأها بالشرط المعتبر عند العلماء في أي مكان حل وفي أي قطر نزل ، وأخبرته بأنني قد تلقيتها من شيخي محمد عبد الحميد خليل شيخ مقارئ الإسكندرية الذي تلقاها من الشيخة نفيسة بنت أبي العلا بن أحمد محمد ضيف الله وهي أخبرته أنها تلقتها عن الشيخ/ عبد العزيز بن علي كحيل وهو عن الشيخ محمد سابق وهو عن الشيخ خليل بن عامر المطوبسي وهو على الشيخ علي الحلو إبراهيم السمنودي وهو عن الشيخ سليمان الشهداوي وهو عن الشيخ مصطفى الميهي وهو عن الشيخ سليمان الجمزوري ، وأخبره أيضا بأنني تلقيتها من الشيخ عبد الباسط هاشم وأجازني بها بسنده وكذلك تلقيتها من الشيخة سميعة بنت أبي بكر بسندها وسند التحفة مقطوع إلى المؤلف رحمه الله تعالى كما قال أفذاذ الأسانيد واجتهد بعض الأفذاذ الآخرين وصله والله أعلم رحم الله الجميع.

وأوصي المجاز بتقوى الله تعالى في السرّ والعلن والمداومة على تلاوة القرآن والتخلق بأخلاقه والبحث عن دقائقه ، وأن يجتهد في طلب العلم وأن يعمل بما علم سائلاً المولى الكريم أن ينفع به الإسلام والمسلمين .

حررت هذه الإجازة في :
الثامن والعشرين من شهر ذي القعدة سنة 1433هـ الموافق الرابع عشر من أكتوبر سنة 2012 مـ

المجيز
الشيخ أبو إسحاق
سعد الدين محمد كمال رزيقه حسنين المصري الشافعي

Some Isnāds of the Author

Isnad 1

13. Abū Zayd أبو زيد

12. Sa'd al-Dīn Ḥasanayn سعد الدين رزيقه حسنين

11. 'Abd al-Bāsiṭ Ḥāshim عبد الباسط هاشم

10. Aḥmad 'Abd al-Ghanī al-Asyūṭī أحمد عبد الغني الأسيوطي

9. Maḥmūd b. Uthmān Farrāj محمود بن عثمان فرّاج

8. Ḥasan Bayūmī al-Karrāk حسن محمد بيومي الكرّاك

7. Muḥammad Sābiq محمد سابق

6. Muḥammad Khalīl al-Muṭawbisī محمد خليل المطَوبِسي

5. 'Alī al-Ḥulw al-Samnūdī علي الحلو السمنودي

4. Aḥmad b. Muḥammad Salamūnah أحمد بن محمد سَلَمُونَة

3. Sulaymān al-Baybānī سليمان بن مصطفى البيباني

2. Aḥmad al-Mīhī أحمد الميهي

1. Sulaymān al-Jamzūrī سليمان بن حسين الجمزوري

Isnad 2

13. Abū Zayd أبو زيد

12. Sa'd al-Dīn Ḥasanayn سعد الدين رزيقه حسنين

11. 'Abd al-Bāsiṭ Ḥāshim عبد الباسط هاشم

10. Maḥmūd Khabbūṭ محمود بن محمد خَبُّوط

9. 'Abd al-Majīd al-Asyūṭī عبد المجيد الأسيوطي

8. Ḥasan Bayūmī al-Karrāk حسن محمد بيومي الكراك

7. Muḥammad Sābiq محمد سابق

6. Muḥammad Khalīl al-Maṭūbisī محمد خليل المطَوبسي

5. 'Alī al-Samnūdī علي الحلو السمنودي

4. Aḥmad Salmūnah أحمد بن محمد سَلَمُونة

3. Sulaymān al-Baybānī سليمان بن مصطفى البيباني

2. Aḥmad al-Mīhī أحمد الميهي

1. Sulaymān al-Jamzūrī سليمان بن حسين الجمزوري

Isnad 3

11. Abū Zayd أبو زيد

10. Saʿd al-Dīn Ḥasanayn سعد الدين رزيقه حسنين

9. Muḥammad ʿAbd al-Ḥamīd Khalīl محمد عبد الحميد خليل

8. Nafīsah bint Abi'l-ʿUlā Ḍayfullah نفيسة بنت أبي العلى

7. ʿAbd al-ʿAzīz bin ʿAlī Kuḥīl عبد العزيز بن علي كحيل

6. Muḥammad Sābiq محمد سابق

5. Khalīl b. ʿĀmir al-Maṭūbisī خليل بن عامر المطوبسي

4. ʿAlī al-Ḥulw al-Samnūdī علي الحلو السمنودي

3. Sulaymān al-Shahdāwī سليمان الشهداوي

2. Muṣṭafā al-Mīhī مصطفى الميهي

1. Sulaymān al-Jamzūrī سليمان بن حسين الجمزوري

Isnad 4

9. Abū Zayd أبو زيد

8. Saʿd al-Dīn Ḥasanayn سعد الدين رزيقه حسنين

7. Samīʿah al-Bināsī سميعة بنت محمد بكر البناسي

6. Ibrāhīm al-Bināsī إبراهيم بن مرسي محمد بكر البناسي

5. Ghunaym b. Muḥammad Ghunaym غُنَيْم بن محمد غنيم

4. Ḥasan Budayr al-Juraysī حسن بن محمد بُدَيْر الجُرَيْسي الكبير

3. Muḥammad al-Mutawallī محمد بن أحمد المتولي

2. Unknown

1. Sulaymān al-Jamzūrī سليمان بن حسين الجمزوري

Isnad 5

9. Abū Zayd أبو زيد

8. Sa'd al-Dīn Ḥasanayn سعد الدين رزيقه حسنين

7. Samī'ah al-Bināsī سميعة بنت محمد بكر البناسي

6. Muṣṭafā al-'Anūsī مصطفى بن محمود العَنُوسي

5. Maḥmūd al-'Anūsī محمود العَنُوسي

4. Yūsuf 'Ajjūr يوسف عَجُّور

3. 'Alī Ṣaqr al-Jawharī علي صقر الجوهري المرحومي

2. Muṣṭafā al-Mīhī مصطفى الميهي

1. Sulaymān al-Jamzūrī سليمان بن حسين الجمزوري

Isnad 6

7. Abū Zayd أبو زيد

6. Walīd Idrīs al-Manīsī وليد إدريس المنيسي

5. Muḥammad Zuhayr Shāwīsh محمد زهير الشاويش

4. Badr al-Dīn al-Ḥasanī بدر الدين الحسني

3. Ibrāhīm b. 'Alī al-Siqā إبراهيم بن علي بن حسن السقا

2. Naṣr al-Hūrīnī أبو الوفا نصر بن نصر الوفائي الهوريني

1. Sulaymān al-Jamzūrī سليمان بن حسين الجمزوري

Isnad 7

9. Abū Zayd أبو زيد

8. Walīd Idrīs al-Manīsī وليد إدريس المنيسي

7. Samī'ah al-Bināsī سميعة بنت محمد بكر البناسي

6. Ibrāhīm al-Bināsī إبراهيم بن مرسي محمد بكر البناسي

5. Ghunaym b. Muḥammad Ghunaym غُنَيْم بن محمد غنيم

4. Ḥasan Budayr al-Juraysī حسن بن محمد بُدَيْر الجُرَيْسي الكبير

3. Muḥammad al-Mutawallī محمد بن أحمد المتولي

2. Unknown

1. Sulaymān al-Jamzūrī سليمان بن حسين الجمزوري

Isnad 8

9. Abū Zayd أبو زيد

8. Walīd Idrīs al-Manīsī وليد إدريس المنيسي

7. Samī'ah al-Bināsī سميعة بنت محمد بكر البناسي

6. Muṣṭafā al-'Anūsī مصطفى بن محمود العَنُوسي

5. Maḥmūd al-'Anūsī محمود العَنُوسي

4. Yūsuf 'Ajjūr يوسف عَجُّور

3. 'Alī Ṣaqr al-Jawharī علي صقر الجوهري المرحومي

2. Muṣṭafā al-Mīhī مصطفى الميهي

1. Sulaymān al-Jamzūrī سليمان بن حسين الجمزوري

Isnad 9

8. Abū Zayd أبو زيد

7. 'Alī Tawfīq al-Nuḥās علي بن محمد توفيق النحاس

6. Muḥammad Tawfīq al-Nuḥās محمد توفيق النحاس

5. Bakhīt al-Muṭī'ī بخيت المطيعي

4. 'Abd al-Raḥmān al-Sharbīnī عبد الرحمن الشربيني

and Ḥasan al-Ṭawīl حسن الطويل

and Muḥammad al-Basyūnī محمد البسيوني

3. Ibrahīm al-Siqā إبراهيم السقا

2. Naṣr al-Hūrīnī نصر الهوريني

1. Sulaymān al-Jamzūrī سليمان بن حسين الجمزوري

Isnad 10

7. Abū Zayd أبو زيد

6. ʿAlī Tawfīq al-Nuḥās علي بن محمد توفيق النحاس

5. Muḥammad Tawfīq al-Nuḥās محمد توفيق النحاس

4. Bakhīt al-Muṭīʿī بخيت المطيعي

3. Ibrahīm al-Siqā إبراهيم السقا

2. Naṣr al-Hūrīnī نصر الهوريني

1. Sulaymān al-Jamzūrī سليمان بن حسين الجمزوري

Isnad 11

7. Abū Zayd أبو زيد

6. Muḥammad Yūnus al-Ghalbān محمد يونس الغلبان

5. Abū Laylah al-Dasūqī الفاضلي أبو ليلة الدسوقي

4. ʿAbdullah al-Dasūqī عبد الله عبد العظيم الدسوقي

3. ʿAlī al-Ḥaddādī علي الحدادي

2. Ibrāhīm al-ʿUbaydī إبراهيم العبيدي

1. Sulaymān al-Jamzūrī سليمان بن حسين الجمزوري

NOTE: Any reader of this book that is studying, has studied, or memorized, the Tuḥfatul Aṭfāl text and is interested in receiving Ijāzah from the author may reach out to him at drabuzayd@gmail.com.

THE TEXT OF CHILDRENS BEQUEST

متن تحفة الأطفال

المُقَدِّمَةُ

Introduction

يَقُولُ رَاجِي رَحمَةِ الغَفُورِ

دَومًا سُلَيمَانُ هُوَ الجَمْزُورِى

Says he who longs for the grace of the One who does forgive,
Sulaymān Ḥusain Muḥammad,
who in the land of Jamzūr did live.

اَلحَمدُ لِلّٰهِ مُصَلِّيًا عَلَى

مُحَمَّدٍ وَّ آلِهِ وَ مَنْ تَلاَ

Praise be to Allah for allowing me to send prayers and reverence,
Upon Muḥammad, his kin and those who followed him in deference.

وَ بَعدُ هٰذَا النَّظْمُ لِلمُرِيدِ

فِي النُّونِ وَ التَّنْوِينِ وَ المُدُودِ

Following that, this poem is for those who yearn to know,
the Nūn, Tanwīn and Madd rules as they go.

سَمَّيتُهُ بِتُحفَةِ الأَطْفَالِ

عَنْ شَيخِنَا المِيهِيِّ ذِى الكَمَالِ

I have resolved to title it *the Children's Bequest,*
relating from our shaykh al-Meehī, masterful, adept.

أَرْجُو بِهِ اَنْ يَّنفَعَ الطُّلَّابَا

وَالأَجْرَ وَ القَبُولَ وَ الثَّوَابَا

I cherish that this proves of worth to its students,
and brings with it reward, reception and recompense

أَحكَامُ النُّونِ السَّاكِنةِ وَالتَّنوِينِ

The Rules of Nūn Sākin and Tanwīn

لِلنُّونِ إِنْ تَسْكُنْ وَ لِلتَّنْوِينِ
اَرْبَعُ أَحكَامٍ فَخُذْ تَبيِيْنِي

For the nūn without vowels and the Tanwīn diction,
exist four basic rules, so take my depiction.

فَالأَوَّلُ الإِظْهَارُ قَبْلَ أَحْرُفِ
لِلحَلْقِ سِتٌّ رُتِّبَتْ فَلتَعْرِفِ

The first of these, the rule of Iẓhār, is before the letters hence,
arising from the throat, six in number, in this known sequence:

هَمزٌ فَهَاءٌ ثُمَّ عَينٌ حَاءُ
مُهمَلَتَانِ ثُمَّ غَينٌ خَاءُ

Hamzah and Hā', then 'Ayn and Ḥā',
without the marks, then Ghayn and Khā'.

وَ الثَّانِ إِدغَامٌ بِستَّةٍ أَتَتْ
فِي يَرْمُلُونَ عِنْدَهُمْ قَدْ ثَبَتَت

The second is Idghām, with six it takes effect,
in *yarmuloon,* a mnemonic which they accept.

لَكِنَّهَا قِسمَانِ قِسمٌ يُدغَمَا
فِيهِ بِغُنَّةٍ بِيَنْمُو عُلِمَا

But this is of two types, with the first being verbalized,
with the trait of ghunnah, and by *yanmu* recognized.

إِلاَّ إِذَا كَانَا بِكِلمَةٍ فَلاَ
تُدْغِمْ كَدُنْيَا ثُمَّ صِنْوَانٍ تَلاَ

Except if this occurs within one word, then there is none,
no Idghām in articulation, as in the words *dunya* and *ṣinwān.*

وَالثَّانِ إِدْغَامٌ بِغَيرِ غُنَّهْ
فِي اللاَّمِ وَ الرَّا ثُمَّ كَرِّرَنَّهْ

The second type is Idghām without the ghunnah trait,
in lām and rā, but the latter you must reverberate.

وَالثَّالِثُ الإِقْلاَبُ عِنْدَ البَاءِ

مِيمًا بِغُنَّةٍ مَعَ الإِخْفَاءِ

The third rule is Iqlāb which occurs with the letter bā,
which is converted to meem and pronounced with Ikhfā'.

وَالرَّابِعُ الإِخْفَاءُ عِنْدَ الفَاضِلِ

مِنَ الحُرُوفِ وَاجِبٌ لِلفَاضِلِ

The fourth is Ikhfā' for the respected student,
with specified letters mandatory for the student.

فِي خَمْسَةٍ مِنْ بَعْدِ عَشْرٍ رَمْزُهَا

فِي كِلْمِ هٰذَا البَيْتِ قَدْ ضَمَّنْتُهَا

In fifteen letters it takes effect,
within this prose that I erect:

صِفْ ذَا ثَنَا كَمْ جَادَ شَخصٌ قَدْ سَمَا

دُمْ طَيِّبًا زِدْ فِي تُقًى ضَعْ ظَالِمَا

Relate of the praiseworthy one, how excellent is he who achieves status robust;
Be ever perpetual in virtue, cultivate piety, and fend off the one who is unjust.

أَحكَامُ المِيمِ وَ النُّونِ المُشَدَّدَتَين

The Rules of the Doubled Nūn and Meem

وَ غُنَّ مِيمًا ثُمَّ نُونًا شُدِّدَا

وَسَمِّ كُلاًّ حَرْفَ غُنَّةٍ بَدَا

And articulate ghunnah of the nūn and meem that carries the double accent,
and refer to both as letters of ghunnah, as is obvious and apparent.

أَحكَامُ الميمِ السَّاكِنةِ

The Rules of Meem Sākinah

وَ الميْمُ إنْ تَسْكُنْ تَجِي قَبْلَ الهِجَا

لاَ أَلِفٍ لَّيِّنَةٍ لِّذِي الحِجَا

When stopping on meem before the letters of the alphabet,
but not before the alif layyinah, for he who is intelligent

أَحكَامُهَا ثَلاَثَةٌ لِمَنْ ضَبَطْ

إِخفَاءٌ إِدغَامٌ وَ إِظْهَارٌ فَقَطْ

are three rules for he who would endear them to memory,
and they are the rules of Ikhfā', Idghām and Iẓhār only.

فَالأَوَّلُ الإِخْفَاءُ عِنْدَ البَاءِ

وَ سَمِّهِ الشَّفْوِيَّ لِلقُرَّاءِ

The first is Ikhfā' with the letter bā,
termed by the reciters as Labial Ikhfā'.

وَ الثَّانِ إِدْغَامٌ بِمِثْلِهَا أَتَى

وَ سَمِّ إِدْغَامًا صَغِيرًا يَا فَتَى

The second is Idghām when its likeness appears,
and name it the Smaller Idghām my dears.

وَ الثَّالِثُ الإِظْهَارُ فِي البَقِيَّهْ

مِنْ أَحرُفٍ وَ سَمِّهَا شَفْوِيَّهْ

The third is Iẓhār which occurs with the balance
of the letters, and termed Labial Iẓhār in our parlance.

وَ احذَرْ لَدَى وَاوٍ وَ فَا أَنْ تَخْتَفِي

لِقُـربِهَا وَ الاِتِّـحَادِ فَـــاعْرِفِ

And be wary of making Ikhfā' with wāw and fā when you read,
due to the closeness and unity of its makhraj, so take heed.

أَحكَامُ لَامِ اَل وَ لَامِ الفِعلِ

The Rules of Lām

لِلاَمِ اَلْ حَالَانِ قَبْلَ الأَحْرُفِ
أُولاَهُمَا إِظْهَارُهَا فَلتَعْرِفِ

The lām of the definite article exists in two states before the letters,
the first is its manifest articulation, and should be understood better,

قَبْلَ اربَعٍ مَعْ عَشرَةٍ خُذْ عِلْمَهُ
مِنِ ابْغِ حَجَّكَ وَ خَفْ عَقِيمَهُ

Occurring before fourteen letters, so learn them well,
from this mnemonic: *Seek your goal and vain pursuits repel.*

ثَانِيهِمَا إِدْغَامُهَا فِي أَربَعِ
وَ عَشْرَةٍ أَيضًا وَ رَمْزُهَا فَعِ

The second is its assimilation, which in fourteen does exist,
and likewise, facilitate your recollection of them from this:

طِبْ ثُمَّ صِلْ رُحْمًا تَفُزْ ضِفْ ذَا نِعَمْ
دَعْ سُوءَ ظَنٍّ زُرْ شَرِيفًا لِلْكَرَمْ

Be meritorious, maintain relations for success, and host those who are beneficent;
Shun ill estimation of others, and frequent the noble ones for munificence.

وَ الَّامُ الْأُولَى سَمِّهَا قَمَرِيَّهْ
وَ الَّامُ الأُخْرَى سَمِّهَا شَمْسِيَّهْ

Name the first Lām Qamariyah,
and the latter Lām Shamsiyyah.

وَ أَظْهِرَنَّ لَامَ فِعْلٍ مُطْلَقَا
فِي نَحْوِ قُلْ نَعَمْ وَ قُلْنَا وَ التَقَى

And pronounce with manifestation the verbal lām consistently,
in words like *Qul Na'am, Qulna, Waltaqā* and their variety.

بَابٌ فِي إِدغَامِ المِثلَينِ وَ المُتَقَارِبَينِ وَ المُتَجَانِسَينِ

The Types of Idghām

إِنْ فِي الصِّفَاتِ وَ الْمَخَارِجِ اتَّفَقْ
حَرْفَانِ فَالْمِثلاَنِ فِيهِمَا أَحَقْ

If two letters agree in attribute and point of articulation,
then it is more deserving to use the *Mithlayn* designation.

وَ إِنْ يَكُونَا مَخْرَجًا تَقَارَبَا
وَ فِي الصِّفَاتِ اخْتَلَفَا يُلَقَّبَا

But if the two in their points of articulation be akin,
yet in their attributes varying then use the heading

مُتَقَارِبَينِ أَوْ يَكُونَا اتَّفَقَا
فِي مَخْرَجٍ دُونَ الصِّفَاتِ حُقِّقَا

Mutaqāribayn; And if they so happen to concur
in articulation but not attribute then they deserve

بِالْمُتَجَانِسَينِ ثُمَّ إِنْ سَكَنْ
أَوَّلُ كُلٍّ فَالصَّغِيرَ سَمِّيَنْ

Mutajānisayn; And if its status be unvowelled
of the first letter in each case, then *Lesser* is the title.

أَو حُرِّكَ الحَرْفَانِ فِي كُلٍّ فَقُلْ
كُلٌّ كَبِيرٌ وَ افهَمَنْهُ بِالمُثُلْ

And if both the letters are vowelled in all the situations,
then term it the *Greater*, and learn this with illustrations.

أَقسَامُ المَدِّ

The Types of Madd

وَ المَدُّ أَصْلِيٌّ وَ فَرْعِيٌّ لَهُ
وَ سَمِّ أَوَّلاً طَبِيعِيًّا وَ هُو

Madd exists in two types, Natural and Derived,
so name the first Natural and it is comprised

مَا لاَ تَوَقُّفٌ لَهُ عَلَى سَبَبْ
وَ لاَ بِدُونِهِ الحُرُوفُ تُجتَلَبْ

Of that madd which on a cause does not rely,
and nor can its letters without it be realized.

بَلْ أَيُّ حَرْفٍ غَيرُ هَمزٍ أَو سُكُونْ
جَا بَعْدَ مَدٍّ فَالطَّبِيعِيُّ يَكُونْ

So if any letter, barring hamzah, or sukūn at hand
follows the madd, then arises the Natural brand.

وَ الآخَرُ الفَرْعِيُّ مَوقُوفٌ عَلَى
سَبَبْ كَهَمْزٍ أَو سُكُونٍ مُسْجَلاَ

Second is the Derived madd which rests on top
of a cause—either on the hamzah or the stop.

حُرُوفُهُ ثَلاَثَةٌ فَعِيهَا
مِنْ لَفْظِ وَايٍ وَهْيَ فِي نُوْحِيْهَا

The madd has three letters, so know them as explained,
in the mnemonic *waī* and in the word *nūḥīhā* contained.

وَ الكَسْرُ قَبْلَ اليَا وَ قَبْلَ الوَاوِ ضَمْ
شَرْطٌ وَ فَتْحٌ قَبْلَ أَلْفٍ يُلْتَزَم

And kasrah before the letter yā, and wāw with dhammah preceding,
Is surely a condition, whereas the fatḥah before the alif is binding.

وَ اللِّينُ مِنْهَا اليَا وَ وَاوٌ سُكِّنَا
إِنِ انْفِتَاحٌ قَبْلَ كُلٍّ أُعلِنَا

And from these the Līn letters: wāw and yā unvowelled,
when preceded by the fatḥah, as we should rightly herald.

أَحكَامُ المَدِّ

The Rules of Madd

لِلْمَدِّ أَحْكَامٌ ثَلاَثَةٌ تَدُومْ
وَهْيَ الوُجُوبُ وَ الجَوَازُ وَ اللُّزُومْ

For the derived madd are three rules enduring,
and they are compulsion, permission and binding.

فَوَاجِبٌ إِنْ جَآءَ هَمْزٌ بَعْدَ مَدْ
فِي كِلْمَةٍ وَ ذَا بِمُتَّصِلْ يُعَدْ

Compulsory is when hamzah after a letter of madd does follow,
in a single word, and this is known as Attached Madd also.

وَ جَائِزٌ مَدٌّ وَ قَصْرٌ إِنْ فُصِلْ
كُلٌّ بِكِلْمَةٍ وَ هٰذَا المُنْفَصِلْ

Permissible is when stretching and shortening are both acceptable,
when they are in separate words, and this is Madd Munfaṣil.

وَ مِثْلُ ذَا إِنْ عَرَضَ السُّكُونُ
وَقْفًا كَتَعْلَمُونَ نَسْتَعِينُ

And likewise is the case where the sukūn is created,
from stopping, in the words *ta'lamūn* and *nasta'īn* illustrated.

أَو قُدِّمَ الهَمْزُ عَلَى المَدِّ وَ ذَا
بَدَلْ كَآمَنُوا وَ إِيمَانًا خُذَا

But in those cases the hamzah precedes the madd letter,
arises the Madd Badal, in *āmanū* and *īmānā* illustrated.

وَ لاَزِمٌ إِنِ السُّكُونُ أُصِّلاَ
وَصْلاً وَ وَقْفًا بَعْدَ مَدٍّ طُوِّلاَ

And Lāzim occurs when real is the stop,
after the madd, in flow and stop, and in length there can be no drop.

أَقْسَامُ المَدِّ اللَّازِمِ
The Types of Binding Madd

أَقْسَامُ لَازِمٍ لَدَيْهِمْ أَرْبَعَهْ
وَ تِلْكَ كِلْمِيٌّ وَ حَرْفِيٌّ مَعَهْ

The types of Binding Madd among them are four exactly,
and they are either the Kalimī or Ḥarfī variety.

كِلَاهُمَا مُخَفَّفٌ مُثَقَّلُ
فَهٰذِهِ أَرْبَعَةٌ تُفَصَّلُ

And each of these into the Light or Heavy division,
a total of four, with this subsequent exposition.

فَإِنْ بِكِلْمَةٍ سُكُونٌ اجْتَمَعْ
مَعْ حَرْفِ مَدٍّ فَهْوَ كِلْمِيٌّ وَ قَعْ

If a word embraces sukūn in combination,
with a madd, it carries the Kalimī designation.

أَوْ فِي ثُلَاثِيِّ الْحُرُوْفِ وُجِدَا
وَ الْمَدُّ وَسْطُهُ فَحَرْفِيٌّ بَدَا

And if in three disjointed letters both arise,
with madd at the center, then the Ḥarfī term applies.

كِلَاهُمَا مُثَقَّلٌ إِنْ أُدْغِمَا
مُخَفَّفٌ كُلٌّ إِذَا لَمْ يُدْغَمَا

Both of these are heavy in the case of merging,
and conversely light when there is no merging.

وَ اللَّازِمُ الْحَرْفِيُّ أَوَّلَ السُّوَرْ
وُجُوْدُهُ وَ فِيْ ثَمَانٍ انْحَصَرْ

The Binding Ḥarfī Madd in the start of the chapters
is found, and encompassed in eight distinct letters,

يَجْمَعُهَا حُرُوْفُ كَمْ عَسَلْ نَقَصْ
وَعَيْنُ ذُوْ وَجْهَيْنِ وَالطُّوْلُ أَخَصْ

Contained within the *Kam 'Aṣal Naqaṣ* expression;
and while 'ayn has two ways, preferred is prolongation.

وَ مَا سِوَى الحَرْفِ الثُّلاَثِيْ لاَ أَلِفْ
فَمَدُّهُ مَدًّا طَبِيْعِيًّا أُلِفْ

And those apart from the trilateral, alif excluding,
for their madd, the natural type is more deserving.

وَ ذَاكَ أَيْضًا فِيْ فَوَاتِحِ السُّوَرْ
فِيْ لَفْظِ حَيٍّ طَاهِرٍ قَدِ انْحَصَرْ

And these are also found in the openings of the chapters,
and in the expression *ḥayyun ṭāhirun* captured.

وَ يَجْمَعُ الفَوَاتِحَ الأَرْبَعْ عَشَرْ
صِلْهُ سُحَيرًا مَنْ قَطَعْكَ ذَا اشْتَهَرْ

And the fourteen of the chapter openings do array,
in what they say: *Restore the bonds without delay, of the kin that cut the way*.

خَاتِمَةُ الكِتَابِ

Conclusion

وَ تَمَّ ذَا النَّظْمُ بِحَمْدِ اللهِ
عَلَى تَمَامِهِ بِلاَ تَنَاهِي

This ode comes now to its conclusion,
with profuse thanks to Allah for its completion.

أَبْيَاتُهُ نَدٌّ بَدَا لِذِيْ النُّهَى
تَارِيخُهَا بُشْرَى لِمَنْ يُتْقِنُهَا

Its verses are *fragrant for those who possess ingenuity*,
and its date ... *a salutation for those who commit it to memory*.

ثُمَّ الصَّلاَةُ وَ السَّلاَمُ أَبَدَا
عَلَى خِتَامِ الأَنبِيَاءِ أَحْمَدَا

And eternal may His salutations be,
upon Aḥmad, the Seal of the Prophecy.

وَالآلِ وَ الصَّحْبِ وَ كُلِّ تَابِعِ
وَ كُلِّ قَارِئٍ وَ كُلِّ سَامِعِ

And his kin, Companions and every follower
And upon every reciter and every listener.

INTRODUCTION TO TAJWEED

الْمُقَدِّمَةُ

IN THIS CHAPTER

What is Tajweed?
What does the Qur'ān say about this topic?
How did the Prophet recite the Qur'ān?
What is the ruling on Tajweed?

The Qur'ān is in essence a book, or, as it affirms in its very beginning in simple yet powerful terms—it is *the Book*. All books by definition exist to be read, and so much more so for the greatest Book sent to human beings. It is also well-known that, unlike other books, religious texts of divine revelation, including the Qur'ān, are meant to be recited or chanted in addition to being read, understood and practiced. This recitation is a unique and special feature of divine scripture. No less than 78 verses of the Qur'ān mention the recitation of scripture in various ways and contexts.[1] The particular words used in these numerous verses are varying forms of the words *qirā'ah, tilāwah, tartīl,* and *dhikr,* all of which are references to reciting and reading the verses of Divine scripture.

The term that has been adopted by Muslim scholars to denote the particular methodology of reciting the Noble Qur'ān is *Tajweed.*

The Qur'ān on its Recitation

The Noble Qur'ān being Allah's final revelation to humanity quite naturally invites people to recite it. Allah orders the recitation of His scripture in numerous verses, among which are the following:

اتْلُ مَا أُوحِيَ إِلَيْكَ مِنَ الْكِتَابِ

Recite what has been revealed to you from the Book.
[The Qur'ān 29:45]

وَاتْلُ مَا أُوحِيَ إِلَيْكَ مِن كِتَابِ رَبِّكَ

And recite what has been revealed to you from your Lord.
[The Qur'ān 18:27]

And in no uncertain terms it commands the Prophet Muḥammad and by extension, the generality of the Muslims, to recite the Qur'ān in a particular manner:

وَرَتِّلِ الْقُرْآنَ تَرْتِيلًا

And recite the Qur'ān with tartīl.
[The Qur'ān 73:4]

[1] For instance, see the following verses of the Qur'ān— 2:44, 2:113, 2:121, 2:129, 2:151, 2:252, 3:58, 3:93, 3:101, 3:108, 3:113, 3:164, 4:127, 5:1, 5:27, 6:151, 7:175, 7:204, 8:2, 8:31, 10:15, 10:16, 10:61, 10:71, 10:94, 11:17, 13:30, 16:98, 17:45, 17:93, 17:106, 17:107, 18:27, 18:83, 19:58, 19:73, 22:30, 22:72, 23:66, 23:105, 25:32, 26:69, 26:199, 27:92, 28:45, 28:53, 28:59, 29:45, 29:48, 29:51, 31:7, 33:34, 34:43, 35:29, 37:3, 39:71, 45:6, 45:8, 45:25, 45:31, 46:7, 46:29, 50:45, 54:17, 54:22, 54:40, 62:2, 65:11, 68:15, 73:4, 73:20, 75:18, 83:13, 84:21, 87:6, 96:1, 96:3, 98:2.

As to the precise meaning of this term *tartīl* in this verse, Muslim scholars have offered a variety of interpretations, all of them linked by a common underlying thread. The majority of the Qur'ānic commentators are of the view that it simply refers to reciting slowly and with deliberation.[2] The reason and wisdom given for this method of recitation is that such a technique is more conducive to understanding and reflection, which is the ultimate purpose of recitation.[3] Imām al-Ṭabarī narrates that Ibn 'Abbās, al-Ḥasan, and Qatādah held the view that tartīl refers to a recitation that is clear and distinct (in Arabic, *bayyinah*). Ibn Kathīr relates from al-Ḍaḥāk that it refers to reciting each letter distinctly. Mujāhid is narrated to have held the view that it refers to systematic ordering and beautiful arrangement. Imām 'Alī b. Abī Tālib is reported to have defined tartīl as the perfection of the letters (in terms of articulation) and knowledge of the stops.[4] These views are not altogether different and certainly not contradictory, for the common underlying notion in all of them is the recitation of the Noble Qur'ān slowly—without haste—and with due deliberation.

These views are aptly summarized by a contemporary commentator of the Qur'ān in his explanation of the aforementioned verse on tartīl:

> Do not recite it quickly and in haste, but slowly and distinctly. Pause at every verse so that the mind understands the meaning and purport of Divine Revelation well and takes effect from it. If it contains mention of Allah's Being and Attributes, it may awe-inspire the heart with His Glory and Majesty. If it expresses His Mercy, the heart may be filled with feelings of gratitude to Him. If it mentions His Wrath and His Punishment, the heart may be overwhelmed by fear of Him. If it enjoins something or forbids something, one may understand what has been enjoined and what has been forbidden. In short, the recital does not only consist of uttering the words with the tongue, but it should involve thoughtful consideration of the meaning.[5]

---

[2] In Arabic, the words used are *tamahhul* [تمهّل] or *muhl* [مهل].

[3] For details, please refer to the commentaries of Ibn Kathīr, al-Qurṭubī, and al-Sa'dī among others.

[4] In Arabic: تجويد الحروف و معرفة الوقوف .

[5] Pg 121, Sayyid Abul A'lā Maudūdī, *The Meaning of the Qur'an.*

The Prophetic Practice of Qur'ānic Recitation

Secondly, a comprehensive understanding of Qur'ānic recitation would invariably remain incomplete unless this conceptual exposition is followed by a glimpse at its practical expression. So while the Noble Qur'ān informs us about the concept and method of reciting the Qur'ān, what is it in practice?

Indeed the Book comes with a guide. Humanity's Creator did not deem it sufficient to merely send a work of divine revelation to human beings, but He sent along with that Book a teacher and guide for it—Muḥammad the Messenger of Allah. And faithful to the divine Book, the Messenger recited it and taught its recitation in the way that it truly deserved. Thus, any study of Tajweed or the concept of tartīl deserves a detailed look at the practice of the one who was responsible for conveying that revelation to us in all of its details, which includes its exact manner of recitation.

Umm Salamah the wife of the Prophet relates that he would recite the verses of the Qur'ān separately by pausing at the end of each verse.[6] That is, he would recite all the verses separately rather than joining them. She also described that he articulated each single letter of the Qur'ān clearly and distinctly.[7] Once the Prophet, in the company of Abu Bakr and 'Umar, praised the recitation of 'Abdullah Ibn Mas'ūd by saying, *Whoever desires to hear the Qur'ān as it was freshly revealed should listen to the recitation of Ibn Umm 'Abd.* That very night, 'Umar rushed over to the home of Ibn Mas'ūd to inform him of these words and to listen to his recitation. He found that Abu Bakr, as usual, had beaten him there. They both listened to Ibn Mas'ūd's recitation and described that it was clear and distinct, down to the articulation of each letter.[8] This tremendous precision and attention to detail—down to the last letter—illustrates the great care and diligence that the recitation of the Noble Qur'ān deserves.

In addition, it was clearly the practice of the Prophet, as described by all who observed him, that he would never recite the Qur'ān in a swift and rapid manner. On the contrary, he would recite with tremendous deliberation and interact with

---

[6] Ḥadīth of Umm Salamah recorded by Aḥmad 25371, al-Tirmidhī 2851, Abū Dāwūd 3487 and al-Dāruquṭnī, and authenticated by Ibn Ḥajr in *Hidāyah al-Ruwāt*, Aḥmad Shākir in *'Umdah al-Tafsīr* and by Nāṣiruddīn al-Albānī in *Irwā al-Ghalīl* and *Aṣl Ṣifah al-Ṣalāh*. Please note that the numbering of ḥadīth narrations in this work– where provided, usually follows the al-'Ālamiyyah enumeration system.

[7] Multiple narrations on the authority of Umm Salamah recorded by al-Tirmidhī 2847, al-Nasā'ī 1012, 1611, Abū Dāwūd 1254, Aḥmad 25317, 25353, al-Baghawī in *Sharḥ al-Sunnah,* Ibn Khuzaymah and others, most of which have been authenticated by the scholars of ḥadīth, including Ibn Ḥajr in *Hidāyah al-Ruwāt* and al-Albānī in *Ṣifah al-Ṣalāh* and his checking of the book *Mishkāt al-Maṣābīḥ*.

[8] Ḥadīth of 'Ammār b. Yāsir reported in *al-'Ilal al-Tirmidhī al-Kabīr* and authenticated by al-Bukhārī as *hasan* in the same work. This incident has also been narrated on the authority of several Companions in various works, including Ibn Mājah 135, Aḥmad 35, 256, 4035, 4112, 17729, al-Bazzār, Ibn 'Asākir, and al-Hindī in *Kanz al-'Ummāl,* and authenticated by Aḥmad Shākir and al-Albānī in their various works.

the content of the recitation in various ways. His recitation was a dynamic one that conveyed a deep bond and attachment with the meanings of its words and passages. The Companion Ḥudhayfah b. al-Yamān once watched the Prophet in the voluntary night prayer (*Qiyām al-Layl*) and noted the overall length of his prayer and the recitation within the prayer, as well as his unhurried and measured pace. He then made the following observation: "I noticed that he glorified Allah when reciting verses of glorification, invoked and supplicated to Allah where the verses called for that, and sought refuge in Allah where the verses called for that."[9] In fact, his prayer was so lengthy that Ḥudhayfah had difficulty keeping up with him and commented, in one narration, that he felt as if his legs were about to break.[10] Anas b. Mālik described the recitation of the Prophet in this way: "The Messenger stretched the words when reciting them."[11] For example, when he recited *Bismillahir-Rahmānir-Rahīm*, he would stretch and prolong the vowels of *Allāh, al-Raḥmān* and *al-Raḥīm*.

In summary, the Prophetic recitation of the Qur'ān had the following features:

Reciting each verse separately
Articulating each letter distinctly
Reciting at a slow pace
Understanding the verses
Conveying a sense of deliberation and contemplation
Interacting with the verses
Repeating some of the verses or passages
Stretching out certain words
Enjoying the words of Allah
Reciting frequently and abundantly

---

[9] Ḥadīth of Ḥudhayfah b. al-Yamān recorded by Muslim 1291, al-Tirmidhī 243, Nasā'ī 998, 999, 1121, 1646, Abū Dāwūd 737, Ibn Mājah 1341, Aḥmad 22156, 22175, 22222, 22254, 22278, 22309, and al-Dārimī 1273 among others.

[10] Narration of Aḥmad 22274, which has been commented on by al-Albānī in *Ṣifah al-Ṣalāh,* where he states that its chain appears to be authentic, consisting of narrators accepted by Imām Muslim save for one person—a cousin of Ḥudhayfah who remains unnamed in the narration and is thus unknown to the scholars of Ḥadīth. Being a cousin of Ḥudhayfah, however, he may have been a Companion, in which case the chain becomes among the most authentic, or at the very least, he was a Follower (Tābi'ī) who is related to a Companion, in which case he is most likely a reliable transmitter of Ḥadīth.

[11] Ḥadīth of Anas b. Mālik related by al-Bukhārī 4657, al-Nasā'ī 1004, Abū Dāwūd 1253, Ibn Mājah 1343 and Aḥmad 11753, 11835, 11891, 12532, 12577, 13562.

It is quite clear, based upon the Qur'ānic injunctions and the Prophetic practice, that the recitation of the Qur'ān is a mandated religious act that has a precise manner and method. The term adopted by scholars to refer to this general manner and method is Tajweed.

PHOTO 2: Remnants of a Qur'ānic School in Chellah, destroyed by an earthquake in the 18th century, present-day Rabat, Morocco. Photo taken by the author in 2014.

The Meaning of Tajweed

The term *Tajweed* is related to the word *jayyid* meaning "excellent" and literally refers to the beautification or embellishment of something. The technical definition of Tajweed offered by scholars of recitation is usually as follows:

إِعطَاءُ كُلِّ حَرفٍ حَقَّهُ وَ مُستَحَقَّهُ

Reciting the Qur'ān by granting each letter its due, from its intrinsic properties and extrinsic ones (those features governed by its placement and relation to other letters).[12]

[12] Pg 14, al-Maseery, *Al-Jāmi' Fī Tajweed al-Qur'ān al-Karīm.*

Qur'ānic scholars centered the definition on the most basic level of speech—the individual letters—and Tajweed is basically reciting each letter properly. Each letter has intrinsic properties and characteristics associated with it which must be fulfilled**, as well as extrinsic properties—which are the variable** rules and regulations that are affected by the placement and sequence of the letters in relation to one other.

The great scholar and authority in Tajweed Ibn al-Jazarī (died 833AH/1429CE) formulated the following definition in his own poetic treatise on Tajweed entitled *al-Muqaddimah al-Jazarīyyah:*

وَ هُوَ أَيـضًا حِليَـةُ التِّـلاوَةِ
وَ زِيـــنَةُ الأَدَاءِ وَ القِرَاءَةِ

وَ هُوَ إِعطَاءِ الحرُوفِ حَقَّهَا
مِن صِفَـةٍ لَهَا وَ مُستَحَقَّـهَا

It is also beautifying the recitation and adorning its effort and delivery

And granting the letters their due, from each intrinsic and acquired quality

A more practical and contemporary definition would be as follows: Tajweed is *the precise methodology of reciting the Qur'ān, based upon a body of rules and principles developed by those well-versed in its recitation, as it was transmitted from the Prophet to subsequent generations.*

The Ruling on Tajweed

There is general agreement that Tajweed is a right of the Qur'ān and its ruling is that of obligation.[13] Ibn al-Jazarī also had something to say on the obligation of Tajweed which is widely quoted and deserves mention:

وَ الأَخْذُ بِالتَّجْوِيدِ حَتمٌ لاَزِمُ
مَنْ لَمْ يُجَوِّدِ القُرْآنَ آثِمُ

لِأَنَّهُ بِـهِ الإِلَـهُ أَنزَلَـا
وَ هَكَذَا مِنهُ إِلَينَا وَصَلاَ

And utilizing Tajweed is matter obligatory,
for whosoever does not, is a sinner assuredly

Because with Tajweed God revealed it so,
and through Tajweed, to us He did bestow.

[13] Among the many scholars that transmitted this view is the great ḥadīth commentator Ibn Ḥajar al-'Asqalānī (died 852AH/1449CE).

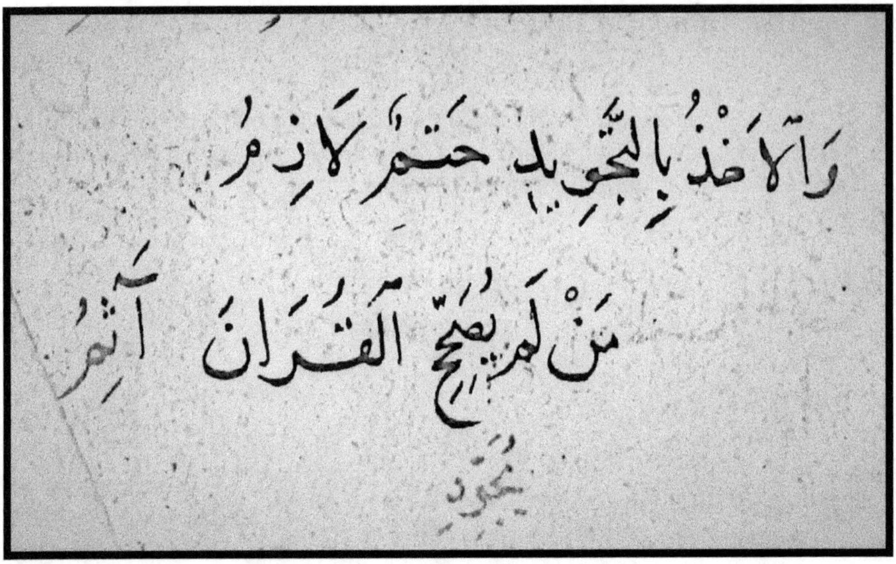

PHOTO 3: A portion from an original manuscript of Ibn al-Jazarī's Ṭayyibat al-Nashr showing the popular verse, courtesy of Princeton University, Mudd Manuscript Library, procured by the author.

Many scholars of Tajweed further specify the nature of this obligation by dividing the knowledge of Tajweed into two types: theoretic knowledge [عِلم نَظَري] and its practical application [تَطبِيق عَمَلِي]. The former is the detailed knowledge of the rules and principles of Tajweed and is considered to be a communal obligation [*farḍ kifāyah*]—that is, some individuals in the community must preserve and transmit this knowledge—while the latter is the proper recitation of the Qur'ān in practice and is considered an individual obligation upon each and every believer [*farḍ 'ayn*].

The Prophet himself had much to say on the issue of the obligation or imperative of Tajweed. Among his exhortations to proper recitation of the Qur'ān are the following:

زَيِّنُوا الْقُرْآنَ بِأَصْوَاتِكُمْ ، فَإِنَّ الصَّوْتَ الْحَسَنَ يَزِيْدُ الْقُرْآنَ حُسْنًا

"Beautify the Qur'ān with your voices, for indeed a beautiful voice adds to the beauty of the Qur'ān."[14]

لَيْسَ مِنَّا مَنْ لَمْ يَتَغَنَّ بِالْقُرْآنِ

"He is not from us who does not recite the Qur'ān beautifully."[15]

تَعَلَّمُوا كِتَابَ اللهِ وَ تَعَاهَدُوهُ وَ تَغَنَّوا بِهِ فَوَالَّذِي نَفْسِي
بِيَدِهِ لَهُوَ أَشَدُّ تَفَلُّتًا مِنَ الْمَخَاضِ فِي الْعُقُلِ

"Learn the Qur'ān, review it, and recite it beautifully, for I swear by the One in Whose Hands is my soul, indeed it slips away more readily than a fully pregnant she-camel from a leash."[16]

تَعَلَّمُوا الْقُرْآنَ وَسَلُوا بِهِ الجَنَّةَ قَبْلَ أَنْ يَتَعَلَّمَهُ قَوْمٌ يَسْأَلُونَ
بِهِ
الدُّنْيَا ، فَإِنَّ الْقُرْآنَ يَتَعَلَّمَهُ ثَلاَثَةٌ : رَجُلٌ يُبَاهِي بِهِ
، وَ رَجُلٌ يَسْتَأْكِلُ بِهِ وَ رَجُلٌ يَقْرَأُ لِلَّهِ عَزَّ وَ جَلَّ

[14] Ḥadīth of al-Barā' b. 'Āzib that has been narrated in three variations: the above text related by 'Alī al-Muttaqī al-Hindī in *Kanz al-'Ummāl* and Ibn Ḥayyān in *Ṭabaqāt al-Muḥaddithīn* and authenticated by al-Albānī in *al-Silsilah al-Aḥādīth al-Ṣaḥīḥah* and *Saḥīḥ al-Jāmi',* the second version containing the text [زَيِّنُوا الْقُرْآنَ بِأَصْوَاتِكُمْ] alone, related by Ibn Mājah 1332, al-Nasā'ī 1005, 1006, Abū Dāwūd 1256, Aḥmad 17763, 17960, al-Dārimī 3364, al-Mundhirī in *al-Targhīb,* Ibn Kathīr in *Faḍāil al-Qur'ān* and authenticated by Ibn Taymiyyah in *Majmū' al-Fatāwā* and by al-Albānī in *Saḥīḥ al-Targhīb* and *Saḥīḥ al-Jāmi'*, and the third version with the text [حَسِّنُوا الْقُرْآنَ بِأَصْوَاتِكُمْ ، فَإِنَّ الصَّوْتَ الْحَسَنَ يَزِيْدُ الْقُرْآنَ حُسْنًا] in al-Dārimī 3365, al-Bayhaqī in *al-Shu'b al-Īmān*, and authenticated by al-Albānī in *Saḥīḥ al-Jāmi'*.

[15] Ḥadīth from Abū Hurayrah recorded by al-Bukhārī 6973, al-Dāruquṭnī and al-Hindī in *Kanz al-'Ummāl* and from Sa'd b. Abī Waqqāṣ in Abū Dāwūd 1257, Aḥmad 1396, 1430, 1467, al-Dārimī 1452, 3352, al-Bazzār, 'Abd al-Razzāq in his *Muṣannaf* and from Abū Lubābah al-Anṣārī in Abū Dāwūd 1258 and al-Bayhaqī in *al-Sunan al-Kubrā.* These various chains have been authenticated by al-Nawawī in *al-Tibyān,* Ibn Taymiyyah in *Majmū' al-Fatāwā,* Ibn Kathīr in his tafseer, al-Haythamī in *Majma' al-Zawāid,* Aḥmad Shākir in his footnotes to *Musnad Aḥmad* and al-Albānī in *Saḥīḥ al-Jāmi'* and *Saḥīḥ Abī Dāwūd.*

[16] Ḥadīth of 'Uqbah b. 'Āmir al-Juhanī recorded by Aḥmad 16679 and al-Hindī in *Kanz al-'Ummāl,* and with slightly different wording through the same Companion by Aḥmad 16721, 16753, al-Dārimī 3214, 3215 and authenticated by al-Haythamī in *Majma' al-Zawāid* and al-Albānī in *Ṣaḥīḥ al-Jāmi'* and *al-Silsilah al-Aḥādīth al-Ṣaḥīḥah.*

"Learn the Qur'ān and seek Paradise by means of it, before a people come who will learn it seeking the world, for indeed only three types learn the Qur'ān—one who boasts through it, one who seeks livelihood by it, and one who recites it solely for Allah the Majestic and Exalted."[17]

[17] Ḥadīth of Abū Sa'īd al-Khudrī related by al-Bayhaqī in *Shu'b al-Īmān*, al-Hindī in *Kanz al-'Ummāl*, al-Qāsim b. Sallām in F*aḍā'il al-Qur'ān* and others, and authenticated by al-Ḥākim, Ibn Ḥajar and al-Albānī in *al-Silsilah al-Ṣaḥīḥah*.

THE RULES OF ISTI'ĀDHA AND BASMALAH

أَحكَامُ الإِستِعَاذَةِ وَ البَسمَلَةِ

IN THIS CHAPTER

How do we begin the recitation of the Qur'ān?
What is the Isti'ādha?
What is the Basmalah?
Why must we begin our recitation in a particular way?
How do we join two chapters of the Qur'ān?

The issue of how to approach the Qur'ān and interact with it is a very important one and traditionally serves as the starting point in all works and classes dealing with the rules and etiquette of Qur'ānic recitation.[18] Basically the recitation of the Qur'ān must begin with two supplications:

1. The *isti'ādhah* [The Seeking of Refuge] الإِستِعَاذَة

2. The *basmalah* [The Use of the Name of Allah] البَسمَلَة

The isti'ādhah supplication involves seeking refuge from the devil (shayṭān) while the basmalah is invoking the name of Allah prior to beginning the recitation of the Qur'ān.

The Isti'ādhah

When we open this very Book, we find that it commands us to begin its reading in a particular way:

فَإِذَا قَرَأْتَ الْقُرْآنَ فَاسْتَعِذْ بِاللَّهِ مِنَ الشَّيْطَانِ الرَّجِيمِ

When you recite the Qur'ān, seek refuge in Allah from the accursed Shayṭān (devil).

[The Qur'ān 16:98]

This refuge being enjoined in this verse is a supplication known as the *isti'ādhah* whose formula from the verse is in the following form:

أَعُوذُ بِاللهِ مِنَ الشَّيطَانِ الرَّجِيمِ

I seek refuge in Allah from the accursed shayṭān.

This is the default form of the supplication, but it may also be done in a number of other forms found in authentic Prophetic reports, such as the following:

أَعُوذُ بِاللهِ السَّمِيعِ العَلِيمِ مِنَ الشَّيطَانِ الرَّجِيمِ

[18] This section has been adapted from the beautiful words and nightly Ramaḍān lessons of Shaykh Muḥammad Yūsuf Iṣlāḥī, from a lecture on September 10, 2008.

With respect to the exact legal ruling of the isti'ādhah, scholars are divided between the view that it is obligatory [wājib] prior to beginning one's recitation of the Qur'ān, and the view that it is recommended and encouraged [mustaḥabb] rather than obligatory. However, from a practical perspective, since the Qur'ān itself demands it, one should obviously adopt this practice.

The isti'ādhah is to be uttered once at the beginning of one's recitation, even if one is reciting multiple chapters or passages in continuity. However, if there is a significant interruption in one's recitation, then it should be redone when resuming recitation. The isti'ādhah should be uttered silently in the congregational prayers and when one is reciting alone. In other settings such as group or public recitation and in teaching situations, it should be done aloud. In collective recitation involving multiple individuals reciting continuously, the one who begins reciting first should recite the isti'ādhah, which suffices for the rest of them, so long as there is no significant interruption.

What is the spiritual significance of these supplications?

Human beings enjoy innumerable blessings bestowed upon them by their Creator. Undoubtedly the greatest of them all is the blessing of guidance represented first and foremost by the Qur'ān. A very important part of showing gratitude for this great blessing of the Qur'ān is to recite it, understand it and apply it in our lives, and also to begin our reading of it in the proper manner. That proper manner includes these supplications.

Furthermore, the Qur'ān is pure guidance. The isti'ādhah is a recognition of the fact that the archenemy of guidance is Shayṭān, whose job is to continually divert us from that guidance. The Qur'ān is the primary means of guiding us to the Straight Path, while Shayṭān's primary mission is to divert us from that path. When Allah ejected Shayṭān from the Garden of Paradise, he promised Allah this:

قَالَ فَبِمَا أَغْوَيْتَنِي لَأَقْعُدَنَّ لَهُمْ صِرَاطَكَ الْمُسْتَقِيمَ
ثُمَّ لَآتِيَنَّهُم مِّن بَيْنِ أَيْدِيهِمْ وَمِنْ خَلْفِهِمْ وَعَنْ أَيْمَانِهِمْ وَعَن شَمَائِلِهِمْ ۖ وَلَا تَجِدُ أَكْثَرَهُمْ
شَاكِرِينَ

He said: Now, because Thou hast sent me astray, verily I shall lurk in ambush for them on Thy Right Path. Then will I assault them from before them and behind them, from their right and their left: Nor wilt thou find, in most of them, gratitude.

[The Qur'ān 7:16-7]

Because of this fact, we are enjoined to always begin our interaction with the Book of Guidance by seeking refuge from Shayṭān, who is described in the supplication as *wretched* or *cursed* due to his opposition to the truth.

Secondly and perhaps more importantly, the isti'ādhah is an affirmation of something far greater. It is quite obvious that in order to study the Qur'ān and derive its benefit one must rely on certain well-known means and tools, such as the Arabic language, proper works of tafsīr (commentary and explanation), knowledge of the life-history of the Holy Prophet, sufficient time, etc. But there is one tool that is more indispensible than all of these—Allah's assistance and support.

So the isti'ādhah is an affirmation that the greatest resource and means of deriving benefit from the Noble Qur'ān is supplicating and seeking the help of the One who revealed it. It is an expression of our utter dependence upon and complete need for Allah's mercy and support. Hence we should constantly supplicate Allah to help us in all our affairs, especially if it involves His Noble Book.

The Basmalah

For this reason, we also begin our recitation in Allah's name, with a formula known as the *basmalah:*

بِسْمِ اللَّهِ الرَّحْمَٰنِ الرَّحِيمِ

It appears from a study of the Qur'ān and Islamic traditions as well the previous scriptures that it has always been a divinely ordained methodology to begin all matters with Allah's name. The Prophet Nūḥ (Noah) rode his ark with Allah's name— *"And he said: Embark therein! In the name of Allah be its course and its mooring. Lo! my Lord is Forgiving, Merciful;"*[19] and likewise, the Prophet Sulaymān began his letter to the Queen of Sheba with Allah's name.[20]

Similarly, all chapters of the Noble Qur'ān also begin with the basmalah (except for Sūrah al-Tawbah), although whether it is an actual verse belonging to those chapters or merely a means to distinguish between them is subject to a well-known difference among scholars. The scholars of the classical Shāfi'ī and Ḥanbalī juridical schools in general consider the basmalah to be a part of the Qur'ānic chapters and thus recite the basmalah aloud before each sūrah in prayer, while those of the Ḥanafī and Mālikī schools consider the basmalah to be a continual and separate verse of the Qur'ān that should be recited at the beginning of recitation and the beginning of the chapters in order to distinguish them, but is not necessarily the first verse of each chapter.

[19] The Qur'ān, 11:41.
[20] The Qur'an 27:30

In any case, we have been commanded to recite beginning with the basmalah in the very first verse ever revealed:

اقْرَأْ بِاسْمِ رَبِّكَ الَّذِي خَلَقَ

Read! In the name of your Lord . . .
[The Qur'ān 96:1]

The beauty of the basmalah expression is that it contains three of Allah's noble names (*Allah, al-Raḥmān* and *al-Raḥīm*) and two of His key attributes (*al-Raḥmān* and *al-Raḥīm*), and so any deed beginning with it is truly blessed and worthy of Divine support. *Al-Raḥmān* is the root of all Divine attributes, and the logical culmination of this attribute relating to the mercy of Allah is the Noble Qur'ān. As He Himself says:

الرَّحْمَٰنُ عَلَّمَ الْقُرْآنَ

Al-Raḥmān (The Most Gracious One) is He who has taught the Qur'ān.
[The Qur'ān 55:1-2]

خَلَقَ الْإِنسَانَ عَلَّمَهُ الْبَيَانَ

He created man, and taught him the faculty of speech.
[The Qur'ān 55:3-4]

The beauty of this sequence of initial verses in this moving and eloquent chapter of the Qur'ān is that it begins by affirming Allah's fundamental Name and Attribute of *al-Raḥmān,* and then immediately mentions its logical culmination—the Qur'ān—followed then by mention of the creation of man and endowing him with the blessing of speech. In this very subtle and most eloquent manner, Allah is hinting that His mercy necessitated the teaching of the Qur'ān, and that human beings were created for this very Qur'ān (since the Qur'ān is mentioned before human creation). Following that, the faculty of speech is mentioned as an implication that the Qur'ān be verbally recited by them.

Therefore, when one intends to recite any portion of the Qur'ān, whether it is in the beginning or middle of a sūrah, one must first recite the isti'ādhah and then the basmalah and then the verses one is choosing to recite.

← ← direction of recitation ← ←

	Basmalah	Isti'ādhah
← ﴿ ٱلْحَمْدُ لِلَّهِ رَبِّ ٱلْعَٰلَمِينَ ﴾	بِسْمِ اللهِ الرَّحْمٰنِ الرَّحِيمِ	أَعُوذُ بِاللهِ مِنَ الشَّيْطَانِ الرَّجِيمِ

Ways of Beginning with Isti'ādhah and Basmalah

The preferred and natural method is to recite each component separately by stopping fully between them. In other words, you recite the isti'ādhah, stop, then recite the basmalah, stop, then begin the verses. This method is referred to as Complete or Total Stopping [*Qaṭ' al-Jamī'*]. [*Please refer to Figure 1 below*]

Although stopping is preferred at these points, it is also possible to join rather than stop at these points and thus recite the two components in continuity without a stop or pause. For instance, one may stop after the isti'ādhah but then join the basmalah with the beginning of the verses in continuity.

There are a combination of four ways of combing the isti'ādhah and basmalah with the beginning of one's recitation, depending upon whether one stops or joins at the breaks. These four techniques are summarized as follows, in order of preference:

←← direction of recitation ←←

	← ﴿ ٱلْحَمْدُ لِلَّهِ رَبِّ ٱلْعَٰلَمِينَ ﴾		Basmalah بِسْمِ اللهِ الرَّحْمٰنِ الرَّحِيمِ		Isti'ādhah أعُوذُ بِاللهِ مِنَ الشَّيطَانِ الرَّجِيمِ
		↑		↑	
1	قَطعُ الجَمِيع *Total Stopping*	Stop		Stop	
2	قَطعُ الأوَّل وَ وَصلُ الثاني وَ الثَّالِث *Initial Stopping and Subsequent Joining*	Join		Stop	
3	وَصلُ الأوَّل بِالثَّاني وَ قَطعُ الثَّالِث *Initial Joining and Subsequent Stopping*	Stop		Join	
4	وَصلُ الجَمِيع *Total Joining*	Join		Join	

FIGURE 1—WAYS OF BEGINNING A SURAH

With respect to beginning one's recitation from the middle of a sūrah rather than its beginning, the basmalah may be left out since it is a feature of the beginning of the sūrahs. However, many scholars still recommend reciting it in those cases due to its beautiful meanings and implications, and due to the general guidelines of beginning every task in Allah's Name.

So if one chooses to recite the basmalah before beginning recitation in the middle of a chapter, then the four ways of joining the isti'ādhah and basmalah with the recitation are identical to the above. However, if one chooses to leave the basmalah and recite only the isti'ādhah then there are two ways to do so—either breaking or joining the isti'ādhah with the verses:

←← direction of recitation ←←

	← ﴿ إِنَّ لِلْمُتَّقِينَ مَفَازًا ﴾		Isti'ādhah أعُوذُ بِاللهِ مِنَ الشَّيطَانِ الرَّجِيمِ
1	القَطعُ	stop	
2	الوَصلُ	join	

FIGURE 2—STARTING WITHIN A SURAH

Exceptions

An important note must be made with respect to the ninth chapter of the Qur'ān known as al-Tawbah or Barā'ah. The only exception to the basmalah beginning the Qur'ānic chapters is this chapter, which does not begin with it due to two possible reasons: its stern content relating to themes of warfare, fighting and dealing with pagans and hypocrites; or its thematic continuity with the previous chapter al-Anfāl. This omission of the basmalah here is in fact proof of the meticulous preservation and transmission of the Qur'an by the Companions and successive generations, for had it been a careless matter or related to our logic, the chapter should logically have begun with the basmalah, like all other chapters, in order to preserve the apparent "coherence" and continuity of the Qur'an.

Therefore, when you recite Sūrah al-Tawbah, you should recite the isti'ādhah, then either stopping or joining it with the beginning of the sūrah, without the basmalah.

It should also be noted that the basmalah is embodied within a chapter of the Qur'ān, where it appears as part of a verse:

إِنَّهُ مِن سُلَيْمَانَ وَإِنَّهُ بِسْمِ اللَّهِ الرَّحْمَٰنِ الرَّحِيمِ

Indeed it (the letter) is from Sulaymān and it begins with the name of Allah, the Most Gracious, Most Merciful.

[The Qur'ān 27:30]

In addition to this, there are a number of other advanced considerations. In some cases, it is not proper to join the isti'ādhah or the basmalah with certain verse due to their meanings and the potential for adverse associations. Obviously, this can only be fully comprehended and implemented by one who understands what is being recited.

Examples would include joining the isti'ādhah, which ends with the name of the accursed Shayṭān, with a verse that begins with mentioning the name of Allah or the Prophet Muḥammad.

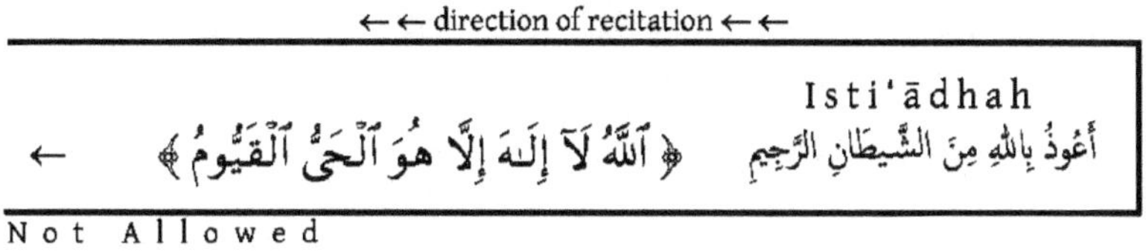

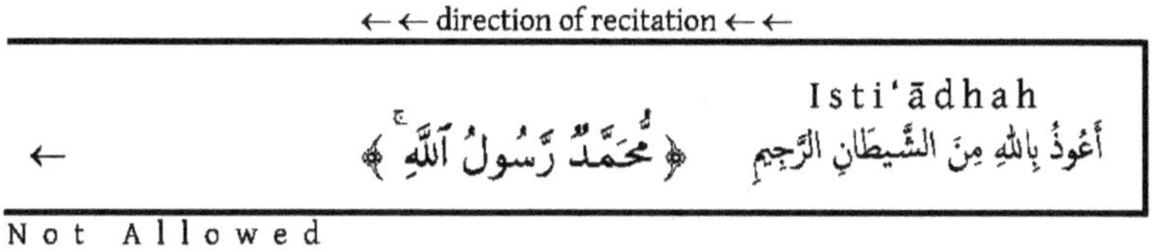

Alternately, it would be reprehensible to join the basmalah, which ends with Allah's attributes, with a verse that begins with the name of Shayṭān.

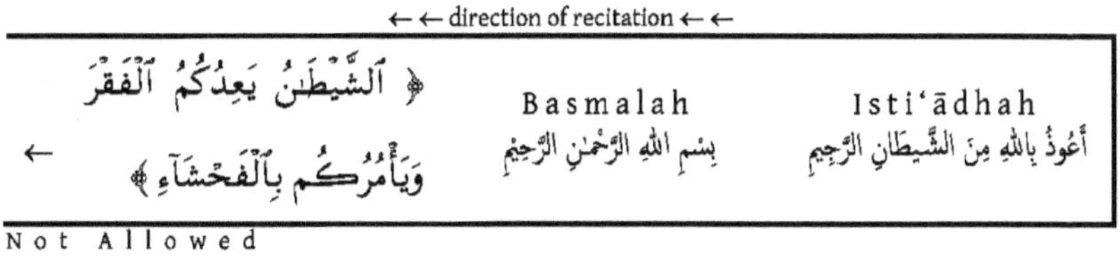

Joining Between Two Chapters

Finally, for those reciting more than one chapter, how does one combine the end of one sūrah with the beginning of the next? There are three basic ways to do so:

1. Complete Stopping [*Qaṭ' al-Jamī'*]: Stop at the end of the first sūrah, recite the basmalah, stop, and then start the next sūrah.

2. Initial Stopping [*Qaṭ' al-Awwal*]: Stop at the end of the first sūrah, then recite the basmalah joined with the beginning of the next sūrah.

3. Complete Joining [*Waṣl al-Jamī'*]: Recite the end of the first sūrah with the basmalah with the beginning of the next sūrah in continuity.

← ← direction of recitation ← ←

	al-Baqarah		Basmalah		al-Fātiḥah end
←	﴿ الٓمٓ ۝ ذَٰلِكَ ٱلۡكِتَٰبُ لَا رَيۡبَۛ فِيهِ ﴾		بِسْمِ اللهِ الرَّحْمَٰنِ الرَّحِيمِ		﴿ غَيۡرِ ٱلۡمَغۡضُوبِ عَلَيۡهِمۡ وَلَا ٱلضَّآلِّينَ ﴾
1	قطعُ الجميع	stop		Stop	
2	قطعُ الأوّل وَ وَصلُ الثاني وَ الثّالِث	join		Stop	
3	وَصلُ الجميع	join		Join	

FIGURE 3—JOINING 2 SURAHS

Note that one of the original four scenarios—that of joining the sūrah end with the basmalah, then stopping before reciting the next sūrah—is not allowed because it joins the basmalah with the previous sūrah that one has finished reciting and cuts it off from the beginning of the next sūrah, to which it really belongs. Hence this possibility is discounted on logical grounds, and we are left with three valid scenarios. These are illustrated below, with the joining of the first and second chapters of the Qur'ān (al-Fātiḥah and al-Baqarah):

Joining Sūrah al-Anfāl and al-Tawbah

These three scenarios apply to joining between all adjacent sūrahs of the Qur'ān, save for that of al-Anfāl and al-Tawbah (since al-Tawbah does not include basmalah in its beginning). Since there is no basmalah between them, there are recited in continuity without any intervening elements. So how are the chapters distinguished from one another, when being recited together? There are thus three ways to join al-Anfāl and al-Tawbah:

1. Complete Stopping [*Qaṭ'*]: Completely stop at the end of sūrah al-Anfāl, and then begin reciting sūrah al-Tawbah.

2. Pausing [*Sakt*]: Briefly pause at the end of sūrah al-Anfāl, without taking another breath, and then begin reciting sūrah al-Tawbah.

3. Joining [*Waṣl*]: Join the end of sūrah al-Anfāl with al-Tawbah in one continuous, uninterrupted recitation.

These ways are illustrated below:

	Beginning al-Tawbah		End of al-Anfāl
←	﴿ بَرَآءَةٌ مِّنَ ٱللَّهِ وَرَسُولِهِۦٓ إِلَى ٱلَّذِينَ عَـٰهَدتُّم مِّنَ ٱلْمُشْرِكِينَ ﴾		﴿ إِنَّ ٱللَّهَ بِكُلِّ شَىْءٍ عَلِيمٌۢ ﴾ ←
1	القَطعُ	Stop	
2	السَّكت	Pause	
3	الوَصل	Join	

FIGURE 4—JOINING SURAH ANFĀL AND TAWBAH

THE TEXT OF CHILDRENS BEQUEST

WITH BRIEF COMMENTARY

متن تحفة الأطفال مع الشرح

المُقَدِّمَةُ

Introduction

يَقُولُ رَاجِي رَحمَةِ الغَفُورِ

دَومًا سُلَيمَانُ هُوَ الجَمْزُورِي

1 Says he who longs for the grace of the One who does forgive,
Sulaymān Ḥusain Muḥammad, [21]
who in the land of Jamzūr[22] did live.

اَلحَمدُ لِلّٰهِ مُصَلِّيًا عَلَى

مُحَمَّدٍ وَّ آلِهِ وَ مَنْ تَلاَ

2 Praise be to Allah for allowing me to send prayers and reverence,
Upon Muḥammad, his kin and those who followed him in deference.

وَ بَعدُ هٰذَا النَّظْمُ لِلمُرِيدِ

فِي النُّونِ وَ التَّنْوِينِ وَ المُدُودِ

3 Following that, this poem is for those who yearn to know,
the Nūn, Tanwīn and Madd rules as they go. [23]

---

[21] He was Sulaymān b. Ḥusain b. Muḥammad al-Affendī al-Jamzūrī, a Shāfi'i scholar from the twelfth Hijrī century, who was born in Rabī' al-Awwal near Ṭanṭā, Egypt close to the year 1160H and wrote this poem in the year 1198H. We don't know the exact year of his demise. He left behind a small number of works, including this treatise on Tajweed named *Tuḥfat al-Aṭfāl,* a commentary on this same text named *Fatḥ al-Aqfāl,* and *al-Fatḥ al-Rabbāni,* a work on the modes of recitation. This is the extent of the limited knowledge we possess today of this author, who lived a humble, largely anonymous life but was blessed by Allah's grace—just as he supplicated for in the opening lines—to leave some works behind that have been benefiting generations of students of the Qur'ān.

[22] A city near Ṭanṭā in present-day Egypt, also known as Abi'l-Nādhim, in the Manūfiyah province.

[23] The author states that the subject-matter of this text consists of the rules of the letter nūn, tanwīn, and the madd, but only by way of example or allusion to the bulk of the Tajweed rules. It is not literally intended that the text is only about these rules—but mostly about them, in addition to some others.

سَمَّيتُهُ بِتُحفَةِ الأَطْفَالِ

عَنْ شَيخِنَا المِيهِيِّ ذِى الكَمَالِ

I have resolved to title it *the Children's Bequest,* [24]
relating from our shaykh al-Meehī, [25] masterful, adept. [26]

أَرْجُو بِهِ اَنْ يَّنفَعَ الطُّلَّابَا

وَالأَجْرَ وَ القَبُولَ وَ الثَّوَابَا

I cherish that this proves of worth to its students,
and brings with it reward, reception and recompense. [27]

أَحكَامُ النُّونِ السَّاكِنةِ وَالتَّنوِينِ

The Rules of Nūn Sākin and Tanwīn

لِلنُّونِ إِنْ تَسْكُنْ وَ لِلتَّنْوِينِ

اَربَعُ أَحكَامٍ فَخُذْ تَبيِيْنِي

For the nūn without vowels and the Tanwīn[28] diction,
exist four basic rules, so take my depiction.

---

[24] The full title of the text is *Tuḥfat al-Aṭfāl wa'l Ghilmān,* which literally means "A gift for the children and youth."

[25] Nūr al-Dīn 'Alī b. 'Alī b. Aḥmad b. 'Umar b. Nājī al-Meehī (named so from his city of birth next to Shibīn al-Kawm, the capitol of the province of Manūfiyah in Egypt), who lived a life of learning and scholarship in various institutions including al-Azhar University, and died in 1204H.

[26] As a mark of humility and devotion to one's teachers that is characteristic of the Muslim tradition, the author ascribes the work to his own teacher—from whom he learned the rules of Tajweed, and describes him with the characteristics of perfection (*kamāl*), which obviously is not meant in an absolute sense as that would clash with the theologic purity of Islam which ascribes absolute perfection to Allah alone.

[27] Being one of the most, if not *the* most, widely read texts on Tajweed today, it has certainly attained the highest degree of acceptance imaginable among the ummah. We can only pray that Allah accepts the rest of the author's heartfelt prayers and reward him profusely for his humble work.

[28] The tanwīn is a double vowel construct at the end of some Arabic words, corresponding to the sounds *–an/-un/-in.* Since it ends with an unvowelled nūn sound, it is included with the rules of the unvowelled nūn. See chapter one for more details on this.

فَالأَوَّلُ الإِظْهَارُ قَبْلَ أَحْرُفِ
لِلحَلْقِ سِتٌّ رُتِّبَتْ فَلتَعرِفِ

The first of these, the rule of Iẓhār, [29] is before the letters hence,
arising from the throat, six in number, in this known sequence:

هَمزٌ فَهَاءٌ ثُمَّ عَينٌ حَاءُ
مُهمَلَتَانِ ثُمَّ غَينٌ خَاءُ

Hamzah and Hā', then 'Ayn and Ḥā',
without the marks, [30] then Ghayn and Khā'.

وَ الثَّانِ إِدغَامٌ بِسِتَّةٍ أَتَتْ
فِي يَرْمُلُونَ عِنْدَهُمْ قَدْ ثَبَتَت

The second is Idghām, [31] with six it takes effect,
in *yarmuloon,* [32] a mnemonic which they accept.

لَكِنَّهَا قِسمَانِ قِسمٌ يُدغَمَا
فِيهِ بِغُنَّةٍ بِيَنْمُو عُلِمَا

But this is of two types, with the first being verbalized,
with the trait of ghunnah, and by *yanmu* [33] recognized.

إِلاَّ إِذَا كَانَا بِكِلمَةٍ فَلاَ
تُدْغِمْ كَدُنْيَا ثُمَّ صِنْوَانٍ تَلاَ

Except if this occurs within one word, then there is none,
no Idghām in articulation, as in the words *dunya* and *ṣinwān.* [34]

---

[29] *Iẓhār* literally means *manifestation,* and refers to the default and original articulation of each letter.

[30] It is quite common in classical Arabic works to describe the punctuation and pronunciation of certain letters in order to minimize mistakes that naturally arise in the process of printing, duplication and transmission or works. The term *muhmalatān* means "without the dots" and here refers to the letters (ح/ع) to distinguish them from (خ/غ), which can easily be mixed up in the course of printing.

[31] *Idghām* means *merging* or *assimilation,* and refers the complete merging of one letter (in this context, the unvowelled nūn) into another.

[32] This is popularly pronounced as *yarmuloon* or as *yarmaloon.* The use of mnemonics and other memory aids is very prominent in Islamic works.

[33] An alternate mnemonic, also quite common is *yoomin* (يومن).

[34] Though the author mentions two words here by way of illustration, there are a total of four words in the Qur'ān in which an unvowelled nūn occurs within one

وَالثَّانِ إِدْغَامٌ بِغَيرِ غُنَّهْ

فِي اللاَّمِ وَ الرَّا ثُمَّ كَرِّرَنَّهْ

The second type is Idghām without the ghunnah trait, [35]
in lām and rā, but the latter you must reverberate. [36]

وَالثَّالِثُ الإِقْلاَبُ عِنْدَ البَاءِ

مِيمًا بِغُنَّةٍ مَعَ الإِخْفَاءِ

The third rule is Iqlāb[37] which occurs with the letter bā,
which is converted to meem and pronounced with Ikhfā'. [38]

وَالرَّابِعُ الإِخفَاءُ عِنْدَ الفَاضِلِ

مِنَ الحُرُوفِ وَاجِبٌ لِلفَاضِلِ

The fourth is Ikhfā'[39] for the respected student,
with specified letters mandatory for the student.

فِي خَمْسَةٍ مِنْ بَعْدِ عَشْرٍ رَمْزُهَا

فِي كِلْمِ هٰذَا البَيْتِ قَدْ ضَمَّنْتُهَا

In fifteen letters it takes effect,
within this prose that I erect: [40]

---

word followed by one of these six letters of assimilation. The other two words not mentioned here are *bunyān* (بُنيَان) and *qinwān* (قِنوَان). Refer to chapter one for details.

[35] Ghunnah is the nasalized sound naturally associated with the letters nūn and meem.

[36] The author is referring here to the quality of the letter rā known as *tikrār* (reverberation), which is the trilling, reverberating quality of the *r* sound.

[37] *Iqlāb* means *conversion,* and refers to the conversion of the nūn sound to a meem as described in the same couplet.

[38] *Ikhfā* means *hiding* or *concealment,* and here refers to the suppressed, concealed manner of articulating the meem sound in the rule of Iqlāb.

[39] *Ikhfā* here refers to the fourth of the Nūn Sākin rules: the suppressed, concealed manner of articulating the nūn sound in these cases.

[40] Here the author has cleverly constructed a poem within a poem—unrelated in meaning to the main text itself—but in which case the first letter of each word in this 15-word couplet is a letter of *Ikhfā'.* This technique is common in classical Islamic works and serves to provide a convenient way to remember more complex pieces of information.

صِفْ ذَا ثَنَا كَمْ جَادَ شَخصٌ قَدْ سَمَا
دُمْ طَيِّبًا زِدْ فِي تُقًى ضَعْ ظَالِمَا

Relate of the praiseworthy one, how excellent is he who achieves status robust;
Be ever perpetual in virtue, cultivate piety, and fend off the one who is unjust.

أَحكَامُ المِيمِ وَ النُّونِ المُشَدَّدَتَينِ

The Rules of the Doubled Nūn and Meem

وَ غُنَّ مِيمًا ثُمَّ نُونًا شُدِّدَا
وَسَمِّ كُلاً حَرْفَ غُنَّةٍ بَدَا

And articulate ghunnah of the nūn and meem that carries the double accent, [41]
and refer to both as letters of ghunnah, as is obvious and apparent.

أَحكَامُ المِيمِ السَّاكِنةِ

The Rules of Meem Sākinah

وَ المِيْمُ إِنْ تَسْكُنْ تَجِي قَبْلَ الهِجَا
لاَ أَلِفٍ لَّيِّنَةٍ لِّذِي الحِجَا

When stopping on meem before the letters of the alphabet,
but not before the alif layyinah, [42] for he who is intelligent

أَحكَامُهَا ثَلاَثَةٌ لِمَنْ ضَبَط
إِخفَاءٌ إِدغَامٌ وَ إِظْهَارٌ فَقَطْ

are three rules for he who would endear them to memory,

[41] Here the author is referring to the formal Tajweed term *ghunnah,* which is the prolonged nasalized sound that must be extended to a duration of two time units, covered in more detail in chapter two.

[42] *Alif layyinah* refers to the unvowelled alif preceded by a letter carrying the fatḥah vowel, which produces the extended *–aa* sound. For obvious reasons such a letter, which is unvowelled, cannot be preceded by an unvowelled meem, as there cannot be two adjacent unvowelled letters in the Arabic language.

and they are the rules of Ikhfā', Idghām and Iẓhār only. [43]

فَالأَوَّلُ الإِخْفَاءُ عِنْدَ البَاءِ

وَ سَمِّهِ الشَّفْوِيَّ لِلقُرَّاءِ

The first is Ikhfā' with the letter bā,
termed by the reciters as Labial Ikhfā'. [44]

وَ الثَّانِ إِدْغَامٌ بِمِثْلِهَا أَتَى

وَ سَمِّ إِدْغَامًا صَغِيرًا يَا فَتَى

The second is Idghām when its likeness[45] appears,
and name it the Smaller Idghām my dears.

وَ الثَّالِثُ الإِظْهَارُ فِي البَقِيَّهْ

مِنْ أَحرُفٍ وَ سَمِّهَا شَفْوِيَّهْ

The third is Iẓhār which occurs with the balance
of the letters, and termed Labial Iẓhār in our parlance.

وَ احذَرْ لَدَى وَاوٍ وَ فَا أَنْ تَخْتَفِي

لِقُـرِبـهَا وَ الاِتِّـحَادِ فَــاعْرِفِ

And be wary of making Ikhfā' with wāw and fā when you read,
due to the closeness and unity of its makhraj, so take heed. [46]

---

[43] These terms have the same basic meanings as the corresponding terms from the rules of the unvowelled nūn.

[44] The term labial (*shafawī*) is often used in the context of the letter meem because the meem is pronounced from the lips.

[45] i.e. the letter meem.

[46] Because the articulation site (makhraj) of the letter meem is very close to that of the letter fā (the meem is articulated from the two lips while the fā is articulated from the lower lip combined with the edge of the upper teeth) and identical to that of the letter wāw (both are articulated from the lips), it is very easy to mistakenly blend the two letters together in articulation, when they are adjacent to one another. Therefore, extra care must be exerted to ensure that the meem in these states is articulated properly, with full manifestation.

أَحكَامُ لَامِ اَل وَ لَامِ الفِعلِ

The Rules of Lām

لِلاَمِ اَلْ حَالَانِ قَبْلَ الأَحْرُفِ
أُولَاهُمَا إِظْهَارُهَا فَلْتَعْرِفِ

The lām of the definite article exists in two states before the letters,
the first is its manifest articulation, [47] and should be understood better,

قَبْلَ ارْبَعٍ مَعْ عَشْرَةٍ خُذْ عِلْمَهُ
مِنِ ابْغِ حَجَّكَ وَ خَفْ عَقِيمَهُ

Occurring before fourteen letters, so learn them well,
from this mnemonic: *Seek your goal and vain pursuits repel.* [48]

ثَانِيهِمَا إِدْغَامُهَا فِي أَربَعِ
وَ عَشْرَةٍ أَيضًا وَ رَمْزُهَا فَعِ

The second is its assimilation, which in fourteen does exist,
and likewise, facilitate your recollection of them from this:

طِبْ ثُمَّ صِلْ رُحْمًا تَفُزْ ضِفْ ذَا نِعَمْ
دَعْ سُوءَ ظَنٍّ زُرْ شَرِيفًا لِلْكَرَمْ

Be meritorious, maintain relations for success, and host those who are beneficent;
Shun ill estimation of others, and frequent the noble ones for munificence. [49]

وَ الَّامُ الْأُولَى سَمِّهَا قَمَرِيَّهْ
وَ الَّامُ الأُخْرَى سَمِّهَا شَمْسِيَّهْ

Name the first Lām Qamariyah,
and the latter Lām Shamsiyyah.

---

[47] i.e. Iẓhār.

[48] Another clever verse consisting of fourteen letters which are all letters of manifestation—[ابْغِ حَجَّكَ وَ خَفْ عَقِيمَهُ]. Therefore, when they follow an unvowelled lām, it is pronounced as a distinct lām, i.e. with manifestation.

[49] Another poem within this poem, consisting of fourteen words, in which the first letter of each word is a letter of merging or assimilation. When these fourteen letters follow an unvowelled lām, that lām is merged into them and is no longer pronounced separately.

وَ أَظْهِرَنَّ لَامَ فِعْلٍ مُطْلَقَا

فِي نَحْوِ قُلْ نَعَمْ وَ قُلْنَا وَ التَقَى

And pronounce with manifestation the verbal lām consistently,
in words like *Qul Na'am, Qulna, Waltaqā* and their variety. [50]

بَابٌ فِي إِدغَامِ المِثلَينِ وَ المُتَقَارِبَينِ وَ المُتَجَانِسَينِ

The Types of Idghām

إِنْ فِي الصِّفَاتِ وَ الْمَخَارِجِ اتَّفَقْ

حَرْفَانِ فَالْمِثلاَنِ فِيهِمَا أَحَقْ

If two letters agree in attribute and point of articulation, [51]
then it is more deserving to use the *Mithlayn* designation.

وَ إِنْ يَّكُونَا مَخْرَجًا تَقَارَبَا

وَ فِي الصِّفَاتِ اخْتَلَفَا يُلَقَّبَا

But if the two in their points of articulation be akin,
yet in their attributes varying then use the heading

مُتَقَارِبَيْنِ أَوْ يَكُونَا اتَّفَقَا

فِي مَخْرَجٍ دُونَ الصِّفَاتِ حُقِّقَا

Mutaqāribayn; And if they so happen to concur
in articulation but not attribute then they deserve

بِالْمُتَجَانِسَينِ ثُمَّ إِنْ سَكَنْ

أَوَّلُ كُلٍّ فَالصَّغِيرَ سَمِّيَنْ

[50] These preceding rules generally apply to the lām of the definite article and not to other types of lām, such as those that occur in verbs (three examples of which are provided in the text). These other types of unvowelled lām are always pronounced with manifestation except in two cases— when followed by another lām or the letter rā. In addition, though not mentioned here, the lām of the particle (or instance, *hal* and *bal*) also follows the verbal lām in that it is not assimilated, except if followed by the letter rā or another lām.

[51] In other words, they are identical letters (e.g. two meems, two lāms, etc.).

Mutajānisayn;[52] And if its status be unvowelled
of the first letter in each case, then *Lesser* is the title.

أَو حُرِّكَ الحَرْفَانِ فِي كُلٍّ فَقُلْ
كُلٌّ كَبِيرٌ وَ افهَمَنْهُ بِالمُثُلْ

And if both the letters are vowelled in all the situations,
then term it the *Greater*, and learn this with illustrations. [53]

أَقسامُ المَدِّ

The Types of Madd

وَ المَدُّ أَصْلِيٌّ وَ فَرْعِيٌّ لَهُ
وَ سَمِّ أَوَّلاً طَبِيعِيًّا وَ هُو

Madd[54] exists in two types, Natural and Derived,
so name the first Natural and it is comprised

مَا لاَ تَوَقُّفٌ لَهُ عَلَى سَبَبْ
وَ لاَ بِدُونِهِ الحُرُوفُ تُجتَلَبْ

Of that madd which on a cause does not rely, [55]

---

[52] It should be noted that there are considerable differences among scholars and Tajweed books as to which letters are considered Mutaqāribayn or Mutajānisayn. This is because these categories differ only in the degree of closeness of two letters, which is a matter that is somewhat subjective and hence inevitably lends itself to result in some differences. Nevertheless, the principles are sound and highly useful.

[53] This entire section is highly technical in nature and explained in detail in chapter seven. In general it deals with the rules governing the assimilation (idghām) of two adjacent letters. These rules are built upon two foundations— the vowel configurations of the two adjacent letters as well as the nearness of the two letters with respect to their properties.

[54] Madd is a type of vowel elongation, of varying durations, that occurs in the case of certain letters and vowels. The rules of madd are built upon the madd letters, which are: the unvowelled alif preceded by the vowel fatḥah, the unvowelled wāw preceded by the vowel dhammah and the unvowelled yā preceded by the vowel kasrah.

[55] The rules of madd are built upon the madd letters and further affected by the presence of certain additional elements, known as “causes” (*sabab,* plural

and nor can its letters without it [56] be realized. [57]

بَلْ أَيُّ حَرْفٍ غَيرُ هَمزٍ أَو سُكُونْ
جَا بَعْدَ مَدٍّ فَالطَّبِيعِيُّ يَكُونْ

So if any letter, barring hamzah, or sukūn at hand
follows the madd, then arises the Natural brand. [58]

وَ الآخَرُ الفَرْعِيُّ مَوقُوفٌ عَلَى
سَبَبْ كَهَمْزٍ أَو سُكُونٍ مُسْجَلاَ

Second is the Derived madd which rests on top
of a cause—either on the hamzah or the stop.

حُـرُوفُـهُ ثَـلاَثَـةٌ فَعِيـهَـا
مِنْ لَفْظِ وَايٍ وَهْيَ فِي نُوْحِيْهَا

The madd has three letters, so know them as explained,
in the mnemonic *waī* and in the word *nūḥīhā* contained.

وَ الكَسْرُ قَبْلَ اليَا وَ قَبْلَ الوَاوِ ضَمْ
شَرْطٌ وَ فَتْحٌ قَبْلَ أَلْفٍ يُلْتَزَم

And kasrah before the letter yā, [59] and wāw with dhammah preceding,
Is surely a condition, whereas the fatḥah before the alif is binding. [60]

وَ اللِّينُ مِنْـهَا اليَا وَ وَاوٌ سُكِّنَا
إِنِ انْفِتَاحٌ قَبْلَ كُلٍّ أُعلِنَا

---

asbāb) of madd following these madd letters (or preceding them in the case of hamzah in some situations). There are two causes of madd—the hamzah letter or sukūn (the stop).

[56] Referring to the madd or lengthening.

[57] What the author means here is that this madd elongation is a necessary part of these madd letters, for without this elongation the letters become something else and the meanings of the words they are used in change.

[58] Therefore the Natural Madd is the default madd, elongated to a duration of two standard units (ḥarakahs), associated with the three madd letters, in the absence of any additonal cause (hamzah or sukūn).

[59] Sākin.

[60] Here the author is elucidating, at the end of the section, what the three madd letters are. If this is understood prior to the beginning of this section, however, then the section becomes more comprehensible for the layman.

And from these the Līn letters: wāw and yā unvowelled,
when preceded by the fatḥah, as we should rightly herald. [61]

أَحكَامُ المَدِّ

The Rules of Madd

لِلْمَدِّ أَحْكَامٌ ثَلاثَةٌ تَدُومْ
وَهْيَ الوُجُوبُ وَ الجَوَازُ وَ اللُّزُومْ

For the derived madd are three rules enduring, [62]
and they are compulsion, permission and binding.

فَوَاجِبٌ إِنْ جَآءَ هَمْزٌ بَعْدَ مَدْ
فِي كِلْمَةٍ وَ ذَا بِمُتَّصِلْ يُعَدْ

Compulsory is when hamzah after a letter of madd does follow,
in a single word, and this is known as Attached Madd also. [63]

وَ جَائِزٌ مَدٌّ وَ قَصْرٌ إِنْ فُصِلْ
كُلٌّ بِكِلْمَةٍ وَ هٰذَا المُنْفَصِلْ

Permissible is when stretching and shortening are both acceptable,
when they are in separate words, [64] and this is Madd Munfaṣil. [65]

وَ مِثْلُ ذَا إِنْ عَرَضَ السُّكُونُ
وَقْفًا كَتَعْلَمُونَ نَسْتَعِينُ

And likewise is the case where the sukūn is created,

[61] The madd līn letters are a modified form of the the madd letters and produce the *–aw* and *–ay* sounds.

[62] This section now deals with the exact types and durations of lengthening of the various forms of derived madd.

[63] Therefore, when hamzah follows a madd letter within a word, its madd elongation becomes compulsory (*wājib*), to an prolonged duration of four time units (ḥarakahs).

[64] i.e. hamzah after a letter of madd.

[65] Therefore, when hamzah follows a madd letter in a separate word, its madd is optional, or permissible. In other words, it may be kept to its default of two durations or lengthened to four or five durations.

from stopping,[66] in the words *ta'lamūn* and *nasta'īn* illustrated.[67]

أَو قُدِّمَ الهَمْزُ عَلَى المَدِّ وَ ذَا
بَدَلْ كَآمَنُوا وَ إِيمَانًا خُذَا

But in those cases the hamzah precedes the madd letter,
arises the Madd Badal, in *āmanū* and *īmānā* illustrated.[68]

وَ لَازِمٌ إِنِ السُّكُونُ أُصِّلَا
وَصْلًا وَ وَقْفًا بَعْدَ مَدٍّ طُوِّلَا

And Lāzim occurs when real is the stop,
after the madd, in flow and stop, and in length there can be no drop.[69]

أَقسَامُ المَدِّ اللَّازِم

The Types of Binding Madd

أَقْسَامُ لَازِمٍ لَدَيْهِمْ أَرْبَعَهْ
وَ تِلْكَ كِلْمِيٌّ وَ حَرْفِيٌّ مَعَهْ

---

[66] In other words, when one stops on a word in recitation, its ending vowel is usually dropped, thereby creating an effective, or presented, sukūn.

[67] Here the author is describing another type of permissible madd, which is the madd letter followed by a presented sukūn (one caused by a stop on the word), as in the words *ta'lamūna* and *nasta'īnu* which become *ta'lamūn* and *nasta'īn,* with the ending vowels dropped due to stopping on them. These are cases of permissible madd, which means that both shortening (at least two durations) and lengthening are allowed. This is known as *Madd 'Āriḍ li'l-Sukūn.*

[68] Here the author is mentioning the third type of permissible madd— Madd Badal, where hamzah precedes the madd letter. In this case, both shortening and lengthening are allowed. It must be noted, however, that even these cases of permissible madd are subject to further rules of recitation according to the modes of reading and are not arbitrary decisions. The Madd Badal, for instance, is recited with two durations only (like the Natural Madd) in the dominant rendition of Ḥafṣ and is only allowed to be lengthened in some other modes of readings, such as Warsh.

[69] The final type of madd is the Binding (Lāzim) Madd, in which a real (not presented) sukūn occurs after the madd letter. This is lengthened to the maximum duration— six ḥarakahs.

The types of Binding Madd among them [70] are four exactly,
and they are either the Kalimī [71] or Ḥarfī [72] variety.

كِلاَهُمَا مُخَفَّفٌ مُثَقَّلُ

فَهٰذِهِ أَرْبَعَةٌ تُفَصَّلُ

And each of these into the Light or Heavy division,
a total of four, with this subsequent exposition.

فَإِنْ بِكِلْمَةٍ سُكُونٌ اجْتَمَعْ

مَعْ حَرْفِ مَدٍّ فَهْوَ كِلْمِيٌّ وَ قَعْ

If a word embraces sukūn in combination,
with a madd, it carries the Kalimī designation.

أَوْ فِيْ ثُلاَثِيِّ الحُرُوْفِ وُجِدَا

وَ الْمَدُّ وَسْطُهُ فَحَرْفِيٌّ بَدَا

And if in three disjointed letters both arise,
with madd at the center, then the Ḥarfī term applies.

كِلاَهُمَا مُثَقَّلٌ إِنْ أُدْغِمَا

مُخَفَّفٌ كُلٌّ إِذَا لَمْ يُدْغَمَا

Both of these [73] are heavy in the case of merging, [74]
and conversely light when there is no merging.

وَ اللاَّزِمُ الحَرْفِيُّ أَوَّلَ السُّوَرْ

وُجُوْدُهُ وَ فِيْ ثَمَانٍ انْحَصَرْ

The Binding Ḥarfī Madd in the start of the chapters
is found, and encompassed in eight distinct letters,

---

[70] The scholars of Tajweed.

[71] If these occur within words, they are termed *Kalimī* (literally, "related to words").

[72] If these occur within the disjointed letters that open certain Qur'ānic chapters, they are term *Ḥarfī* (literally, "related to letters").

[73] Both types of madd: Kalimī and Ḥarfi.

[74] i.e. after the madd letter. In other words, if the unvowelled letter following the madd merges into the next letter (by virtue of it being the same letter), becoming doubled (*mushaddad*) as a result, then the Madd is considered heavy; otherwise it is light. It should be noted that this division is merely theoretical and does not affect the duration of the madd, which remains at six ḥarakahs, nor any other aspect of articulation.

يَجْمَعُهَا حُرُوْفُ كَمْ عَسَلْ نَقَصْ

وَعَيْنُ ذُوْ وَجْهَيْنِ وَالطُّوْلُ أَخَصْ

Contained within the *Kam 'Aṣal Naqaṣ* [75] expression;
and while 'ayn has two ways, [76] preferred is prolongation.

وَ مَا سِوَى الحَرْفِ الثُّلَاثِيْ لَا أَلِفْ

فَمَدُّهُ مَدًّا طَبِيْعِيًّا أُلِفْ

And those apart from the trilateral, alif excluding,
for their madd, the natural type is more deserving. [77]

وَ ذَاكَ أَيْضًا فِيْ فَوَاتِحِ السُّوَرْ

فِيْ لَفْظِ حَيٍّ طَاهِرٍ قَدِ انْحَصَرْ

And these are also found in the openings of the chapters,
and in the expression *ḥayyun tāhirun* [78] captured.

وَ يَجْمَعُ الفَوَاتِحَ الأَرْبَعْ عَشَرْ

صِلْهُ سُحَيْرًا مَنْ قَطَعْكَ ذَا اشْتَهَرْ

And the fourteen of the chapter openings do array,
in what they say: *Restore the bonds without delay, of the kin that cut the way.* [79]

[75] Literally "How little was the honey."

[76] Shortening and lengthening.

[77] Those letters whose names consist of two letters, one of them a madd letter, are articulated with the natural two durations. Alif is excluded though it appears among the disjointed letters for the simple reason that its name does not include any madd letter.

[78] This expression of two words captures the disjointed letters that are articulated with a natural madd of two durations: [ح ي ط ه ر].

[79] Literally: "Meet in the early morning the one who severed relations with you." This expression captures all fourteen disjointed letters that appear throughout the Qur'ān in its chapter openings.

خَاتِمَةُ الْكِتَابِ

Conclusion

وَ تَمَّ ذَا النَّظْمُ بِحَمْدِ اللهِ

عَلَى تَمَامِهِ بِلاَ تَنَاهِي

This ode comes now to its conclusion,
with profuse thanks to Allah for its completion.

أَبْيَاتُهُ نَدٌّ بَدَا لِذِيْ النُّهَى

تَارِيخُهَا بُشْرَى لِمَنْ يُتْقِنُهَا

Its verses are *fragrant for those who possess ingenuity,* [80]
and its date ... *a salutation for those who commit it to memory.* [81]

ثُمَّ الصَّلاَةُ وَ السَّلاَمُ أَبَدَا

عَلَى خِتَامِ الأَنبِيَاءِ أَحْمَدَا

And eternal may His salutations be,
upon Aḥmad, the Seal of the Prophecy.

وَالآلِ وَ الصَّحْبِ وَ كُلِّ تَابِعِ

وَ كُلِّ قَارِئٍ وَ كُلِّ سَامِعِ

And his kin, Companions and every follower
And upon every reciter and every listener.

[80] Here the author is referring to a particular system commonly used in classical Islamic literature, of assigning numerical values to each letter of the alphabet called *Ḥisāb al-Jumal*. Thus the Arabic phrase from our text نَدٌّ بَدَا , according to this system, equals 61 (nūn=50, dāl=4, bā=2, dāl=4, alif=1), and refers to the total of 61 verses. [Refer to the addendum on the following page for details.]

[81] Again, according to this system, the Arabic text بُشرَى لِمَن يُتقِنُهَا refers to the year 1198 of the Hijri calendar (bā=2, sheen=300, rā=200, yā=10, lām=30, meem=40, nūn=50, yā=10, tā=400, qāf=100, nūn=50, hā=5, alif=1; a total of 1198), the year this work was completed.

Addendum: Ḥisāb al-Jumal

حِسَاب الجُمَل

The system of *Ḥisāb al-Jumal* is a commonly used scheme of assigning numerical values to letters of the Arabic alphabet in order to allow them to encode information such as dates and numbers in traditional Islamic texts. It relies upon taking the Arabic alphabet in the following order:

أبجد هوز حطي كلمن سعفص قرشت ثخذ ضظغ

and assigning the following numerical values to them:

الألف	الباء	الجيم	الدال	الهاء
1	2	3	4	5
الواو	الزاي	الحاء	الطاء	الياء
6	7	8	9	10
الكاف	اللام	الميم	النون	السين
20	30	40	50	60
العين	الفاء	الصاد	القاف	الراء
70	80	90	100	200
الشين	التاء	الثاء	الخاء	الذال
300	400	500	600	700
	الضاد	الظاء	الغين	الضاد
	800	900	1000	800

Figure 5 — NUMERICAL SYSTEM OF ḤISĀB AL-JUMAL

Chapter ONE: THE RULES OF NŪN AND NUNNATION

أَحكَامُ النُّونِ السَّاكِنَةِ وَ التَّنوِينِ

IN THIS CHAPTER

What is Nūn Sākinah?
What is Tanwīn?
Why do we start with the letter nūn?
What is ghunnah?
The four rules of Nūn Sākin and Tanwīn

Much of the beauty and charm of Qur'ānic recitation is related to the distinct nasalized sounds associated with certain letters. These are referred to in Tajweed terminology as *ghunnah*. Indeed, it is these vocalizations that set the recitation of the Qur'ān apart from the normal articulation of everyday speech and ordinary prose. Much like humming, the ghunnah is the nasalization that is intrinsically a part of the letters meem (م) and nūn (ن) and occurs in an expanded form in certain situations, to be learned later. It is for this reason that a study of Tajweed generally begins, as in the case of the *Tuḥfah,* with rules related to the letters nūn and meem, similar to the English letters *n* and *m*.

DEFINITIONS

Sukūn/Sākin

In the Arabic language, as in most languages, all letters are necessarily either vowelled (*mutaḥarrik*) or unvowelled (*sākin*). Basically, this means that you must articulate each letter with a vowel or a stop. There are no other possibilities.

For instance, the following are three examples of the letter nūn vowelled with the three possible vowels:

نَ ***sounds like:*** *na*

نُ ***sounds like:*** *nu*

نِ ***sounds like:*** *ni*

The following is an example of the unvowelled nūn:

إِنْ

in

When a letter is designated to be unvowelled, you must stop on it in articulation. This stop or pause is referred to as *sukūn*, and the letter being stopped upon is given the description *sākin (*or more precisely, *sākinah,* the feminine form). Hence an unvowelled nūn would be referred to as Nūn Sākinah, while the unvowelled meem would be Meem Sākinah, the unvowelled rā, Rā Sākinah, etc.

There are a number of common conventions to identify the sukūn on a letter, including a circle-like symbol that sometimes appears over a letter [ـْ] or a semi-circle-like symbol [ْ]. Often, even the absence of any symbol or vowel on a letter indicates the unvowelled state. It should be noted that these conventions are not absolute or unchangeable as they are later additions to the Arabic script to facilitate its reading and may vary across time and regions.

> **GRAMMAR POINT**
>
> The sukūn can occur in any type of Arabic word, from nouns to verbs to prepositions. Incidentally, it can occur in the middle or end of a verb or noun, and at the **end of prepositions/particles.** However, note that according to the phonetics of the Arabic language, it is impossible for an unvowelled letter to begin a word because an unvowelled letter must always be preceded by a vowelled letter.

Nūn Sākinah

The term *Nūn Sākinah* [نون ساكنة] simply refers to the letter nūn when it appears without a vowel.

Tanwīn

The word *tanwīn* literally means "nunnation," or the process of adding a nūn to the end of a word. The Tanwīn is basically a particular vowel construct that occurs at the end of a noun to designate that noun as indefinite. All nouns are either definite [مُعَرَّف] or indefinite [نَكِرَة]. Definite nouns refer to specific things or objects (*the book*) while indefinite nouns refer to generic rather than specific things (*a book*). Consider the following example of the Arabic word for "book" in both the definite and indefinite forms:

Indefinite		Definite	
كِتَابٌ *kitābun*	"a book"	الكِتَابُ *al-kitābu*	"the book"

The Tanwīn can occur with either of the three vowels- *fatḥah, ḍammah* or *kasrah*, and it ends with the phonetic equivalent of a Nūn Sākinah. It is written out as a double vowel, as follows:

	Vowel	Tanwīn	Sounds like
Fatḥah	ـَ	ـً	*–an*
Ḍammah	ـُ	ـٌ	*–un*
Kasrah	ـِ	ـٍ	*–in*

This ending nūn sound in the Tanwīn is only evident during pronunciation and is not written out in the text. Moreover, it is pronounced only in states of continuation. In other words, when you don't stop on the word but continue with its recitation/pronunciation into the next word, the end of the tanwīn sounds like a Nūn Sākinah. But when you stop on a word which ends with Tanwīn (or any vowel), the ending vowels are usually dropped.

Because the Tanwīn is effectively a Nūn Sākinah in pronunciation, it is lumped together with it in Tajweed rules. This chapter, therefore, deals with the rules pertaining to the ending nūn sound of certain words.

Ghunnah

The Ghunnah is the nasal sound that is normally part of the letter nūn and meem. In Tajweed terminology it refers to the prolonged nasal sound that is emitted in certain circumstances based upon certain rules. It is primarily the Ghunnah that lends Qur'ānic recitation its melody and charm. It is akin to the concept of humming, which is usually defined as the emission of *a continuous low droning sound like that of the speech sound (m) when prolonged.*[82]

[82] *The American Heritage® Dictionary of the English Language, Fourth Edition.*

The Ghunnah is traditionally described as having two basic characteristics: its point of articulation [*makhraj*] is in the nasal cavity (which basically means that the ghunnah sound is articulated from the nose); and secondly, its standard duration is two *ḥarakahs*. The *ḥarakah* is the standard unit of time duration and length in Tajweed, and each ḥarakah is the approximate time it takes to extend or flex one finger.

So the Ghunnah (nasalization) in essence is the prolonged nasal tone that is emitted when continually emitting the *n* or *m* sound.

Now we turn to the rules of Nūn Sākinah and Tanwīn, which revolve around one basic issue– how do we pronounce the ending nūn?

The Rules

The exact manner of pronouncing this final nūn in cases of Nūn Sākinah and Tanwīn depends upon the letter following that nūn. Based upon that, there are four basic Tajweed rules governing the Nūn Sākinah and Tanwīn:

1. Manifestation [Iẓhār] إظهار
2. Merging [Idghām] إدغام
3. Conversion [Qalb or Iqlāb] إقلاب
4. Concealment [Ikhfā'] إخفاء

Rule One: MANIFESTATION [IẒHĀR]

The term *iẓhār* is derived from the root word *ẓahara*, which means *to become obvious or apparent.* Therefore, linguistically iẓhār means *to make something clear, obvious or apparent*. In Tajweed rules, it refers to the pronunciation of each letter in its default state—from its normal articulation point and without extended ghunnah or any other departure from its natural, inherent characteristics. There are six letters associated with this rule:

ء ه ع ح غ خ

These six letters are called the guttural (or throat) letters (ḥurūf ḥalqiyyah الحُرُوف الحَلقِية) because their point of articulation (makhraj مَخرَج) is from the deep portion of the throat (ḥalq حَلق).

The rule of Iẓhār essentially means that when the Nūn Sākinah or Tanwīn are followed by any of these six letters, the ending nūn is pronounced clearly and naturally without any additional characteristics.

For instance, consider the following Qur'ānic word:

المُنْخَنِقَةُ

In this case, the fourth letter is an unvowelled nūn (Nūn Sākinah) which is followed by the letter khā (one of these six letters). Hence, the nūn is pronounced normally and the word is articulated as: *munkhaniqah.*

For an example of Tanwīn, consider the following two words:

عِلمًا عَلَىٰ

The first word ends with Tanwīn while the second one immediately begins with the letter 'ayn, which is one these six letters. Therefore, the ending nūn of that Tanwīn is pronounced normally and the two words would be articulated as: *'ilman 'alā.*

PHONETICS

Arabic is a highly acoustic and musical language, and many of its rules of reading and recitation are related to this auditory element.

Linguistic scholars note that the wisdom behind the rule of Iẓhār in these guttural letters is the great physical, anatomical difference in the points of articulation of these letters— arising from deep inside the throat, and the nūn sound— which arises from the tip of the tongue. These guttural letters and the nūn/meem arise from near opposite portions of the oropharynx and thus are difficult to blend or join together, making the natural default articulation of the nūn (Iẓhār) easy on the tongue.

These six letters are further classified according to the exact position of their articulation in the throat into three levels (discussed in more detail in Chapter Five):

1. *The farthest letters* [حروف أقصَى الحَلق] are those that arise from deep inside the throat:

   ء هـ

2. *The middlemost letters* [حروف وَسَطِ الحَلق] arise from higher up in the throat:

   ح ع

3. *The closest letters* [حروف أدنَى الحَلق] are those who articulation is closest to the mouth:

   خ غ

Examples of Iẓhār

Please note the following examples of the rule of Iẓhār for each of these letters:

Within one word		Between two words	
أ	يَنْأَوْنَ	إِنْ أُوتِيتُمْ	جَنَّاتٍ أَلْفَافًا
هـ	أَنْهَارٌ	مِنْهَا	قَوْمٍ هَادٍ
ع	أَنْعَمْتَ	مِنْ عَيْنٍ	سَوَاءٌ عَلَيْهِمْ
ح	وَانْحَرْ	مِنْ حَيْثُ	عَزِيزٌ حَكِيمٌ
غ	فَسَيُنْغِضُونَ	مِنْ غِلٍّ	عَمَلٌ غَيْرُ
خ	الْمُنْخَنِقَةُ	مَنْ خَفَّتْ	لَطِيفٌ خَبِيرٌ

Rule Two: MERGING [IDGHĀM]

Idghām linguistically means to *insert or submerge one thing into another*. In Tajweed terminology it simply refers to the complete joining or assimilation of two letters. More precisely, it is the submersion of a non-vowelled (sākin) letter into a vowelled letter, causing both to be articulated as one single, doubled [*mushaddad*] letter. The letters of Idghām are six and remembered by the mnemonic *yarmulūn*:

ي ر م ل و ن

يَرمُلُون

So based on this rule, if the Nūn Sākinah or Tanwīn is followed by any of these six letters, the rule of Idghām applies: the ending nūn of Nūn Sākinah or Tanwīn is submerged into the following letter, which becomes doubled as a result (*mushaddad*).

There are two subtypes of Idghām:

1. Merging with Nasalization [Idghām with Ghunnah] إدْغام بِغُنَّة
2. Merging without Nasalization [Idghām without Ghunnah] إدْغام بِغَيْر غُنَّة

Idghām with Ghunnah

The first type of Idghām— that with Ghunnah, applies in the following four letters, remembered by the mnemonic *yanmū*:

ي ن م و

يَنمُو

In these cases, the nūn of Nūn Sākinah and Tanwīn is submerged into these subsequent letters, and they are articulated as single letters without the nūn, but with the characteristic of ghunnah (nasalization). This ghunnah is considered a remnant of the nūn which has been assimilated into these letters.

For instance, consider the combination of the following two words:

مَنْ + يَعْمَلْ

In combination, they are pronounced as:

مَــيَّعْمَلْ

The first word ends with Nūn Sākinah and the following letter in the beginning of the second word is yā, which is one of the letters of Idghām with Ghunnah. Hence that nūn is not pronounced as it merges into the subsequent yā, which is pronounced in a doubled way along with ghunnah. In other words, the yā is pronounced with a prolonged nasalization of two durations. This example is found in the following verse of the Qur'ān:

مَــــن يَــــعْمَلْ سُوءًا يُجْزَ بِهِ وَلَا يَجِدْ لَهُ مِن دُونِ اللَّهِ وَلِيًّا وَلَا نَصِيرًا

Whosoever works evil, will have the recompense thereof, and he will not find any protector or helper besides Allah.

[The Qur'ān 4:123]

Consider the following example with the letter wāw:

مِنْ + وَلِيٍّ

becomes pronounced as:

مِـوَّلِيٍّ

Here the Nūn Sākinah is followed by the letter wāw, and so the nūn is merged into the subsequent wāw, and articulated as a doubled wāw with the ghunnah nasalization. It appears in the Qur'ān in the following verse:

وَمَــــن يُــــضْلِلِ اللَّهُ فَمَا لَهُ مِن وَلِيٍّ مِّن بَعْدِهِ

For any whom Allah leaves astray, there is no protector thereafter.

[The Qur'ān 42:44]

The following are examples for the letters nūn and meem respectively:

مِنْ + نَفْسٍ

becomes pronounced as:

مِنَّفْسٍ

وَهُوَ الَّذِي أَنشَأَكُم مِّن نَّفْسٍ وَاحِدَةٍ فَمُسْتَقَرٌّ وَمُسْتَوْدَعٌ

It is He Who has produced you from a single person, and here is a place of sojourn (birth) and a place of departure (death).

[The Qur'ān 6:98]

مِنْ + مَاءٍ

becomes pronounced as:

مِمَّاءٍ

خُلِقَ مِن مَّاءٍ دَافِقٍ

He has been created out of a seminal fluid.

[The Qur'ān 86:6]

The following are examples of Idghām with Ghunnah involving Tanwīn:

Letter	Pronounced as:	Example:
ي	وَيلُيَّوْمَ	وَيْلٌ يَوْمَئِذٍ لِّلْمُكَذِّبِينَ *Woe, that Day, to those that deny!* [The Qur'ān 83:10]
ن	رِجَالَنُّوحِي	وَمَا أَرْسَلْنَا قَبْلَكَ إِلَّا رِجَالًا نُّوحِي إِلَيْهِمْ ۖ فَاسْأَلُوا أَهْلَ الذِّكْرِ إِن كُنتُمْ لَا تَعْلَمُونَ *And We sent not before you but men to whom We sent revelation. So ask the people of the Reminder if you do not know.* [The Qur'ān 21:7 and 16:43]

م	رَسُولُمِّنَ اللهِ	رَسُولٌ مِّنَ اللَّهِ يَتْلُو صُحُفًا مُّطَهَّرَةً *A Messenger from Allah reciting purified pages.* [The Qur'ān 98:2]
و	مَالُوَّ لا	يَوْمَ لَا يَنفَعُ مَالٌ وَلَا بَنُونَ *The Day neither wealth nor progeny will avail [you].* [The Qur'ān 26:88]

Idghām without Ghunnah

The second type of Idghām occurs without the characteristic of ghunnah in the case of the letters lām and rā'.

For instance, consider the following two words:

مِنْ + رَبِّهِمْ

becomes pronounced as:

مِرَّبِهِمْ

This appears in the following verse:

أُولَٰئِكَ عَلَىٰ هُدًى مِّن رَّبِّهِمْ

They are on true guidance from their Lord.

[The Qur'ān 2:5]

The following is an example with the tanwīn followed by the letter lām:

رِجَالٌ + لَا

becomes pronounced as:

رِجَالُلَّا

رِجَالٌ لَّا تُلْهِيهِمْ تِجَارَةٌ وَلَا بَيْعٌ عَن ذِكْرِ اللَّهِ

They are men who do not let business nor trade distract them from the remembrance of Allāh.

[The Qur'ān 24:37]

In these cases, the nūn is completely assimilated into the subsequent letters, and there is no ghunnah nasalization. Also, do not forget to pronounce the letter in the emphatic, double way (*mushaddad*).

Complete versus Deficient Merging

The ghunnah is a natural, intrinsic characteristic of the letters nūn and meem. In case of the letters wāw and yā, the idghām occurs with ghunnah. Since ghunnah is not a feature of these letters, it represents a retention of the ghunnah of the preceding nūn. In these cases, although the nūn has been assimilated into the following wāw or yā', it has been not been done completely, since its ghunnah is still retained. Therefore, the Idghām is termed incomplete (*Idghām Nāqis*).

For the rest of the letters, since the nūn is completely submerged into them and even loses the ghunnah trait, the Idghām in these cases is termed complete (*Idghām Kāmil*).

Note that for the letters meem and nūn, the ghunnah does exist in the case of idghām, but most scholars consider this ghunnah to be from the natural characteristics of these letters (meem and nūn) themselves and not from the preceding nūn of the Nūn Sākinah or Tanwīn. Hence it is considered complete merging. However, in the final analysis, the difference is more of semantics than of practical value. If the nasalization is considered to be from the previous Nūn Sākinah or Tanwīn the merging would be considered incomplete, while if it is considered to be from the letters nūn or meem which are being assimilated into, the merging would be considered complete. The important point is that there is ghunnah in these cases.

Exceptions

Note that there are two exceptions to this rule of Idghām in the Qur'an. In both these cases, the nūn is pronounced manifestly (*Iẓhār*) and not assimilated into the following letter.

The first case is based upon the principle, as noted in the text of the *Tuḥfah*, that the rule of Idghām can only take place between two separate words and not within one single word. In other words, if these letter combinations (the Nūn Sākinah or Tanwīn followed by a letter of Idghām) occur within one word, then there is no merging of the letter nūn but it is pronounced in its normal state (i.e. with Iẓhār). There are only four Qur'ānic examples of such words:

دُنيَا

صِنوَانٌ

قِنوَانٌ

بُنيَانٌ

The second case involves the beginning of the following two chapters of the Qur'ān:

يس وَالْقُرْآنِ الْحَكِيمِ

Yā Sīn. By the wise Qur'ān.
[The Qur'ān, Sūrah Yāsīn 36:1-2]

ن ۚ وَالْقَلَمِ وَمَا يَسْطُرُونَ

Nūn. By the pen and that which they write . . .
[The Qur'ān, Sūrah al-Qalam 68:1]

These chapters begin with the disjointed letters, which are articulated in the Qur'ān with the names of the letters. In both of these examples, the ending of the opening letters of the chapter is effectively a Nūn Sākinah in pronunciation (*Yā Sīn* and *Nūn*) while the following word begins with a letter of Idghām. However, although these examples fulfill all of the criteria of this rule and involves two separate words, there is no Idghām in these cases according to the rendition of Ḥafṣ, the predominant mode of recitation prevalent in the world today.[83] Why is this the case? This is simply the way it has been transmitted to us, and since Tajweed is a transmitted science we observe its conventions as meticulously as possible.

And so, in both of these cases, the ruling is Iẓhār (manifest articulation of the nūn).

[83] There are other modes of reading such as the Reading of Shu'bah in which there is assimilation rather than manifestation in these verses. Moreover, there is a transmission of the Ḥafṣ reading as well that involves assimilation rather than manifestation in these same verses. But since it is transmitted as manifestation by the majority of reciters, we present it as such.

NOTE

This *Iẓhār* articulation in these disjointed letters is further termed Iẓhār Muṭlaq (meaning *absolute manifestation*) in some works. It is qualified with the term Muṭlaq simply to distinguish this case from the previous cases of Iẓhār involving the guttural letters (also called Iẓhār Ḥalqī).

Rule Three: CONVERSION [IQLĀB]

Iqlāb, also referred to as Qalb, literally means conversion or transformation. In Tajweed terminology it refers to the conversion of the letter nūn to meem when the Nūn Sākinah or Tanwīn is followed by the letter bā'. This can occur within one word or in separate words. This conversion has two necessary characteristics: nasalization (ghunnah) and a suppressed pronunciation of the meem (known as *ikhfā'*).

PHONETICS

The wisdom behind this rule is the fact that the makhraj (point of articulation) of meem lies between that of the nūn and the bā'. Therefore, when the nūn (articulated by the tip of the tongue with the mouth open) is followed by the bā' (articulated with the lips closed), the natural sound that comes out in this combination is extremely close to the meem letter (articulated with lips closed and the nasal sound).

For the rule of Iqlāb, when the Nūn Sākinah or Tanwīn is followed by bā', three steps must be taken:

1. The nūn is converted to meem.
2. The meem is pronounced with a slightly suppressed pronunciation (Ikhfā').
3. The nasalized sound (ghunnah) is articulated, along with its necessary duration of two ḥarakahs.

The meem of Iqlāb must not be pronounced overtly but with a slight suppression to distinguish this from the overt letter meem. According to some scholars of Tajweed, the way to do this is to leave a slight opening in one's lips when articulating this meem, unlike the normal articulation of the meem which is done with completely closed lips.

For instance, consider the combination of the following two words:

Pronounced as:		
مِمْبَعْدِ	←	مِنْ + بَعْدِ
mimba'di		*min ba'di*

They occur in the following verse among others:

فَمَن تَابَ مِــــن بَــــعدِ ظُلْمِهِ وَأَصْلَحَ فَإِنَّ اللَّهَ يَتُوبُ عَلَيْهِ ۗ إِنَّ اللَّهَ غَفُورٌ رَّحِيمٌ

And whoever repents after his crime and does righteous deeds, then Allah will pardon him. Verily Allah is Oft-Forgiving, Oft-Merciful.

[The Qur'ān 5:39]

Examples

Here are additional examples of the Iqlāb rule:

عَوَانٌۢ بَــــينَ

عَلِيـــــمٌۢ بِـــــالظَّالِمِينَ

فَـــانۢبَــــــجَسَتْ

فَــــانۢبِـــــذْ

ذَنۢبِــــــهِم

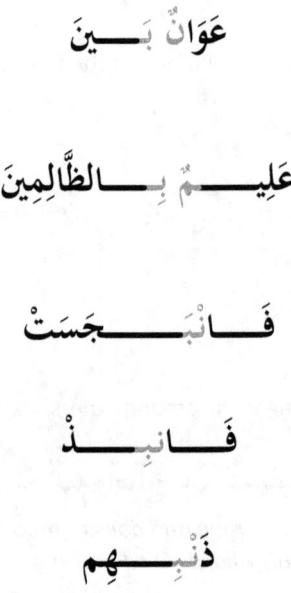

Rule Four: CONCEALMENT [IKHFĀ']

Ikhfā' literally means *to hide something* and in Tajweed terminology refers to the articulation of the ending nūn of the Nūn Sākinah or Tanwīn with a special quality between that of overt manifestation (Iẓhār) and complete assimilation (Idghām). This articulation is to be done without stress (*shaddah*) and with the attribute of ghunnah nasalization. This rule occurs in the case of fifteen letters, which are the remaining letters of the Arabic alphabet apart from the six letters of Iẓhār, the six letters of Idghām and the one letter of Iqlāb. These letters are:

ص ذ ث ك ج ش ق س د ط ز
ف ت ض ظ

These letters are easily remembered by recalling the couplet in the Tuḥfah text, in which the first letter of each word is one of these letters, in this same sequence:

صِفْ ذَا ثَنَا كَمْ جَادَ شَخْصٌ قَدْ سَمَا
دُمْ طَيِّبًا زِدْ فِي تُقًى ضَعْ ظَالِمَا

Relate of the praiseworthy one, how excellent is he who achieves status robust;
Be ever perpetual in virtue, cultivate piety, and fend off the one who is unjust.

> **PHONETICS**
>
> Scholars state that the reason for this rule is the fact that the makhraj (articulation point) of these fifteen letters is not close enough to nūn to merit assimilation (Idghām) nor far enough to merit manifest pronunciation (Iẓhār). Therefore, the pronunciation of the nūn is done in an intermediate manner.

This rule has four basic components:

1. The articulation of nūn with a suppressed, slightly hidden pronunciation between overt manifestation and complete assimilation

2. The lack of emphasis or stress (shaddah) on the nūn

3. The attribute of ghunnah

4. Association with the letter following it in makhraj and attribute

In this rule, the nūn is articulated separately from the subsequent letter, but with a slightly altered articulation. This is done essentially as a nasalized sound (ghunnah) without overtly articulating the nūn. It is done without allowing the tip of the tongue to completely touch the base of the top incisors, for if the tongue were to touch them, a full nūn would be articulated. In addition, the nūn of Ikhfā' is generally understood to be associated with the letter following it and its articulation must reflect that, in both makhraj and attribute. Therefore, if the following letter is a heavy letter, for instance, this Ikhfā' must be pronounced with heaviness as well. If that subsequent letter is light, the Ikhfā' is light as well.

To summarize, the nūn of Ikhfā' is essentially articulated as a ghunnah sound (with its necessary duration of two ḥarakahs), without overt pronunciation, and with the general attributes of the following letter. However, it still remains distinct from that following letter. So this nūn would be articulated from the nasal cavity, and then, the subsequent letter from the mouth in the normal fashion.

CAUTION IN IKHFĀ

In addition, caution must be observed with respect to the vowel of the letter preceding the Ikhfā'. That vowel must not be extended more than one duration (ḥarakah) so as not to alter the meaning of the word. For instance, consider the word *kuntum:*

كُنْتُمْ

This word should be pronounced with extension of the ghunnah of the nūn to two durations (as in *kunnntum*), but care must be observed not to extend the ḍammah vowel of the kāf preceding the nūn (which would make *kuuuntum*), a mistake that can easily slip on the tongue.

Examples

Consider the following examples of Ikfhā' from the Noble Qur'ān:

مِّنَ الْمُؤْمِنِينَ رِجَـــالٌ صَـــدَقُوا مَا عَاهَدُوا اللَّهَ عَلَيْهِ

Among the Believers are men who have been true to their covenant with Allah.

[The Qur'ān 33:23]

مَـــن ذَا الَّذِي يَشْفَعُ عِـــندَهُ إِلَّا بِإِذْنِهِ

Who is there that can intercede in His presence without His permission?

[The Qur'ān 2:255]

خَلَقَ الْإِنسَـــانَ

He created the human being.

[The Qur'ān 55:3]

مِـــن شَـــرِّ الْوَسْوَاسِ الْخَنَّاسِ

From the evils of the whispering of the devil.

[The Qur'ān 114:4]

سَيَصْلَىٰ نَارًا ذَاتَ لَهَبٍ

He will be plunged in flaming fire.

[The Qur'ān 111:3]

وَلَا أَنتُـــمْ عَابِدُونَ مَا أَعْبُدُ

And you do not worship what I worship.

[The Qur'ān 109:3]

الَّذِينَ هُمْ عَـــن صَـــلَاتِهِمْ سَاهُونَ

Those who are negligent about their prayers.

[The Qur'ān 107:5]

الَّذِي أَطْعَمَهُم مِّـــن جُـــوعٍ وَآمَنَهُم مِّنْ خَوْفٍ

The one who has fed them against hunger and made them safe from fear.

[The Qur'ān 106:4]

Chapter TWO: RULES OF THE DOUBLED NŪN AND MEEM

أَحكَامُ المِيمِ وَ النُّونِ المُشَدَّدَتَينِ

IN THIS CHAPTER

What is the doubled nūn and meem?
What is its rule?

Definitions

The shaddah refers to the doubling of a letter and is denoted by the symbol [ـّ] over the relevant letter. From a basic linguistic perspective, an accented or doubled (known in Arabic as *mushaddad*) letter actually consists of two letters—the first unvowelled (sākin) and the second vowelled, with the first being assimilated into the second and pronounced as a single, doubled letter.

What this rule means is that when the nūn or meem letter is doubled (*mushaddad*), it must be pronounced with two durations, whether one is continuing or stopping on the letter. In other words, the sound of the letter nūn or meem, which includes the nasalization known as ghunnah, must be prolonged to two durations.

A notable example is the word:

إِنَّ

which would be pronounced as *inna,*
with doubled emphasis on the n sound
to sound like *innnnna.*

Examples

إِنَّ اللَّهَ عَلَىٰ كُلِّ شَيْءٍ قَدِيرٌ

Indeed Allah has power over all things.
[The Qur'ān 2:20]

كَانَ النَّاسُ أُمَّةً وَاحِدَةً

Humanity was previously a single nation.
[The Qur'ān 2:213]

Please note that the above verse contains two examples of this rule.

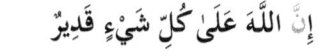

Chapter THREE: RULES OF MEEM SĀKIN

أَحكَامُ المِيمِ السَّاكِنَةِ

IN THIS CHAPTER

What is Meem Sākin?
What are its three rules?
Which of the corresponding rules of Nūn Sākinah is missing from these rules and why?

Definitions

Having covered the bulk of the rules related to the letter nūn in the first chapter and touching on the letter meem in the second chapter, we now turn to the remaining rules pertaining to the other letter of ghunnah: meem. We begin with the rules of the unvowelled meem (*meem sākinah*). They are very similar to the rules of the unvowelled nūn and tanwīn except that, unlike nūn, there are only three rules associated with the unvowelled meem—concealment (Ikhfā), merging (Idghām) and manifestation (Iẓhār). To distinguish these rules from their counterparts from the rules of nūn, they are usually named as follows:

1. Labial Concealment (*Ikhfā' Shafawī*) إخفاء شفوي

2. The Lesser Merging of Two Identical Letters (*Idghām Mithlayn Ṣaghīr*) إدغام مثلين صغير

3. Labial Manifestation (*Iẓhār Shafawī*) إظهار شفوي

Rule One: Labial Concealment [Ikhfā' Shafawī]

This rule is invoked only in the case of one letter: bā (ب). When the letter bā follows the unvowelled meem, the meem is articulated with a suppressed pronunciation (*ikhfā'*) along with nasalization (*ghunnah*). It is termed *labial* because the letters meem and bā are both articulated from the lips. Incidentally, this rule can only occur between two words and not within one word.

Note that this rule is nearly identical to the Rule of Conversion (Iqlāb) from the rules of Nūn Sākinah and Tanwīn, which—as covered previously—is the conversion of the nūn to a meem before the letter bā and its articulation with concealment (ikhfā') and nasalization (ghunnah).

> **PHONETICS**
>
> The wisdom for this rule is the similarity between the letters bā and meem. They are identical in their makhraj and share most of their attributes, and thus the Ikhfā' is the easiest way of articulating the two in combination.

Examples

إِنَّ رَبَّهُـــم بِـــهِمْ يَوْمَئِذٍ لَّخَبِيرٌ

On that day will their Lord be perfectly informed concerning them.

[The Qur'ān 100:11]

وَمِنَ النَّاسِ مَن يَقُولُ آمَنَّا بِاللَّهِ وَبِالْيَوْمِ الْآخِرِ وَمَا هُـــم بِـــمُؤْمِنِينَ

And from the people are those who say 'We believe in Allah and the Last Day' but they do not really believe.

[The Qur'ān 2:8]

تَرْمِيهِـــم بِـــحِجَارَةٍ مِّن سِجِّيلٍ

. . . which pelted them with stones of baked clay.

[The Qur'ān 105:4]

Rule Two: Merging [Idghām Mithlayn Ṣaghīr]

This rule is invoked in the simple case of the unvowelled meem being followed by another meem. In this case, the first meem is assimilated into the second one and they are pronounced in turn as one doubled meem. Remember to pronounce this meem with full ghunnah and its necessary duration of two ḥarakahs.

Incidentally, this only occurs between two words.

Note that this rule is functionally identical to the doubled meem rule from chapter 2. The only real difference is in its origin as an unvowelled meem at the end of one word being assimilated into the initial meem of the following word and articulated as one double meem.

This merging is titled *Idghām Mithlayn Ṣaghīr* (The Lesser Merging of Two Identical Letters) in order to distinguish it from other types of assimilation. The term *Idghām* is due to the assimilation of two meems, and *Mithlayn* due to the fact that it involves two identical letters, and *Ṣaghīr* because the first meem is unvowelled while the second is vowelled (this will be covered in more detail in chapter 8).

Examples

كَــــم مِّـــــن فِئَةٍ قَلِيلَةٍ غَلَبَتْ فِئَةً كَثِيرَةً بِإِذْنِ اللَّهِ

How often, by Allah's will, has a small army vanquished a larger one?
[The Qur'ān 2:249]

الَّذِي أَطْعَمَهُــــــم مِّـــــن جُوعٍ وَآمَنَهُم مِّنْ خَوْفٍ

The one who protected them from hunger and protected them from fear.
[The Qur'ān 106:4]

تَنَزَّلُ الْمَلَائِكَةُ وَالرُّوحُ فِيهَا بِإِذْنِ رَبِّهِــــــم مِّـــــن كُلِّ أَمْرٍ

The angels and the Spirit descend therein, by Allah's will, with all decrees.
[The Qur'ān 97:4]

Rule Three: Labial Manifestation [Iẓhār Shafawī]

The Iẓhār rule occurs with the remaining 26 letters of the Arabic alphabet. In those cases, the meem is pronounced in its normal manner with no alterations. This can occur within one word (there are 8 such letters) or between two words (in the case of the remaining 18 letters).

> **PHONETICS**
>
> The wisdom for this rule is that the makhraj of meem is so different from that of these letters that it does not allow for any alterations from the default articulation of meem, such as assimilation or suppressed pronunciation.

Examples

الحَـــمْدُ لِلَّهِ رَبِّ الْعَالَمِينَ

Praise is due to Allah, the Lord of the worlds.

[The Qur'ān 1:2]

صِرَاطَ الَّذِينَ أَنْعَـــمْتَ عَلَيْهِمْ غَيْرِ الْمَغْضُوبِ عَلَيْهِـــمْ وَلَا الضَّالِّينَ

The path of those whom You favored, not those who incurred Your wrath, nor those who went astray.

[The Qur'ān 1:7]

عَلَّمَ الْإِنسَانَ مَا لَـــمْ يَـــعْلَمْ

He taught man what he did not know.

[The Qur'ān 96:5]

Caution with the Letters Wāw and Fā

A note of caution is in order with respect to the letters wāw [و] and fā [ف]. These are letters that necessitate the rule of Manifestation (Iẓhār) for the letter meem when it precedes them. However, the makhraj (articulation point) of meem is very close to that of the letter fā and identical to that of wāw. Because of this similarity between these three letters, it is somewhat natural for the tongue to blend the unvowelled meem into these letters with either a suppressed articulation as in ikhfā' or like assimilation or merging as in idghām. However, that would be incorrect, so great care must be exerted by the reciter to pronounce the meem in these cases with full manifestation (Iẓhār).

In the verse below, an example of this is the last instance of meem sākin towards the end of the verse, where meem is followed by wāw.

صِرَاطَ الَّذِينَ أَنْعَمْتَ عَلَيْهِمْ غَيْرِ الْمَغْضُوبِ عَلَيْهِـــمْ وَلَا الضَّالِّينَ

The path of those whom You favored, not those who incurred Your wrath, nor those who went astray.

[The Qur'ān 1:7]

Chapter FOUR: RULES OF LĀM

أَحكَامُ اللاَّم

IN THIS CHAPTER

What are the types of lām?

What are the rules pertaining to this letter?

Having covered all the rules associated with the letters nūn and meem, we now turn to the letter lām. Much like nūn and meem, the letter lām is also articulated in varying ways based upon its context.

We specifically examine the rules related to the unvowelled lām (*lām sākinah*), which are two—manifestation (*iẓhār*) and merging (*idghām*).

There are three types of words in the Arabic language: nouns, verbs and particles. In other words, every word in the Arabic language is either a noun [إسمٌ] or a verb [فِعلٌ] or a particle [حَرفٌ]. The unvowelled lām can occur in any of these three types of words:

1. The Lām of the Noun لام الإسم

2. The Lām of the Verb لام الفعل

3. The Lām of the Particle (لام هَلْ و بَلْ) لام الحرف

With respect to nouns, the unvowelled lām most commonly appears in the definite article, which is the *al-* prefix attached to nouns to make them definite. Note that nouns end in tanwīn (a type of double vowel) if they are indefinite or with a single vowel if they are definite. Therefore, nouns can never end with an unvowelled lām, but it can appear in the prefix attached to nouns. This unvowelled lām prefix in nouns is called:

The Lām of the Definite Article لام التعريف or لام ال

This chapter is divided into three sections—we shall first look at the rules pertaining to the lām of the definite article, followed by the rules pertaining to the remaining types of lām, and we end with the rules pertaining to the lām of the Grand Word (*Allah*).

Part One: The Lām of the Definite Article

The definite article in the Arabic language is merely the prefix *al-* (الـ) attached to nouns in order to make them particular or definite. For instance:

كِتَابٌ ⟷ اَلْكِتَابُ

"a book" "the book"

Hamzah al-Waṣl

The definite article is a fundamental feature of the Arabic language and consists of a hamzah al-waṣl followed by an unvowelled lām. The hamzah al-waṣl is unlike a regular hamzah in that it is pronounced with a fatḥah vowel only when beginning with that word, but in continuation it is silent.

For instance, consider the word اَلْحَقُّ (*al-ḥaqq*). It begins with hamzah al-waṣl and so, if this word begins a sentence, this hamzah would be pronounced with the fatḥah vowel, as in the following verse:

الْحَقُّ مِن رَّبِّكَ ۖ فَلَا تَكُونَنَّ مِنَ الْمُمْتَرِينَ

The truth is from your Lord, so be not at all in doubt.
[The Qur'ān 2:147]

pronounced: *al-haqqu mirrabbika . . .*

In the following verse, however, the same word (*al-ḥaqq*) is within the sentence and not beginning it, and therefore its beginning hamzah is not pronounced but takes the vowel of the last letter preceding it—in this case kasrah (thus pronounced as *il-ḥaqqu*) :

وَقُلِ الْحَقُّ مِن رَّبِّكُمْ

Say: "The truth is from your Lord.
[The Qur'ān 18:29]

pronounced: *Wa qulil haqqu mirrabbikum.*

As for the lām, which is our lesson here, there are two possible rules for this unvowelled lām of the definite article: manifestation and assimilation.

Manifestation of Lām [Iẓhār]

In the case of fourteen letters of the alphabet, the lām of the definite article is pronounced with a normal, overt pronunciation. In other words, when the lām of the definite article is followed by any of these fourteen letters, the lām is simply articulated as a normal lām.

These fourteen letters are termed *al-Ḥurūf al-Qamariyyah* (The Moon Letters) and are as follows:

أ ب غ ح ج ك و خ ف ع

ق ي م هـ

They are captured in the mnemonic:

إِبْغِ حِجَّكَ وَ خَفْ عَقِيمَهُ

This rule is also sometimes referred to as *Iẓhār Qamarī* due to its association with the Moon Letters.

PHONETICS

The reason for being called the Moon Letters is the fact that the stars in the skies, in the presence of the moon, retain their visibility (as opposed to the presence of the sun, in which case they disappear). Similarly, these fourteen letters retain their manifest identity in the presence of the lām of the definite article.

Examples

الْحَمْدُ لِلَّهِ رَبِّ الْعَالَمِينَ

pronounced: *Al-ḥamdu lillahi rabbil-'ālamīn.*

Praise is due to Allah, the Lord of the worlds..

[The Qur'ān 1:2]

Note that this verse contains two examples of this rule, in the first and last word.

ذَٰلِكَ الْكِتَابُ لَا رَيْبَ ۛ فِيهِ

pronounced: *Dhālikal-kitābu . . .*

This is the Book, there is no doubt in it.

[The Qur'ān 2:2]

خَلَقَ الْإِنسَانَ مِنْ عَلَقٍ

pronounced: *Khalaqal-insāna . . .*

He created man from a clot.

[The Qur'ān 96:2]

Merging of Lām [Idghām]

On the other hand, when the lām of the definite article precedes the remaining fourteen letters of the alphabet, it is fully assimilated into them. As noted previously, the technical definition of idghām is the merging of one letter into another, and the subsequent articulation of one single doubled letter of the latter type. In other words, the first letter is merged into the second, which is doubled, and the end result is the articulation of the second letter doubled.

These fourteen letters are called *al-Ḥurūf as-Shamsiyyah* (The Sun Letters), and they are:

ط ث ص ر ت ض ذ ن د س

ظ ز ش ل

They are conveniently remembered from the following lines of poetry (or not so conveniently, depending on how much you like the couplet). In this couplet, the first letter of each word is a Sun Letter.

طِب ثُمَّ صِل رُحمًا تَفُز ضِف ذَا نِعَم

دَع سُوءَ ظَنٍّ زُر شَرِيفًا لِلكَرَم

Be meritorious, maintain relations for success, and host those who are beneficent;
Shun ill estimations of others, and frequent the noble ones for munificence.

This rule is also known as *Idghām Shamsī* due to its association with the Sun Letters.

> **PHONETICS**
>
> These letters are named after the shining sun which, with its sheer radiance, absorbs all elements around it, including the stars. Likewise, the Sun Letters fully absorb the lām of the definite article within themselves.

Let us look at the following two verses, from the opening chapter of the Qur'ān:

الْحَمْدُ لِلَّهِ رَبِّ الْعَالَمِينَ

Praise is due to Allah, the Lord of the worlds.

الرَّحْمَٰنِ الرَّحِيمِ

The Most Gracious, the Most Merciful.
[The Qur'ān 1:2-3]

In the first verse above, the lām of the first word is pronounced overtly due to its being followed by a Moon Letter (the ḥā) and is articulated as *al-ḥamdu,* while the lām of the last word is also pronounced overtly due to its being followed another Moon Letter ('ayn). In contrast, the two words in the second verse both begin with a lām that is followed by a Sun Letter (the rā) and therefore, that lām is merged into the subsequent rā, making the articulation as *ar-raḥmān-ir-raḥīm* rather than *al-raḥmān-il-raḥīm.*

NOTE

One quick way to tell the difference in the normal muṣḥaf between Sun and Moon Letters is to look for the shaddah (stress) on the letter following the lām of the definite article. Remember, the shaddah is part of the idghām rule, which is for the Sun Letters. Therefore, whenever you see a shaddah you can assume it is a Sun Letter requiring idghām. In the above verses, note the lack of shaddah over the ḥā of *al-ḥamdu* in the first verse, and the shaddah over the two rā letters in the two words of the second verse.

Part Two: Other Types of Lām

There are four other types of unvowelled lām: the lām of verbs, commands, nouns and particles. The general rule for these types of lām in most cases is normal, overt articulation (iẓhār). The only exception is when the unvowelled lām is at the end of a word and is followed by the letter rā or another lām in the next word, in which case the rule is assimilation (idghām) of the lām into the following letter. The reason for the assimilation of lām into lām is inherently obvious—it is the same letter. The assimilation of lām into rā is because of the fact that both of them are articulated from a similar point within the mouth (see chapter on makhārij) and thus their merging is natural.

Note that the unvowelled lām can occur at the end of verbs, commands and particles but not nouns, since nouns always end with vowels, such as tanwīn.

To summarize, there are only two rules for all of these types of lām:

1. Manifestation (*iẓhār*): In nearly all cases

2. Merging (*idghām*): When the unvowelled lām is followed by lām or rā

Let us look at specific examples, arranged by the various types of lām. From the perspective of Tajweed, it is not necessary to distinguish these types as the rules for all of them are the same. Nevertheless, we are listing the examples according to the types of lām for purposes of arrangement.

The Lām of the Verb لام الفعل

Iẓhār:	Idghām [followed by ل or ر]:
قَالَ أَلَمْ أَقُــــــلْ إِنَّكَ لَن تَسْتَطِيعَ مَعِيَ صَبْرًا *He (Khidr) said: "Did I not tell you, that you would not be able to have patience with me?"* [The Qur'ān 18: 72]	قَالَ أَلَمْ أَقُــــــل لَّــــكَ إِنَّكَ لَن تَسْتَطِيعَ مَعِيَ صَبْرًا *(Khidr) said: "Did I not tell you that you can have no patience with me?"* [The Qur'ān 18: 75]

The Lām of Commands لام الأمر

Iẓhār:	Idghām [followed by ل or ر]:
قُــــلْ هُــــوَ اللَّهُ أَحَدٌ *Say, He Allah is one.* [The Qur'ān 112:1]	وَقُــــل رَّبِّ زِدْنِي عِلْمًا *O my Lord, increase me in knowledge.* [The Qur'ān 20: 114]
قُــــلْ إِنَّ هُدَى اللَّهِ هُوَ الْهُدَىٰ *Say: "The Guidance of Allah, that is the (only) Guidance."* [The Qur'ān 2: 120]	قُــــل لَّــــوْ كَانَ الْبَحْرُ مِدَادًا لِّكَلِمَاتِ رَبِّي لَنَفِدَ الْبَحْرُ قَبْلَ أَن تَنفَدَ كَلِمَاتُ رَبِّي وَلَوْ جِئْنَا بِمِثْلِهِ مَدَدًا *Say: "If the ocean were ink (wherewith to write out) the words of my Lord. Sooner would the ocean be exhausted than would the words of my Lord, even if we added another ocean like it, for its aid."* [The Qur'ān 18:109]

The Lām of the Particle (لام الحرف (لام هَلْ و بَلْ)

There are only two particles that end with lām in the Qur'ān:

بَلْ

هَلْ

Iẓhār:	Idghām [followed by ل or ر]:
بَلْ نَقْذِفُ بِالْحَقِّ عَلَى الْبَاطِلِ فَيَدْمَغُهُ فَإِذَا هُوَ زَاهِقٌ ۚ وَلَكُمُ الْوَيْلُ مِمَّا تَصِفُونَ *Nay, We hurl the Truth against falsehood, and it knocks out its brain, and behold, falsehood doth perish! Ah! woe be to you for the (false) things ye ascribe (to Us).* [The Qur'ān 21:18]	بَل رَّفَعَهُ اللَّهُ إِلَيْهِ ۚ وَكَانَ اللَّهُ عَزِيزًا حَكِيمًا *Nay, Allah raised him (Jesus) up unto Himself; and Allah is Exalted in Power, Wise.* [The Qur'ān 4: 158]
بَلْ كَذَّبُوا بِالسَّاعَةِ ۖ وَأَعْتَدْنَا لِمَن كَذَّبَ بِالسَّاعَةِ سَعِيرًا *Nay, they deny the Hour (of the Judgment to come): but We have prepared a Blazing Fire for such as deny the Hour.* [The Qur'ān 25: 11]	وَقَالُوا قُلُوبُنَا غُلْفٌ ۚ بَل لَّعَنَهُمُ اللَّهُ بِكُفْرِهِمْ فَقَلِيلًا مَّا يُؤْمِنُونَ *Nay, Allah's curse is on them (Israelites) for their blasphemy: little is it they believe.* [The Qur'ān 2: 88]
هَلْ جَزَاءُ الْإِحْسَانِ إِلَّا الْإِحْسَانُ *Is there any reward for good other than good?* [The Qur'ān 55: 60]	فَقُلْ هَل لَّكَ إِلَىٰ أَن تَزَكَّىٰ *And say (O Mūsā) to him (Pharoah): "Would you purify yourself (from the sin of disbelief by becoming a believer)?"* [The Qur'ān 79:18]

Part Three: The Lām of the Grand Word [ALLĀH]

اللّٰه

The word *Allāh* is a unique and special word in the Arabic language that denotes the proper name of God. It has a distinct appearance, and is written with two lām letters along with a shaddah over them. Scholars refer to this word as the Grand Word [*Lafẓ al-Jalālah*] in order to allow for discussing the word more freely in the context of grammar and rules of Tajweed in a manner that is venerable and respectful of Allah.

When the Grand Word is preceded by a fatḥah or ḍammah vowel, it is pronounced in a distinct heavy manner that is unlike any other case of lām. This attribute of heaviness is referred to as *tafkhīm* and will be discussed in detail in the chapter on attributes. This heavy articulation features the elevation of the tongue towards the roof of the mouth in order to force a thick and heavy sound that fills the mouth. This heavy lām is thus articulated with the entire body of the tongue rather than its tip alone. Keep in mind that this must be practically demonstrated by a teacher to be understood fully.

In the following verse, the Grand Word appears twice and is preceded by the vowels ḍammah and fatḥah respectively. As such, its lām is articulated in a heavy manner in both instances:

أُولَٰئِكَ حِزْبُ اللَّهِ ۚ أَلَا إِنَّ حِزْبَ اللَّهِ هُمُ الْمُفْلِحُونَ

They are the Party of Allah, and indeed the Party of Allah will be victorious.

[The Qur'ān 58:22]

On the other hand, when the Grand Word is preceded by the kasrah vowel, it is articulated in a light manner, with the tip of the tongue alone, as in the case of the basmalah:

بِسْمِ اللَّهِ الرَّحْمَٰنِ الرَّحِيمِ

Here the Grand Word is preceded by the vowel kasrah and hence its lām is articulated lightly. Again, bear in mind that these variations in articulation can only be demonstrated verbally and are impossible to describe fully in writing.

Examples

Heavy Lām:

إِذَا جَاءَ نَصْرُ اللَّهِ وَالْفَتْحُ

When Allah's help and victory comes . . .

[The Qur'ān 110:1]

نَارُ اللَّهِ الْمُوقَدَةُ

The fire of Allah kindled.

[The Qur'ān 104:6]

رَسُولٌ مِّنَ اللَّهِ يَتْلُو صُحُفًا مُّطَهَّرَةً

A messenger from Allah reciting purified pages.

[The Qur'ān 98:2]

Light Lām:

الْحَمْدُ لِلَّهِ رَبِّ الْعَالَمِينَ

Praise is due to Allah, the Lord of the worlds..

[The Qur'ān 1:2]

وَرَأَيْتَ النَّاسَ يَدْخُلُونَ فِي دِينِ اللَّهِ أَفْوَاجًا

And see the multitudes of people entering into the religion of Allah.

[The Qur'ān 110:2]

إِنَّمَا نُطْعِمُكُمْ لِوَجْهِ اللَّهِ لَا نُرِيدُ مِنكُمْ جَزَاءً وَلَا شُكُورًا

Verily we feed you for the sake of Allah and seek from you neither reward nor gratitude.

[The Qur'ān 76:9]

Chapter FIVE: THE MAKHĀRIJ (POINTS OF ARTICULATION)

مَخَارِجُ الحُرُوفِ

IN THIS CHAPTER

What is the makhraj (plural makhārij)?

How do you demonstrate a letter's makhraj?

How many makhārij are there?

The topic of makhārij occupies a central place in the study of Tajweed. In fact, it would be no exaggeration to assert that the entire science of Tajweed revolves around one central pivot—the makhārij.

The makhārij refer to the exact physical articulation of each letter of the Arabic alphabet. Now, the Qur'ān itself is entirely constructed from these letters. Therefore, according to many Qur'ānic scholars the disjointed letters that open many chapters of the Qur'ān (such as *alif lām meem*) are essentially a reminder of this fact along with an implied divine challenge to produce something similar to the Qur'ān from these same letters.

It is for this reason among others that many works on Tajweed begin with the makhārij before all other topics. However, since the topic is technical by nature and somewhat difficult, particularly for non-Arabic speakers, we choose to cover it after other more basic topics, much like the author of the *Tuḥfah*.

Linguistically *makhraj* (plural, *makhārij*) is a point of exit, while in the terminology of Tajweed, it refers to the distinct articulation site of each letter. In other words, the makhraj is the exact location within the oro-nasopharynx (the region of the mouth, nose and throat) that produces the distinct sound of each letter.

The technique used to clearly illustrate the makhraj of each letter is to make that letter unvowelled (sākin) and preceded by a vowelled hamzah. Although articulating a letter in any manner illustrates its makhraj, this technique has traditionally been used by teachers because it highlights the makhraj in a clearer way that is more helpful for the purposes of instruction. So, for instance, to illustrate the makhārij of the following letters:

ق ك ل م ن

Write them as follows:

اَقْ اَكْ اَلْ اَمْ اَنْ

The scholars of Arabic have identified precise locations within the oro-nasopharynx that correspond to the makhraj of each letter. Although the exact number of makhārij is subject to some dispute among linguists, the dominant opinion—including that of Ibn al-Jazarī—is that there are a total of seventeen makhārij grouped into five locations, or divisions, of the oro-nasopharynx. Ibn al-Jazarī alludes to that in his work in the following couplet:

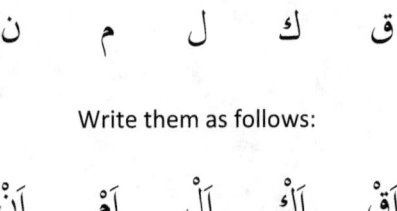

مخارج الحروف سبعة عشر

على الذي يختاره من اختبر

The makhārij of the letters are seventeen in number,
for those who choose it by examination

These locations are as follows:

1. The Oral Cavity (*al-Jawf*): which contains one makhraj

2. The Throat (*al-Ḥalq*): which contains three makhārij

3. The Tongue (*al-Lisān*): which contains ten

4. The Lips (*al-Shafatayn*): which contains two

5. The Nasal Cavity (*al-Khayshūm*): which contains one makhraj.

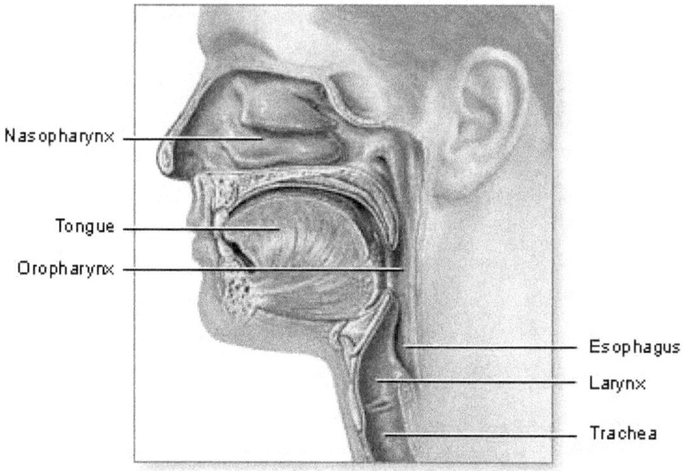

ADAM.

Figure 6 — ANATOMY OF THE OROPHARYNX

Other scholars such as Imām al-Shāṭibī (died 590H) and the grammarian al-Sībawayh (died 180H) have held that there are sixteen makhārij in four locations. In essence, they don't acknowledge the oral cavity (al-Jawf) as a separate makhraj in and of itself. Yet a third opinion held by the noted grammarian al-Farrā' (died 207H) and others is that there are fourteen makhārij dispersed among four locations in the oro-nasopharynx. Like the second group, they also do not acknowledge the oral cavity as a makhraj, but additionally, they differ in the exact makhraj of some of the letters.

1. The Oral Cavity الجوف

This refers to the hollow cavity in the center of the mouth and throat. This location is the makhraj of the madd letters, which are:

1. The unvowelled alif (ا) preceded by the vowel fatḥah, as in:

قَال

2. The unvowelled yā (ي) preceded by the vowel kasrah, as in:

قِيل

3. The unvowelled wāw (و) preceded by the vowel ḍammah, as in:

يَقُول

These are referred to as madd letters because their articulation is slightly prolonged as compared to other letters. The three madd letters are remembered by the mnemonic واي and demonstrated in the word نُوحِيهَا.

2. The Throat الحلق

The throat is the makhraj of the six guttural letters covered previously. They are:

أ ه ع ح غ خ

They are divided into three locations within the throat according to the place of their articulation:

1. **The Farthest Portion of the Throat** أقصى الحلق :

أ ه

By farthest we mean from the opening of the mouth. Note that the vocal cords are used for the letter hamzah (أ) producing a sound while this is not the case for the hā (ه), whereby only breath is emitted.

2. **The Middle of the Throat** وسط الحلق :

ح ع

Note that the vocal cords are used for the letter ‘ayn (ع) producing a sound while this is not the case for the ḥā (ح), whereby only breath is emitted.

3. **The Closest Portion** أدنى الحلق :

خ غ

Note that the vocal cords are used for the letter ghayn (غ) producing a sound while this is not the case for the khā (خ), whereby only breath is emitted.

3. The Tongue اللسان

The tongue is the division of the oro-nasopharynx with the most letters arising from it. It is usually subdivided into:

1. **The Posterior Tongue** أقصى اللسان

The posterior portion (root) of the tongue is further subdivided into two positions, each associated with one letter. The absolute farthest portion of the tongue touches the soft palate (the soft portion of the roof of the mouth in the back) to produce the letter qāf (ق). Slightly anterior to that, a portion of the tongue closer to the front joins the hard palate (the hard portion of the roof of the mouth in the center) to produce the letter kāf (ك). The makhraj of both is essentially the same, except that their position is separated slightly.

2. **The Middle Portion** وسط اللسان

The middle portion of the tongue is involved with three letters: jīm (ج), shīn (ش), and yā (ي). Note that this is the actual letter yā (sometimes referred to as *yā lafdhiyyah*) and not the madd letter yā (*yā maddiyyah*), which is an unvowelled yā preceded by a letter with the vowel kasrah. These letters are also referred to as the al-Ḥurūf al-Shajariyya (الحروف الشجريّة) because they emanate from the base or middle of the tongue much like a tree (in Arabic شجرة).

3. **The Edge** حافة اللسان

The entire edge of the tongue on either side in association with the roof of the mouth is involved in emitting the letter ḍād (ض). This is perhaps the single most difficult letter to pronounce in the Arabic alphabet. It is a letter unique to the Arabic language, and for this reason Arabic is sometimes called *the language of ḍād* (لغة الضاد). This letter is articulated by firmly joining either side of the tongue to the upper molar teeth. It can be done from either the left or the right side of the tongue or from both simultaneously. The use of the left side is easier and hence more common, followed by the use of the right side. The use of both sides of the tongue is extremely difficult and few can articulate the ḍād in this manner. It is reported that Umar b. al-Khaṭṭāb used to articulate it in this manner.[84]

The anterior edge of the tongue is joined to the gums behind the upper teeth to articulate the letter lām (ل).

4. **The Tip** طرف اللسان

The tip of the tongue contains the makhraj for eleven letters.

---

[84] Shaykh Muḥammad Makkī Naṣr al-Jarīsī, *Nihāyah al-Qawl al-Mufīd fī 'Ilm Tajwīd al-Qur'ān al-Majīd.*

The letter nūn (ن) is articulated from the joining of the tip of the tongue to the base of the upper incisors. The letter rā (ر) is emitted from the same makhraj except that the top of the tongue is also used in addition to the tip, and the tongue does not completely touch the mouth.

The letters lām, nūn and rā all utilize the tip of the tongue (also referred to in Arabic as الذلق) to some extent and are referred to collectively as al-Ḥurūf al-Dhalqiyyah (الحروف الذلقية).

The next three letters are articulated from the top portion of the tip of the tongue in conjunction with the base (or root) of the two top incisors:

ط د ت

These are also called al-Ḥurūf al-Niṭ'iyyah (الحروف النطعية). Of these, the ṭā (ط) is a heavier letter and uses a greater portion of the tongue. These will be covered in more detail in Chapter 6 on the characteristics of the letters.

The next three letters (ص س ز) arise from joining of the top portion of the tip of the tongue to the base of the top incisors but not completely, leaving a slight space. These are also called al-Ḥurūf al-Asaliyyah (الحروف الأسلية) due to their association with the tip of the tongue (also referred to as الأسل) and al-Ḥurūf al-Ṣafīr due their characteristic of resembling a whistle, or flow of breath.

The last three letters are articulated from the tip and the top of the tongue joining the bottom edge of the top incisors. The tongue emerges from the mouth slightly beyond the teeth: ث ذ ظ. These are also called al-Ḥurūf al-Lithawiyyah (الحروف اللثوية) or Interdental Letters.

4. The Lips الشّفتين

Bringing the two lips together forms three letters– ب م و , while bringing the lower edge of the upper teeth to the inside of the lower lip articulates one letter— ف .

The letters bā and meem are both articulated with the lips fully closed (the sound of bā comes from the inner wet portion of both lips, while the sound of meem comes from the outer dry portion of both lips), and the only real difference between them is that there is an additional nasalization with the letter meem (ghunnah). The sound of wāw comes from the incomplete joining (and slight protrusion) of both lips.

5. The Nasal Cavity الخيشوم

The nasal cavity is the makhraj of the ghunnah (nasalization), which was covered in a previous chapter. The ghunnah is an intrinsic characteristic of two letters— ن م , and in Tajweed terminology it refers to the prolonged nasal sound that is emitted in certain circumstances based upon rules of Tajweed. As previously mentioned, it is akin to humming, which is usually defined as the emission *of a continuous low droning sound like that of the speech sound (m) when prolonged.*[85]

[85] *The American Heritage® Dictionary of the English Language, Fourth Edition*. Houghton Mifflin Company, 2004. 16 Jan. 2007.

Chapter SIX: THE ṢIFĀT(ATTRIBUTES OF THE LETTERS)

صِفَاةُ الحُرُوفِ

IN THIS CHAPTER

What are the attributes?
How do they differ from the makhārij?
What are the categories of attributes?

This topic of *ṣifah* (plural *ṣifāt*) is closely related to the previous one involving *makhārij*, being a continuation of a study of the individual letters. While the makhārij are the physical locations where each of the letters is articulated, the ṣifāt are additional characteristics and features related to the sounds of the letters. These two topics illustrate the highly precise and scientific nature of the Arabic language, rendering it a suitable choice to be the medium for Divine Revelation.

While there are certain complex definitions offered by scholars of Tajweed for the attributes, they are cumbersome and not entirely necessary for a proper understanding of the topic. The *ṣifāt* are simply the characteristics and attributes related to the articulation of each letter. The benefit of knowing the attributes is that it allows us to distinguish letters from one another—especially those that have similar or the same articulation points (makhārij), assists us in the rules of assimilation (idghām)—which are dependent to some extent on the attributes, and allows us to perfect the articulation of each letter.

The total number of attributes is subject to some difference of opinion among scholars. According to the majority of them, led by Ibn al-Jazarī (died 833H) and followed by nearly all teachers of Tajweed today, there a total of eighteen attributes. Other minority views include the opinion that they are twenty or fifteen, or even greater than forty.

There are two broad categories of attributes:

1. **the Basic Attributes** [الصِّفَات الذَّاتِيَّة]
2. **the Conditional Attributes** [الصِّفَات العَرَضِيَّة]

The Basic Attributes are those basic, intrinsic attributes that are always associated with the letters in all circumstances. They are also referred to as Fundamental Attributes [الصِّفَات الأَصلِيَّة] in some works. For instance, the heavy and elevated way of articulating the letter qāf (known as *isti'lā'*) or the whispered sound of the letter fā (known as *hams*) are both basic attributes. The basic attributes are the subject of this chapter.

The Conditional Attributes, on the other hand, are those incidental, varying characteristics that are associated with the letters in certain situations only and not permanently a part of them. These include attributes such as manifestation (*iẓhār*), merging (*idghām*), conversion (*iqlāb*), etc. They have been covered in previous chapters and will not be dealt with here.

The Basic Attributes are further divided into two types:

1. **the Paired Attributes** [الصِّفَات المُتَضَادَة]
2. **the Unpaired Attributes** [الصِّفَات غَير المُتَضَادَة]

The Paired Attributes

The Paired Attributes are also known as Essential Attributes [الصِّفَات اللَّازِمَة] and refer to eleven paired attributes (five pairs of attributes making a total of ten plus an intermediate attribute within one pair) which every letter must necessarily possess. In other words, each letter of the Arabic alphabet necessarily has one attribute from each pair. These Paired Attributes are as follows:

	Basic Attribute:		*Its Opposite:*	
Pair 1	الهَمْس	**Whispered**	الجَهْر	**Loud**
Pair 2	الشِّدَّة	**Forceful**	الرَّخَاوَة	**Soft**
	Between these two paired characteristics is an intermediate one: التَّوَسُّط Moderate			
Pair 3	الإِستِعلاء	**Elevated**	الإِستِفَال	**Depressed**
Pair 4	الإِطبَاق	**Closed**	الإِنفِتَاح	**Open**
Pair 5	الإِذلاق	**Flowing**	الإِصمَات	**Sharp**

Let us look at these eleven Paired or Essential Attributes in more detail.

1. The Whisper versus Loudness

The first pair of attributes has to do with the quality of exhalation of breath [جَرَيان النَّفس] during articulation.

Whispered letters

For the letters that have the basic attribute of the Whisper [الهمس], exhalation of air continues while articulating them. These letters are:

ف ح ث ه ش خ ص س ك ت

These are remembered by the mnemonic:

فَحَثَّهُ شَخْصٌ سَكَتْ

When you articulate the sounds of these letters, your breath naturally continues to flow while pronouncing them while the voice is largely silent. In fact, it is possible to prolong some of these sounds for as long as you want by continuing to exhale during their articulation.

For instance, for the letter ف : *ffffffffff* . . .

For the letter ش : *shhhhhhhhhhh* . . .
(as in gesturing someone to be silent)

For the letter ح : *hhhhhhhhhh* . . .

For the letter س : *ssssssssss* . . .

Note that in these letters, you are exhaling quite significantly (use of breath) while the voice box (larynx) is not used much. So there is flow of breath [جريان النفس] but not of sound or voice.

Loud letters

The remaining letters of the alphabet apart from the above have the opposite quality of loudness or apparentness, and exhalation of air stops abruptly during their articulation. Take the letter qāf, for instance. During its articulation, the flow of air abruptly stops to articulate its sound, and it is not possible to prolong its sound. Try it: *qqqqqqqqq* . . . It's not possible to prolong its sound.

PHONETICS

The attribute of the Whisper [*al-hams*] is named so since it is considered a weak attribute from a linguistic perspective and is a result of a weakened association of the letters with their articulation points [*makhārij*].

On the other hand, the attribute of Loudness [*al-jahr*] is named such due to the strong and firm association of these letters with their articulation points, which results in a strong and firm articulation, with no loss or exhalation of air.

2. Forcefulness versus Softness

This pair of attributes pertains to the flow of sound or voice [جَرَيَان الصَّوت].

Forceful letters

The quality of Forcefulness [*al-shiddah*] means the letter is articulated quite forcefully from its makhraj, with complete stopping of the flow of sound. There are eight letters with this quality:

أ ج د ق ط ب ك ت

They are recalled by the mnemonic:

أَجِدُ قَطٍّ بَكَتْ

The articulation of these letters is strong, forceful and involves an abrupt halt to the flow of sound. As such, their articulation comes to a stop and cannot be prolonged.

Soft Letters

Opposite to that is the quality of Softness [*al-rakhāwah*] in which the flow of sound continues to some extent, resulting in a less forceful and softer articulation. The letters of Softness are:

أ، ث، ح، خ، ذ، ز، س، ش، ص، ض، ظ، غ، ف، هـ، و، ي

Moderate Letters

Between these two opposites is an intermediate attribute referred to as the quality of Moderation [*al-tawassuṭ*], in which the articulation, and the flow of sound, is neither fully forceful nor fully soft. There are five letters with this attribute:

ل ن ع م ر

And they are remembered by the mnemonic:

لِنْ عُمَرْ

PHONETICS

The attribute of Forcefulness [*al-shiddah*] is due to the very strong association of these letters with their articulation points [*makhārij*] which results in an abrupt halt to the flow of sound during articulation and a forceful articulation.

On the other hand, the attribute of Softness [*al-rakhāwah*] is named such due to a weaker association of these letters with their articulation points, which results in a softer articulation, with some loss or flow of sound.

3. Elevation versus Depression

Elevated letters

The next pair of qualities has to do with the use of the mouth and tongue in an elevated, heavy form of articulation. The attribute of Elevation [*al-Isti'lā'*] is also called Heaviness or Velarization [*al-fakhm* or *al-tafkhīm*] and refers to the elevation of the tongue towards the palate (roof of the mouth) in articulation. This elevation results in focusing pressure of the letter towards the roof of the mouth in a thick and heavy articulation which reverberates the sound of the letter in the mouth. The shape of the mouth in this state of articulation is full, with the lips protruding as if one is about to whistle or blow out air forcefully. The mouth is thus filled with the sound of the letter.

There are seven letters associated with this attribute:

خ ص ض غ ط ق ظ

They are remembered by the mnemonic:

خُصَّ ضَغْطٍ قِظْ

Depressed letters

The rest of the letters apart from these are pronounced in a normal, light manner, with the tongue largely flat in the mouth and the lips apart as if one is about to smile or grin. The sounds of these letters is lighter and does not fill the entire mouth. They are twenty one in number. This attribute is referred to as the attribute of depression [*al-Istifāl*] or lightness [*al-tarqīq* or *al-riqqah*].

Of these twenty one letters, three letters are variable in their characteristic of lightness, depending on circumstances: lām, rā and the three madd letters. This means that the lām and rā letters are articulated either in a heavy or light manner, based upon certain principles. Basically the lām is sometimes articulated in a heavy manner only in the context of the Grand Word (the word *Allah*), as covered previously in Chapter 4. The rules of determining whether the rā is articulated heavy or light is covered in the next chapter. The attributes of heaviness and lightness are also given more attention at the end of this chapter.

4. Closed versus Open

Closed letters

This attribute is associated with the tongue. The attribute of Adhesion or Closedness [*al-Iṭbāq*] refers the compression of the tongue against the palate in producing the sound of four letters:

ص ض ط ظ

The sound of these letters is articulated with a closed, elevated and compressed quality due to the complete adhesion of the tongue to the palate. These letters vary in the level of strength of this attribute, and their order in level of decreasing strength is as follows:

ط

ض

ظ

ص

Open letters

The remaining twenty four letters are pronounced with the tongue loose and not fully attached to the palate, which results in a more open articulation. This attribute is that of Openness [*al-Infitāḥ*].

5. Flowing versus Sharp

Flowing letters

The final pair of attributes has to do with the tongue as well. The attribute of Flowing [*al-Idhlāq*] refers to the easy, fluent articulation of six letters, which are easy on the tongue and flow swiftly and easily from the lips:

ف ر م ن ل ب

They are remembered by the mnemonic:

فَرَّ مِنْ لُبٍّ

Sharp letters

The remaining twenty two letters carry the attribute of Sharpness [*al-Iṣmāt*], for they are slightly more difficult to articulate and do not flow as smoothly from the tongue and lips.

For example, consider the articulation of the letter jīm [ج] in the following word, which produces a sharper sound :

أَجْمَلُ

PHONETICS

The Flowing letters [*al-Idhlāq*] are easy and light in articulation and flow from the mouth with a high degree of fluency due to the fact that their articulation is from the tip of the tongue or the edge of the lips, which are the closest to the exit of the mouth where speech exits. Since they originate close to where they exit, their articulation is easy and they lend a degree of fluency to speech.

The Arabic language is a highly phonetic and acoustical language. It is a basic principle that any Arabic word that contains more than three letters must necessarily contain a Flowing letter to make the articulation of that word easier! Otherwise, a word with multiple letters that are difficult on the tongue would make for cumbersome speech.

The Unpaired Attributes

The following are additional attributes that are solitary (i.e. they don't exist in pairs) and are associated with some of the letters:

1. **The Whistle or Sibilance** الصَّفِير

The word *ṣafara* literally refers to the hissing, whistling or buzzing sound produced by certain animals. In Tajweed, the quality of *ṣafīr* refers to the whistling or buzzing sound produced by three letters:

ص س ز

These letters emanate a flowing, whistling sound, like the buzzing of a bee in the case of the letter *zā*, or the hissing of a snake in the letters *sīn* and *ṣād*.

2. **The Echo** القَلْقَلَة

Qalqalah means to shake, convulse or agitate, and in Tajweed, it refers to the reverbating or echoing sound produced by five letters. When any of the following five letters are stopped upon (*sākin*), there is an extra sound produced by the release of the tongue, like a single echo or reverberation of that letter:

ق ط ب ج د

Their mnemonic is:

قُطُبُ جَدٍّ

For instance, consider the following words and their transliteration:

قَدْ أَفْلَحَ

qad aflaḥa

The first word ends with an unvowelled letter dāl, which is a letter of the qalqalah attribute. Because of that, when you stop on the articulation of the dāl, you release the tongue slightly, nearly pronouncing it as if it had a vowel but not quite, as in: *qadi aflaḥa.*

The qalqalah is an extremely common feature in the Qur'ān that should be practiced and mastered by anyone seeking to perfect their recitation. It distinguishes expert reciters from beginners.

PHONETICS

Note that these five letters are all letters with the attribute of Forcefulness (al-Shiddah), which are, if you recall:

أَجِدُ قَطٍّ بَكَتْ

This attribute means that the articulation of these letters involves an abrupt stop to the flow of sound from their makhraj. Therefore, when you stop on these letters, the flow of sound completely stops, somewhat awkwardly. To preserve acoustic continuity and smoothness, there must be a slight release mechanism, like a partial vowel, to complete the articulation of these letters in the unvowelled (sākin) state.

This explains the five qalqalah letters from the above group of eight letters, but what about the remaining three letters? With respect to the alif letter, its articulation does not involve any significant component of sound from the oropharynx except for the abrupt *a* sound from the throat, and thus its unvowelled state simply involves an abrupt interruption to the flow of sound, which is natural to the letter. Hence, no release mechanism is necessary. With respect to the letters tā and kāf, their release mechanism is a slight release of breath (not sound) which is a natural attribute of these letters (see the attribute of *al-hams*, or "The Whisper," above).

With regards to its exact articulation, a variety of views have been presented by the scholars of Tajweed, but the strongest appears to be that there are two manners of articulation, depending upon whether the letter is Heavy (bearing the attribute of Tafkhīm or Isti'lā') or Light (the attribute of Tarqīq or Istifāl). The qalqalah of the heavy letters is articulated in a heavy manner (inclining towards the ḍammah vowel), while the qalqalah of the light letters is articulated in a light manner (inclining towards the kasrah vowel). But extreme care must be exerted not to articulate a full vowel during the qalqalah, for otherwise, the word would change. Again, it must be noted that this can only be learned from a teacher by verbal demonstration.

There are varying degrees of qalqalah in terms of strength, depending upon the letter as well as the state of the letters. With respect to the letters themselves, the letter ṭā [ط] has the strongest qalqalah feature, followed by the letter jīm [ج] which has an intermediate strength, followed by the remaining three letters. With respect to the state and position of the letters, there are three levels of qalqalah strength:

1. The strongest level is in the case of a letter of qalqalah that is doubled (*mushaddad*) and is stopped on, as in the case of the following words:

   اَلْحَقُّ → اَلْحَقّْ

   أَشَدُّ → أَشَدّْ

   وَ تَبَّ → وَ تَبّْ

   In these words, you must pause for a brief, extra moment on the doubled letters before releasing the sound of the letter.

2. This is followed by the qalqalah letters that are stopped on but are not doubled:

   خُلِقَ → خُلِقْ

   أَحَدٌ → أَحَدْ

   اَلْكِتَابُ → اَلْكِتَابْ

3. Next are the qalqalah letters that are unvowelled and not doubled, but not stopped on, as they are either in the middle of a word or at the end of a word which you are not stopping on (in other words, you do not end your recitation on that letter):

   يَقْبَلُ

   يَبْتَغِ

   يَجْعَلُ

You must note that in many situations, an unvowelled letter is merged into another and loses its original qualities (the rule of idghām, see chapter on idghām).

If this merged letter happens to a letter of qalqalah, obviously there would be no qalqalah in this case as the letter is merged into the subsequent one and is not articulated. See the following two verses as examples:

وَلَا يَغْتَـــب بَّـــعْضُكُم بَعْضًا

Pronounced: *walaa yaghtab-ba'ḍukum . . .*
[no qalqalah at the bā; no opening or release of lips]
Do not spy on nor backbite one another.
[The Qur'ān 49:12]

قَـد تَّـــبَيَّنَ الرُّشْدُ مِنَ الْغَيِّ

Pronounced: *qattabayyanarr-rushdu . . .*
There is no coercion in faith, for truth is clear from error.
[The Qur'ān 2:256]

3. **Lenience** اللِّين

The attribute of lenience or softness (*līn*) is derived from the word *lāna* which means to soften, become gentle, pliable or supple. It applies to madd letters in the following two cases:

The unvowelled yā preceded by the vowel fatḥah → لَيْسَ *laysa*

The unvowelled wāw preceded by the vowel fatḥah → يَوْمَ *yawma*

It is named such due to the easy and soft manner of articulation, which are essentially like vowels, specifically the *–ay* and *–aw* sounds.

4. **The Drifting or Bending** الإنحِرَاف

This attribute is due to the slight bending of the tip of the tongue towards the roof of the mouth, which causes a slight deviation in the sound of two letters—lām and rā. Scholars point out that the articulation of the letter lām deviates slightly towards the makhraj of nūn, causing some people to slip in their articulation of these two letters, particularly when they are adjacent to each other.

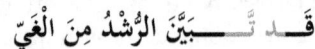

5. **The Repetition** التِّكْرَار

Tikrār comes from the root word *karra* which means to return, turn around or repeat. This is an attribute of the single letter rā and refers to the vibrating, repetitive, trilling quality of the sound produced by this letter, from its tight makhraj—the tip of the tongue being compressed against the roof of the mouth without fully pressing against it. The doubled unvowelled rā has more trill to it than the unvowelled rā, but care must be exerted to not exaggerate in this attribute.

6. **The Spreading Around** التَّفَشِّي

The root word *fashā* means to spread about, diffuse or circulate something, such as air. The attribute of *tafashshī* refers to the expansive sound of the letter shīn caused by its sound extending horizontally throughout the mouth [*shshshshsh* . . . as in the popular gesture for silence].

7. **The Lengthening** الإِستِطَالَة

The word *ṭāla* means to lengthen, extend or draw out, and the attribute of *istiṭālah* refers to the expansive, elongated quality of one letter. This final attribute is associated with the letter ḍād [ض], which is a letter unique to the Arabic language alone and is the single most difficult letter to pronounce in Arabic.

This attribute is named so from the elongated makhraj of ḍād, which is articulated by a compression of the tongue against the roof of the mouth in an expanded, firm manner.

These are the attributes of the letters, and scholars divide them into three categories of their strength:

The Weak Attributes:	***The Intermediate Attributes:***	***The Strong Attributes:***
The Whisper (*al-Hams*) Lenience (*al-Līn*) Openness (*al-Infitāḥ*) Depression (*al-Istifāl*) Softness (*al-Rakhāwah*)	Sharpness (*al-Iṣmāt*) Flowing (*al-Idhlāq*) Moderation (*al-Tawassuṭ*)	Loudness (*al-Jahr*) Forcefulness (*al-Shiddah*) Elevation (*al-Isti'lā'*) Closedness (*al-Iṭbāq*) Echo (*al-Qalqalah*) Repetition (*al-Tikrār*) Drift (*al-Inḥirāf*) Spreading (*al-Tafashshī*) Lengthening (*al-Istiṭālah*) Whistle (*al-Ṣafīr*)

FIGURE 7 — THE ATTRIBUTES SUMMARIZED

Heaviness versus Lightness

Finally, the concept of heavy and light letters deserves a more detailed look. This discussion is based upon attributes already covered—namely, heaviness (*Isti'lā'*, or more commonly referred to as *Tafkhīm*) and its opposite quality of lightness [*Istifāl*, or more commonly, *Tarqīq*]. From the perspective of this pair of attributes, all Arabic letters can be divided into three types:

Those that are always heavy:	*Those that can be either:*	*Those that are always light:*
7 letters from the mnemonic خُصَّ ضَغْطٍ قِظْ	3 letters: ل ر The madd letters (نُوحِيهَا)	All remaining letters

The seven letters of permanent heaviness intrinsically have varying degrees of strength in the following order:

Heaviest:	ط
	ض
	ص
	ظ
	ق
	غ
Least heavy:	خ

Note that the first four letters in this group are letters of Adhesion or Closedness [*al-Iṭbāq*]— ص ض ط ظ , which means that among the heavy letters, the letters of Adhesion are stronger than the others in their quality of heaviness due to the adhesion of the tongue to the roof of the mouth in addition to the elevation of the tongue.

Moreover, there are five degrees of heaviness based upon the states of the letters, as follows:

1. The strongest state of Heaviness is when one of these five letters carries the fatḥah vowel and is followed by alif (i.e. the heavy letter is followed by the madd letter alif), as in the following words:

   قَالَ فَطَالَ ضَآلِّينَ الظَّالِمِينَ

2. The second state of Heaviness involves these letters simply carrying the fatḥah vowel but *not* followed by alif:

   طَلَبًا صَبَرَ ظَلَمَ ضَنكًا

3. The third state of Heaviness involves these letters carrying the ḍammah vowel:

   فَقُطِعَ ظُلِمُوا القُرْآنُ الطُّورَ

4. The fourth state of Heaviness involves an unvowelled letter of this type:

   أَظْلَمَ يَقْدِرُ يَضْحَكُونَ يَخْتَصِمُونَ

5. The fifth and lowest state of Heaviness involves these letters with the kasrah vowel:

   طِفلاً الصِّرَاطَ المستَقِيمَ ظِلاًّ

An alternate point of view regarding the levels of Heaviness is that there are simple three levels of strength, based upon the three vowels—the strongest being the fatḥah, followed by the ḍammah, and finally the kasrah. The letter simply follows the level of strength of its vowel. The unvowelled letter in this scheme simply follows the strength of the vowel preceding it.

The letters that vary between heaviness and lightness include the madd letters, the lām and rā. The madd alif simply follows the attribute of the letter preceding it. That is, if the letter before the alif madd letter is heavy, then the madd letter is articulated in a heavy manner, and vice versa.

The madd alif that is articulated heavy would sound like the beginning of the word *awsome* (the *aw* sound) while the madd alif when it is articulated light sounds like the beginning of the word *apple* or *ask.*

For instance, in the following cases, the madd alif is preceded by a heavy letter and should be articulated such:

قَالَ فَطَالَ الظَّالِمُ

On the other hand, in these words the madd alif is preceded by a light letter and is articulated lightly:

أَقْفَالُهَا الكِتَابُ الأَرحَامِ

With respect to the other madd letters (yā and wāw), the same principles would apply.

The lām in general is always light, save for the case of the Grand Word [Lafẓ Jalālah]— *Allah,* which was covered previously in Chapter 4.

As for the letter rā, it has lengthy rules relating to its attribute of Heaviness/Softness, and shall be covered in the next chapter.

CHAPTER SEVEN: THE RULES OF RĀ

أَحكَامُ الرَّاء

IN THIS CHAPTER

When is the rā pronounced in a heavy manner?

When is it pronounced in a light manner?

What are the principles for determining this?

What are the exceptional cases to these general principles?

The letter rā is among the letters which vacillates between the quality of heaviness [*tafkhīm*] and that of lightness [*tarqīq*] depending upon certain factors. In fact, among these letters with variable qualities the case of the letter rā is the most complex and is contingent upon a number of rules and factors—primarily based upon the loose principle that the fatḥah and ḍammah are "heavy" vowels while the kasrah is a "light" vowel. In other words, it is these vowels on the letter rā in general that determine whether the rā would be articulated in a heavy manner or a light manner.

So while the case of the vowelled rā is quite simple, the unvowelled rā is slightly more complex. In that case, there are a number of scenarios. The basic methodology for determining the heaviness/lightness of the unvowelled rā is that you must look to its preceding vowel (i.e. the vowel on the preceding letter). In the case that the preceding letter is also unvowelled, then you must look to the vowel before that, etc. There are also a number of other factors that additionally influence the state of the unvowelled rā, including the heaviness of adjacent letters and the existence of conditional vowels adjacent to it.

In summary, the heaviness/lightness of rā is determined by its vowel (*if fatḥah/ḍammah → heavy; if kasrah → light*), and when it is unvowelled, by the last vowel preceding it, along with a few other factors such as adjacent heavy letters or conditional vowels. This process is summarized in Figure 8 and detailed thereafter.

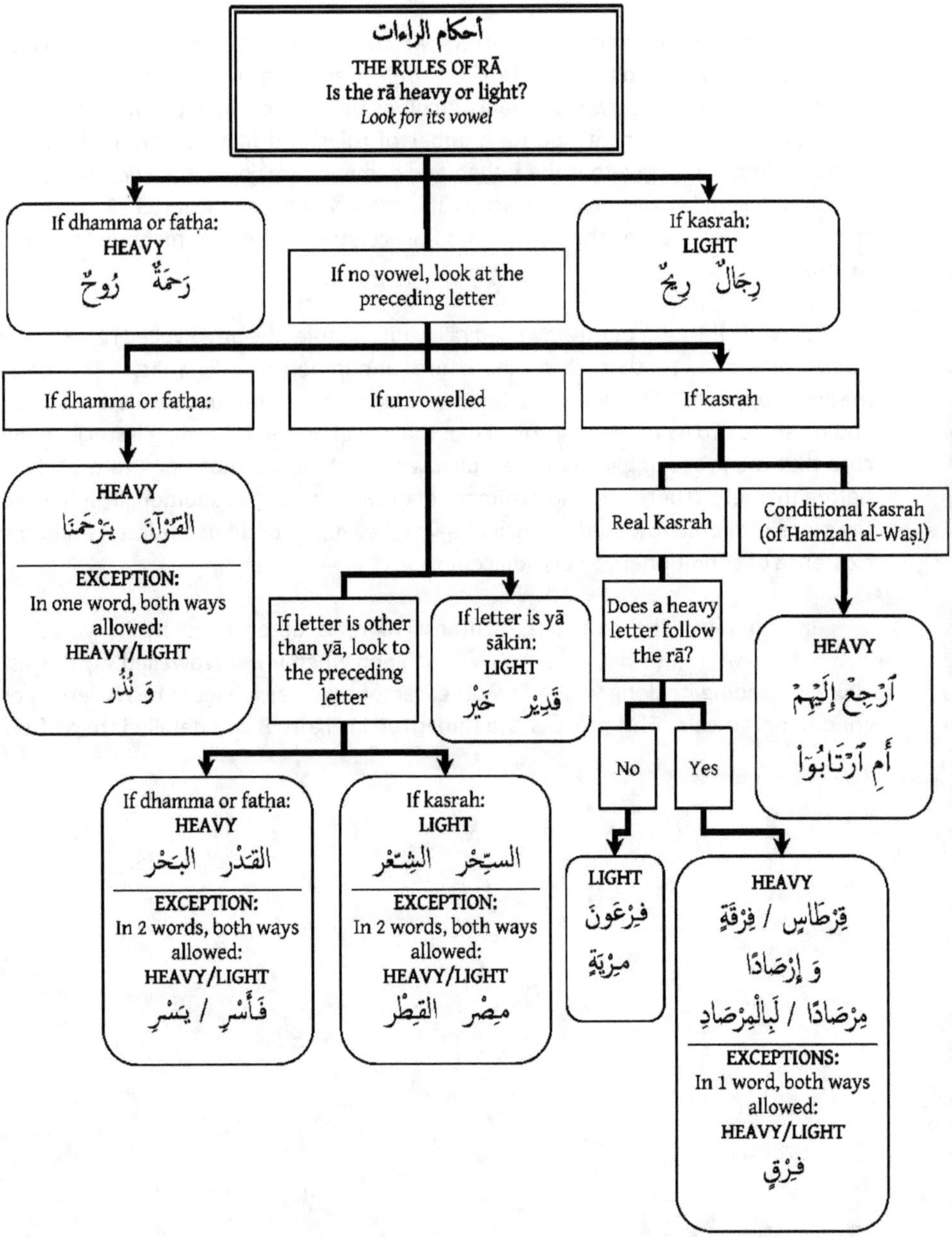

FIGURE 8—RULES OF RĀ

Let us examine these cases in detail, looking first at all the instances of the heavy rā followed by the light rā. The rā is pronounced in a heavy manner in the following five cases:

1. If it carries the fatḥah or ḍammah vowel
2. If it is unvowelled and preceded by the fatḥah or ḍammah vowel
3. If it is unvowelled at the end of a word and preceded by an unvowelled letter (other than yā) which is preceded by the fatḥah or ḍammah vowel
4. If it is unvowelled and preceded by a conditional kasrah vowel (due to a hamzah al-waṣl)
5. If it is unvowelled and preceded by a kasrah vowel, but is followed by a heavy letter

It is pronounced in a light manner in the following four cases:

1. If it carries a kasrah vowel
2. If it is unvowelled following a kasrah vowel, and no heavy letter follows it (in the same word)
3. If it is unvowelled at the end of a word and preceded by an unvowelled letter other than yā which is preceded by the kasrah vowel
4. If it is unvowelled at the end of a word and preceded by an unvowelled yā

The Heavy Rā

Let us look at specific examples for the five cases of the heavy rā.

1. If it carries the fatḥah or ḍammah vowel

The heavy rā occurs primarily when it carries the fatḥah or ḍammah vowel, as in the following words:

الرُّسُلُ   الرَّسُولُ   رُبَّمَا   رَبَّنَا

2. If it is unvowelled and preceded by the fatḥah or ḍammah vowel

When the rā does not have a vowel, on the other hand, you have to look at the preceding vowel. So the second case of the heavy rā involves the unvowelled rā preceded by a fatḥah or ḍammah vowel, as in the following words:

الْعَرْشِ

الأَرْضِ

أَرْسَلَ

الْمُرْسَلِين

الْقُرْآنُ

3. If it is unvowelled at the end of a word and preceded by an unvowelled letter (other than yā) which is preceded by the fatḥah or ḍammah vowel

If the rā has no vowel, and the letter preceding it also has no vowel, then you must look to the letter before both of them to determine the way the rā should be articulated. How can this scenario occur? There is a basic rule in the Arabic language which stipulates that there cannot be two adjacent unvowelled letters in a word because of the difficulty in pronouncing them. However, this case can exist when a letter (in our example the rā) occurs at the end of a word and you are stopping on that word in recitation. Consider the following word:

الْقَدْرِ

The ending rā letter in this word is indeed vowelled while its preceding letter (dāl) is unvowelled, and thus this does not violate the rule forbidding two adjacent unvowelled letters. However, when you stop on this word in recitation, the vowel of the last letter is dropped according to the rules of reading. The word in that case is pronounced as:

الْقَدْرْ

This terminal sukūn is a conditional state due to stopping on the letter, and is known as *al-sukūn al-āriḍ* [السُّكُون العَارِض], which is a conditional sukūn as opposed to a real one.

So the question is—is this terminal unvowelled rā heavy or light? It is the vowel that determines the answer. Obviously, there is no vowel on the rā itself since it is dropped. In that case, look for the vowel of the preceding letter—the letter dāl, which also happens to be unvowelled. Move to the next letter, then—the qāf, which carries fatḥah, a "heavy vowel." Therefore, it is this vowel on the qāf that determines the state of the rā, which would be heavy in this case. This, then, is the third type of heavy rā—the unvowelled rā preceded by another unvowelled letter (other than yā for a reason we shall see later) which is preceded by either fatḥah or ḍammah.

4. If it is unvowelled and preceded by a conditional kasrah vowel (due to a hamzah al-waṣl)

The fourth type of heavy rā involves an unvowelled rā preceded by a conditional kasrah due to a hamzah al-waṣl. This type of hamzah is a special hamzah letter that is usually placed in the beginning of a word and is pronounced only when beginning on that word and not in continuation (when that word is joined to another). It is a part of the *al-* prefix that is a part of definite nouns [See chapter 4 on the rules of lām]. It is also found as a part of the command form of many verbs, as in the following Qur'ānic word:

ارْجِعْ

This is a command (which means *return!*) that begins with a hamzah al-waṣl, as most commands do. According to the rules of reading, this hamzah is silent and not articulated when reading it in continuity with other words, as the following verse demonstrates:

قَالَ ارْجِعْ إِلَىٰ رَبِّكَ فَاسْأَلْهُ مَا بَالُ النِّسْوَةِ اللَّاتِي قَطَّعْنَ أَيْدِيَهُنَّ

He (Yusūf) said: Return unto thy lord and ask him what was the case of the women who cut their hands.

[The Qur'ān 12:50]

In this example, this portion of the verse is pronounced with a heavy rā as follows—*qālarji' ilā*. The hamzah of *irji'* is not pronounced but joined with the lām of the previous word *qāla*. Since that lām has a fatḥah, the rā is heavy as a result.

On the other hand, if this same command is without a preceding word and articulated standing alone, then the rules of articulation are different, as in the following verse:

ارْجِعْ إِلَيْهِمْ فَلَنَأْتِيَنَّهُم بِجُنُودٍ لَّا قِبَلَ لَهُم بِهَا وَلَنُخْرِجَنَّهُم مِّنْهَا أَذِلَّةً وَهُمْ صَاغِرُونَ

Return to them, and be sure we shall come to them with such hosts as they will never be able to meet: We shall expel them from there in disgrace, and they will feel humbled.

[The Qur'ān 27:37]

In this verse, the hamzah of the command is pronounced since it is not being joined to the letter of a previous word. What is its vowel? Its vowel is determined by the next vowel following it—if that vowel is a fatḥah or kasrah, then the hamzah is articulated with a kasrah; if the vowel is a ḍammah then the hamzah is articulated with a ḍammah as well. This kasrah is called a conditional kasrah, or *al-kasrah al-'āriḍah* [الكَسرَة العَارِضَة].

In the above example, the hamzah is followed by a kasrah on the letter jīm (the rā after the hamzah is unvowelled, so you must look to the next letter) and thus it is articulated with a kasrah. This conditional kasrah makes the letter rā heavy, and this word would be pronounced— *irji' ilayhim . . .,* with a heavy rā.

5. If it is unvowelled and preceded by a kasrah vowel, but is followed by a heavy letter

The final type of heavy rā is that of the unvowelled rā which follows a kasrah vowel (which would normally make it light) but is followed by a heavy letter within the same word—those seven letters with the attribute of Elevation [al-Isti'lā], found in the mnemonic:

خُصَّ ضَغْطٍ قِظْ

In this case, the preceding kasrah (which necessitates lightness in the rā) is mitigated by the condition of having a heavy letter following the rā within the same word, which forces the rā to be heavy. The following words are examples:

مِرْصَادًا   قِرْطَاسٍ   فِرْقَةٍ

The Light Rā

1. If it carries a kasrah vowel

The rā is light when it carries the kasrah vowel, as in the words:

رِجَالٌ   رِزْقًا   فَرِحَ

2. If it is unvowelled following a kasrah vowel, and no heavy letter follows it (in the same word)

It is also light when it is unvowelled and preceded by a kasrah (and no heavy letter follows it in the same word, as we just saw in the last type of heavy rā). Examples of this would include:

فِرْعَونَ   شِرْعَةً   فَاطِرِ

3. If it is unvowelled at the end of a word and preceded by an unvowelled letter other than yā which is preceded by the kasrah vowel

Finally the rā is light when it is unvowelled (due to a stop), preceded by an unvowelled letter other than yā which is preceded by a kasrah, as in the following words:

الذِّكْر   السِّحْر   الشِّعْر

4. If it is unvowelled at the end of a word and preceded by an unvowelled yā

It is also light when it is unvowelled and preceded by an unvowelled yā. Note that in this case, the mere presence of the unvowelled yā before the rā makes it light and there is no need to look to the preceding letter's vowel. Examples include:

قَدِير   نَكِير   الطَّير   خَير

Exceptions

Finally, there are a limited number of words in the Qur'ān which are exceptions to these rules, and in their case, the rā may be articulated both ways—heavy or light—in the Ḥafṣ reading.

The first exception is the word [فِرْقٍ] in *al-Shu'arā* 26:63, in which case the unvowelled rā should be heavy due to its being followed by a heavy letter (the 5th type of heavy rā). Therefore, articulating it in a heavy manner is correct. However, due to the fact that the subsequent heavy letter (qāf) is vowelled with a kasrah, which is a "light" vowel that lightens the heaviness of the qāf to some degree, the rā may also be articulated lightly. This is the only example of a word in the Qur'ān that contains an unvowelled rā preceded by kasrah but followed a heavy letter that is vowelled with kasrah.

The second exception involves the two Qur'ānic words [مِصْرَ] and [الْقِطْرِ], in which case the unvowelled rā (when you are stopping on the word) should be light due to it being preceded by an unvowelled letter other than yā which is preceded by the vowel kasrah (3rd type of light rā). Therefore, pronouncing it in a light manner is correct. However, due to the fact that the rā is immediately preceded by a heavy letter, it is also correct to articulate it in a heavy manner. These 2 words appear in the following verses of the Qur'ān– 34:12, 12:21, 12:99 and 43:51.

The third exception involves the word [نُذُرِ] which should be articulated heavy when stopping on it due to it being preceded by the vowel ḍammah (2nd type of heavy rā). However, it may also be articulated lightly due to the linguistic origin of the word, which originally ended with a yā which made the rā vowelled with a kasrah—[نُذُرِي]. This final yā was dropped in writing and articulation but remains a part of the word as an implied linguistic feature of that word.

The fourth and final exception involves the two word [يَسْرِ] and [فَأَسْرِ], which are also normally articulated with the heavy rā when stopping on them due to their being preceded by an unvowelled letter preceded by a fatḥah vowel (2nd type of heavy rā). However, as in the case above, their linguistic origin also involves a terminal yā in a similar fashion—[يَسْرِي] and [فَأَسْرِي], which was dropped but remains implied in the word. As such, it is permissible to recite the rā in these words in a light manner.

It should be noted that these cases are correctly articulated in both ways in the reading of Ḥafṣ, but they should be subject to the further rules of *Riwāyah* (reading the Qur'ān by transmission from your teachers). The reading of Ḥafṣ is transmitted from the Prophet through many chains extending to us today, and each of these chains specifies how these cases are to be articulated.

Chapter EIGHT: THE RULES OF ASSIMILATION

أحكَامُ الإدغام

IN THIS CHAPTER

What are the types of merging?

What are these based upon?

What are the types of adjacent letter pairs?

What are the two types of adjacent vowel combinations?

This chapter discusses the articulation of adjacent letters. The default articulation of each letter is its natural inherent manner (iẓhār). However, adjacent letters are sometimes assimilated or merged into one another in certain circumstances. We have already covered many of these cases involving the letters nūn, meem and lām. This chapter covers the remaining cases in a systematic way.

In essence, this chapter is built upon the basic premise that there are four types of adjacent letter pairs based upon their points of articulation (makhārij) and attributes (ṣifāt), as well as two types of assimilation based upon the vowels of the two adjacent letters.

The four types of adjacent letter pairs, based upon their makhraj and attributes, are:

1. **Mithlayn** (Two Identical Letters): These are two adjacent letters that share the same articulation point (makhraj) and attributes (ṣifāt). In other words, they are identical letters.

2. **Mutaqāribayn** (Two Close Letters): These are two letters that have similar points of articulation and attributes.

3. **Mutajānisayn** (Two Similar Letters): These are two letters that share the same makhraj but differ in attributes.

4. **Mutabā'idayn** (Two Distant Letters): These are letters which have very different points of articulation as well as attributes.

The two types of idghām (assimilation), based upon the vowel configurations of the two letters, are:

1. **Ṣaghīr:** This type of assimilation occurs when the first letter is unvowelled while the second vowelled. It is named such (*Ṣaghīr* meaning *Smaller*) because this type of assimilation—when it occurs—does so quite naturally with little effort. Most cases of idghām are of this type.

   For instance, in the following example, the first word ends with an unvowelled dāl while the second begins with a vowelled dāl, and the two are naturally assimilated:

   قَــد دَّخَلُوا

2. **Kabīr:** This configuration refers simply to two adjacent vowelled letters. In general, two vowelled letters are never assimilated and each letter is pronounced with its respective vowel.

For instance, the first two bā letters of the following word are articulated with their vowels without being assimilated:

بِبَـــعْضِ

However, in some limited cases, assimilation does occur with this configuration of letters (two vowelled letters). It is named *Kabīr* (meaning *Great*) because the assimilation of two vowelled letters requires tremendous effort and is not natural—quite obviously as the first letter must be converted to an unvowelled one and subsequently merged into the second.

Note that the other two possible vowel combinations (a vowelled followed by an unvowelled letter, and two unvowelled letters) does not result in any assimilation in the majority Ḥafṣ reading and is thus not discussed here.

Now let us look at these cases in detail.

Mithlayn المِثْلَين

The Two Identical Letters

Mithlayn (sometimes also referred to as Mutamāthilayn) simply refers to two identical letters, which obviously share the same makhraj and attributes adjacent to one another, as in the following examples:

إِنْ كُنْتُـــمْ مُـــؤْمِنِيْنَ

وَ قَـــدْ دَخَلُوا

مَنَاسِـــكَكُـــمْ

بِبَـــعْضِ

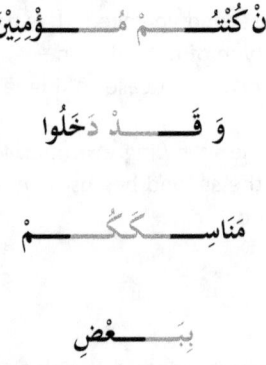

حَيــــــثْ ثَّـــــــقِفْتُمُوهُمْ

Idghām Mithlayn Ṣaghīr

When two identical letters (i.e. Mithlayn letters) appear such that the first is unvowelled while the second is vowelled (i.e. Ṣaghīr configuration), they are assimilated according to all modes of recitation and are referred to as Idghām Mithlayn Ṣaghīr. Examples include the following words, some of which were already shown above (note that they can occur between two words or within one):

إِنْ كُنْتُـــــمْ مُّـــــؤْمِنِيْنَ

وَ قَـــــدْ دَّخَلُوا

يُدْرِككُّـــــمْ

يُكْرِههُّـــنَّ

Note

A question arises—why do we state that Mithlayn letters are *two identical letters that share the same makhraj and attributes,* for don't all identical letters automatically share the same makhraj and characteristics? While this is usually the case, the makhraj of the letters wāw and yā, for instance, vary between their vowelled and unvowelled state. Consider the following cases:

ءَامَنُـــــوْا وَعَمِلُوا

فِـــــيْ يُـــــوسُفَ

In both of these cases, the first letter is unvowelled while the second is vowelled, and they represent the same letter in each case (wāw in the first case and yā in the second). Therefore, it would appear that they should be assimilated as examples of Idghām Mithlayn. However, in reality the first letters are actually slightly different from the second ones in that the former are madd letters (the unvowelled wāw preceded by the ḍammah vowel and the unvowelled yā preceded by the kasrah vowel) whose makhraj is from the oral cavity while the vowelled wāw and vowelled yā have their own distinct makhraj—the wāw comes from the lips while the yā comes from the middle portion of the tongue. Therefore, since these letters don't share the same makhraj they are not assimilated and don't carry the Mithlayn designation. The mandatory and natural assimilation of Mithlayn letters in the Ṣaghīr configuration requires that the letters share identical articulation sites and attributes. That is why we do not define Mithlayn letters as simply two adjacent identical letters but must specify that they are two identical letters that share the same makhraj and attributes.

This is the case with these two madd letters (the unvowelled wāw preceded by ḍammah and the unvowelled yā preceded by kasrah). What about the case of the Madd Līn (which is either an unvowelled wāw preceded by fatḥah or an unvowelled yā preceded by fatḥah) when it is followed by a vowelled wāw or yā? In that case, they do get assimilated and are examples of Idghām Mithlayn Ṣaghīr. An example of that is the following word:

إِذَا مَا اتَّقَـــوا وَّ ءَامَنُوا

Idghām Mithlayn Kabīr

Please note that this section is very advanced and contains information relating to the linguistic origins of words that has little practical bearing upon our recitation from the normal muṣḥaf in use today. It serves to complete our understanding of the types and principles of merging but may be skipped with no detriment to one's recitation.

When two Mithlayn letters appear adjacently and both are vowelled (Kabīr configuration), their default articulation is iẓhār in nearly all cases, as in the following examples:

عُقْدَةُ النِّكَـــاحِ حَـــتَّى

حِـــجَجٍ

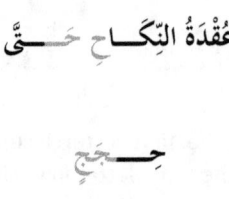

There are only a limited number of exceptions to this default rule of iẓhār in the Qur'ān, where assimilation does occur, and they are referred to as Idghām Mithlayn Kabīr. Please note that these examples are not readily recognizable in the muṣḥaf as they have been written in a modified way to reflect their actual assimilated articulation. Therefore, this discussion is more theoretical than practical, as the following examples illustrate.

The most prominent example in the Qur'ān is the following verse:

﴿ قَالُواْ يَٰٓأَبَانَا مَا لَكَ لَا تَأۡمَ۫نَّا عَلَىٰ يُوسُفَ وَإِنَّا لَهُۥ لَنَٰصِحُونَ ﴾

They said, O our father, why will you not trust us with Yūsuf,
when we are indeed good friends to him?
[The Qur'ān 12:11]

How does this highlighted word reflect Idghām Mithlayn Kabīr? Linguistically, the original word was:

تَأْمَنُنَا

This word has been re-written to reflect its actual assimilated articulation as follows:

تَأْمَنَّا

The diamond-shaped symbol placed over the word indicates this conversion and illustrates the special way of reciting this word referred to in Tajweed terminology as *Ishmām*—while articulating the above nūn, the lips are brought together and puckered as if one is about to pronounce the ḍammah vowel or the wāw sound, but no actual sound is articulated. Rather, the voice articulates the normal nūn despite this exercise of the lips, which is merely a demonstration of the original ḍammah vowel which was lost with the assimilation. This is one of the few features of recitation that must be learned visually from a trained teacher.

Other exceptions involve the following verses:

قَالَ مَا مَكَّنِّي فِيهِ رَبِّي خَيْرٌ فَأَعِينُونِي بِقُوَّةٍ أَجْعَلْ بَيْنَكُمْ وَبَيْنَهُمْ رَدْمًا

He answered, That wherein my Lord has established me is better, so do help me with strength and I shall erect a strong barrier between you and them.

[The Qur'ān 18:95]

Original word		Written as
مَكَّنَنِي	→	مَكَّنِّي

﴿ وَحَآجَّهُۥ قَوْمُهُۥ قَالَ أَتُحَٰٓجُّوٓنِّي فِي ٱللَّهِ وَقَدْ هَدَىٰنِ ﴾

His people disputed with him (Ibrāhīm) and he said, Do you dispute with me about Allah and He has guided me.

[The Qur'ān 6:80]

Original word		Written as
أَتُحَاجُّونَنِي	→	أَتُحَاجُونِّي

﴿ قُلْ أَفَغَيْرَ ٱللَّهِ تَأْمُرُوٓنِّيٓ أَعْبُدُ أَيُّهَا ٱلْجَٰهِلُونَ ﴾

Say, Is it someone other than Allah that you order me to worship, O ignorant ones?

[The Qur'ān 39:64]

Original word		Written as
تَأْمُرُونَنِي	→	تَأْمُرُونِّي

The last example concerns a word that appears in the following two verses:

إِن تُبْدُوا الصَّدَقَاتِ فَنِعِمَّا هِيَ

If you disclose acts of charity, even so it is well.

[The Qur'ān 2:271]

إِنَّ اللَّهَ نِعِمَّا يَعِظُكُم بِهِ

Verily how excellent is the teaching which He gives you.
[The Qur'ān 4:58]

Original word		*Written as*
نِعمَ مَا	→	نِعِمَّا

These rules concerning the assimilation of Mithlayn letters can be summarized as follows:

Mithlayn letters	***Configuration***		***Default Rule***	***Exception***
	Ṣaghīr		Idghām in all cases	None
	Kabīr		Iẓhār	Idghām in 6 verses

Mutaqāribayn الْمُتَقَارِبَيْنِ

The Two Close Letters

These are letters which have similar or identical articulation sites or attributes. This can occur in various scenarios:

- Both the articulation sites and attributes of the two letters are similar—the letters lām and rā [ل ر], and the letters tā and thā [ت ث]
- The attributes are similar but not the articulation sites—the letters kāf and thā [ك ث]
- The articulation sites are close but not the attributes—the letters dāl and sīn [د س], the letters ḍād and rā [ض ر] and the letter qāf and kāf [ق ك]

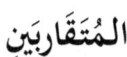

- The attributes are exactly the same while the articulation sites are close—the letters dāl and jīm [د ج], and the letters ḥā and hā [ح هـ]

- The attributes are the same while the articulation sites are far apart—the letters kāf and tā [ك ت], the letters thā and hā [ث هـ], and the letters ḥā and thā [ح ث]

In these letters there is no uniform rule for assimilation but varies case by case.

Let us begin by looking at these letters in the Ṣaghīr configuration (first letter unvowelled, second vowelled).

Idghām Mutaqāribayn Ṣaghīr

The following are four cases where assimilation is mandatory:

1. The unvowelled lām followed by rā

وَقُـــل رَّبِّ زِدْنِي عِلْمًا

Pronounced: *wa qurrabbi zidnī 'ilmā . . .*
[Note that the lām is merged or assimilated into the subsequent rā, which is doubled as a result]
And say, My Lord increase me in knowledge.
[The Qur'ān 20:114]

بَـــل رَّفَعَهُ اللَّهُ إِلَيْهِ

Pronounced: *barrafa 'ahullahu ilayhi . . .*
Nay, Allah raised him (Jesus) up unto Himself.
[The Qur'ān 4:158]

2. The unvowelled lām followed by the Sun Letters

This was covered in Chapter 4, where we learned that when the unvowelled lām is followed by any of the fourteen Sun Letters (al-Ḥurūf al-Shamsiyyah), it is assimilated and merged into them, as the following words demonstrate:

اَلشَّمْس

اَلرَّحِيْم
اَلزَّيْتُون

These fourteen letters are:

ط ث ص ر ت ض ذ ن د س ظ
ز ش ل

Please note that the only exception out of these fourteen letters is the letter lām, which obviously is identical to lām. Therefore the unvowelled lām followed by the Sun Letter lām would be an example of Mithlayn rather than Mutaqāribayn, but is still assimilated.

3. The unvowelled qāf followed by kāf

There is only a single example of this in Qur'ān, in the following verse:

أَلَمْ نَخْلُقكُّم مِّن مَّاءٍ مَّهِينٍ

Pronounced: *alam nakhlukkum mimmā'immahīn . . .*

Did we not create you from a base fluid?

[The Qur'ān 77:20]

In this case, the qāf is fully merged into the kāf, although in some readings, this merging is done in an incomplete way (known as *Idghām Nāqiṣ*) so as to retain some of the characteristics of the qāf.

4. The unvowelled nūn (of nūn sākin or tanwīn) followed by the letters of Idghām

This was covered in the chapter on Nūn Sākin and Tanwīn concerning the letters in the mnemonic yarmulūn [يرملون], five of which are examples of Idghām Mutaqāribayn Ṣaghīr. From these six letters, the only exception is the letter nūn, which would be identical to the unvowelled nūn that precedes it, making it an example of Idghām Mithlayn Ṣaghīr rather than Mutaqāribayn Ṣaghīr. But it is still assimilated and the final result is the same.

Exceptions

One exception from assimilation is the case of the unvowelled nūn followed by the letter wāw in the disjointed letters, which occurs in only two places in the Qur'ān:

﴿ يسٓ ۝١ وَٱلْقُرْءَانِ ٱلْحَكِيمِ ۝٢ ﴾

Pronounced: *yā sīn wal-Qur'ānil-hakīm . . .*
[the articulation of the letter sīn ends with an unvowelled nūn which is followed by the letter wāw in the next verse]

Yā Sīn. By the Qur'ān full of wisdom.
[The Qur'ān 36:1-2]

﴿ نٓ ۚ وَٱلْقَلَمِ وَمَا يَسْطُرُونَ ﴾

Pronounced: *nūn wal qalami wa mā yasṭurūn . . .*
[the articulation of the letter nūn ends with an unvowelled nūn which is followed by the letter wāw in the next verse]

Nūn. By the pen and that which they write.
[The Qur'ān 68:1]

Though the normal ruling should be that of idghām (nūn sākin followed by wāw, a letter of idghām), because of these being disjointed letters, the idghām or assimilation is not mandatory but varies by the various modes of reading. Even in the predominant reading of Ḥafṣ, upon which this work is primarily based, it may be recited with both iẓhār and idghām, depending upon the teacher and chain of transmission. But the dominant way of reading is with manifestion not assimilation.

All other Mutaqāribayn letters in the Ṣaghīr configuration apart from the above four examples are not assimilated but pronounced in their normal state with iẓhār. Examples of Mutaqāribayn Ṣaghīr letters which are not assimilated include:

كَذَّبَتْ ثَمُودُ

[The letters tā and thā are Mutaqāribayn letters that are articulated with iẓhār, and the above words would be articulated in the normal fashion without assimilation, as *kadhdhabat thamūdu*]

Another exception involves the letter dhāl followed by the letter tā, which is assimilated in other modes of reading but *not* in the reading of Ḥafṣ, which is the basis for this work. An example of this is in the following word:

اتَّخَذْتُمْ

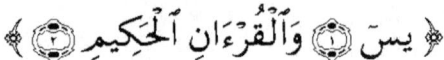

This word is articulated in the normal way as *ittakhadh-tum* in the reading of Ḥafṣ, but is assimilated in other modes of reading, such as the reading of Qālūn as *ittakhattum* (with complete merging of the dhāl into the tā). There are some additional examples relevant to other modes of reading, but that is not our concern in this work.

Mutaqāribayn Kabīr

These Mutaqāribayn letters in the Kabīr configuration (both of them vowelled) are always articulated with iẓhār and never assimilated.

To summarize the Mutaqāribayn letters:

Configuration		***Default Rule***				
Ṣaghīr		No uniform rule, but:	Idghām:	ل		ر
				ل		الحُرُوف الشَّمسِيَّة
				ق		ك
				ن		يرملون
			Iẓhār:	The remaining examples		
Kabīr		Iẓhār				

Mutajānisayn مُتَجَانِسَين

The Two Similar Letters

These are two letters that have identical articulation sites but differ in attributes. They also don't have a uniform rule with regards to assimilation but must be studied with examples.

The following are the five cases where assimilation is mandatory in the Ṣaghīr configuration (first letter unvowelled, second vowelled):

1. The unvowelled dāl followed by a vowelled tā [د . ت]

لَا إِكْرَاهَ فِي الدِّينِ ۖ قَد تَّبَيَّنَ الرُّشْدُ مِنَ الْغَيِّ

Pronounced: *qattabayyanarr-rushdu . . .*

There is no coercion in faith, for truth is clear from error.

[The Qur'ān 2:256]

وَلَا أَنَا عَابِدٌ مَّا عَبَدتُّمْ

Pronounced: *walā ann 'ābidummā 'abattum . . .*

And I do not worship that which you worship.

[The Qur'ān 109:4]

In these cases, the dāl merges into the tā, with the result that only the tā sound is articulated, albeit in a doubled form.

2. The unvowelled tā followed by a vowelled dāl [ت . د]

This case occurs in only the following two verses of the Qur'ān:

فَلَمَّا أَثْقَلَت دَّعَوَا اللَّهَ رَبَّهُمَا لَئِنْ آتَيْتَنَا صَالِحًا لَّنَكُونَنَّ مِنَ الشَّاكِرِينَ

Pronounced: *falamā athqaladda 'awallaha . . .*

When she grows heavy (with pregnancy) they both call unto their Lord, If You give us a goodly child, we shall indeed be from the grateful ones.

[The Qur'ān 7:189]

قَالَ قَدْ أُجِيبَت دَّعْوَتُكُمَا فَاسْتَقِيمَا وَلَا تَتَّبِعَانِّ سَبِيلَ الَّذِينَ لَا يَعْلَمُونَ

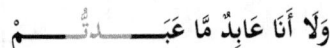

Pronounced: *qāla qad ujībadda'watukumā . . .*
Allah said, Accepted is the prayer of you two (Mūsā and Hārūn), so stand straight and don't follow the path of those who do not know.
[The Qur'ān 10:89]

3. **The unvowelled tā followed by a vowelled ṭā [ت . ط]**

فَآمَنَــــت طَّــــائِفَةٌ مِّن بَنِي إِسْرَائِيلَ وَكَفَرَت طَّــــائِفَةٌ

Pronounced: *fa āmanaṭṭā'ifatummin banī isrā'īla wa kafaraṭṭā'ifah . . .*
A party of the Israelites believed while a party disbelieved.
[The Qur'ān 61:14]

4. **The unvowelled dhāl followed by a vowelled ẓā [ذ . ظ]**

This occurs in only two verses of the Qur'ān:

وَلَن يَنفَعَكُمُ الْيَوْمَ إِذ ظَّــــلَمْتُمْ أَنَّكُمْ فِي الْعَذَابِ مُشْتَرِكُونَ

Pronounced: *walanyanfa'akumul yawma iẓẓalamtum . . .*
It will avail you nothing when you have done wrong, on that Day, that you shall be partners in the punishment.
[The Qur'ān 43:39]

وَلَوْ أَنَّهُمْ إِذ ظَّــــلَمُوا أَنفُسَهُمْ جَاءُوكَ فَاسْتَغْفَرُوا اللَّهَ وَاسْتَغْفَرَ لَهُمُ الرَّسُولُ لَوَجَدُوا اللَّهَ تَوَّابًا رَّحِيمًا

Pronounced: *walaw annahum iẓẓalamū . . .*
If they had only, when they were unjust to themselves, come to you seeking Allah's forgiveness and the Messenger also seeking Allah's forgiveness for them, they would have found Allah indeed accepting of repentance and full of Mercy.
[The Qur'ān 4:64]

5. **The unvowelled ṭā followed by a vowelled tā [ط . ت]**

This occurs in exactly four verses of the Qur'ān:

أَن تَقُولَ نَفْسٌ يَا حَسْرَتَىٰ عَلَىٰ مَا فَرَّطتُ فِي جَنبِ اللَّهِ وَإِن كُنتُ لَمِنَ السَّاخِرِينَ

Pronounced: *. . . 'alā mā farraṭtu fī . . .*

Lest any soul should say, Alas I neglected my duty towards Allah, and was among those that mocked.

[The Qur'ān 39:56]

فَمَكَثَ غَيْرَ بَعِيدٍ فَقَالَ أَحَطتُ بِمَا لَمْ تُحِطْ بِهِ وَجِئْتُكَ مِن سَبَإٍ بِنَبَإٍ يَقِينٍ

Pronounced: *. . . faqāla ahaṭtu bimā . . .*

And he (the hoopoe bird) tarried but for a short while, and said, I have encompassed that which you did not, for I have come to you from Sheba with certain news.

[The Qur'ān 27:22]

قَالَ كَبِيرُهُمْ أَلَمْ تَعْلَمُوا أَنَّ أَبَاكُمْ قَدْ أَخَذَ عَلَيْكُم مَّوْثِقًا مِّنَ اللَّهِ وَمِن قَبْلُ مَا فَرَّطتُمْ فِي يُوسُفَ

Pronounced: *. . . mā farraṭtum fī yūsufa.*

The eldest one said, Don't you know that your father took an oath from you in Allah's name, and how, before this, you did fail in your duty with Yūsuf.

[The Qur'ān 12:80]

لَئِن بَسَطتَ إِلَيَّ يَدَكَ لِتَقْتُلَنِي مَا أَنَا بِبَاسِطٍ يَدِيَ إِلَيْكَ لِأَقْتُلَكَ

Pronounced: *laimbasaṭta ilayya . . .*

If you extend your hand to kill me, I shall not extend mine likewise to kill you, for I fear Allah the Lord of the worlds.

[The Qur'ān 5:28]

It should be noted that these cases of the ṭā merging into the tā is an incomplete merging [idghām nāqiṣ], due to the very strong characteristics of the ṭā [ط] as compared to the tā [ت]. Therefore, in this merging, some remnant of the original ṭā remains, namely the attribute of Adhesion [*Iṭbāq*], which is the firm, compression of the tongue against the palate. Therefore, when articulating these pair of letters, you begin by elevating and compressing the tongue against the roof of the mouth, but then you release the tongue and articulate the normal tā from the tip of the tongue. Basically, you start out with the ṭā [ط] sound (but without the qalqalah) and end with the tā [ت] sound.

In the following two cases assimilation is variable:

1. The unvowelled thā followed by a vowelled dhāl [ث . ذ]

There is only one such example in the Qur'ān:

وَلَوْ شِئْنَا لَرَفَعْنَاهُ بِهَا وَلَٰكِنَّهُ أَخْلَدَ إِلَى الْأَرْضِ وَاتَّبَعَ هَوَاهُ ۚ فَمَثَلُهُ كَمَثَلِ الْكَلْبِ إِن تَحْمِلْ عَلَيْهِ يَلْهَثْ أَوْ تَتْرُكْهُ يَلْهَث ذَّٰلِكَ مَثَلُ الْقَوْمِ الَّذِينَ كَذَّبُوا بِآيَاتِنَا ۚ فَاقْصُصِ الْقَصَصَ لَعَلَّهُمْ يَتَفَكَّرُونَ

Pronounced: *. . . aw tatrukhu yalhadhdhālika . . .*

If it had been Our will, We should have elevated him with Our signs; but he inclined to the earth, and followed his own vain desires. His similitude is that of a dog: if you attack him, he lolls out his tongue, or if you leave him alone, he (still) lolls out his tongue. That is the similitude of those who reject Our signs; So relate the story; perchance they may reflect.

[The Qur'ān 7:176]

Here, the majority of reciters of the Ḥafṣ mode of reading recite with assimilation (idghām), but some do so without assimilation through authentic chains of transmission.

2. The unvowelled bā followed by a vowelled meem [ب . م]

This also occurs in the following Qur'ānic verse only:

وَهِيَ تَجْرِي بِهِمْ فِي مَوْجٍ كَالْجِبَالِ وَنَادَىٰ نُوحٌ ابْنَهُ وَكَانَ فِي مَعْزِلٍ يَا بُنَيَّ ارْكَب مَّعَنَا وَلَا تَكُن مَّعَ الْكَافِرِينَ

Pronounced: *. . . yā bunayyarkamma'anā . . .*

So the Ark floated with them on the waves like mountains, and Noah called out to his son, who had separated himself, "O my son! embark with us, and be not with the unbelievers!"

[The Qur'ān 11:42]

Again, most scholars of the Ḥafṣ mode of reading recite with assimilation while some do not.

All other cases of Mutajānisayn letters in the Ṣaghīr configuration are pronounced with iẓhār, without assimilation. In addition, all cases of Mutajānisayn letters in the Kabīr configuration (i.e. both vowelled) are also pronounced with iẓhār, without assimilation, as in the following example:

اَلصَّالِحَاتِ طُـوبَى

Let us summarize the assimilation rules for Mutajānisayn letters:

Configuration		*Default Rule*				
Ṣaghīr		No uniform rule, but:	Idghām:	د		ت
				ت		د
				ت		ط
				ذ		ظ
				ط		ت
			Both allowed:	ث		ذ
				ب		م
			Iẓhār:	All remaining examples		
Kabīr		Iẓhār				

Mutabā'idayn مُتَبَاعِدَيْنِ

The Two Distant Letters

These are letters which have very different articulation sites as well as attributes. This case applies to the majority of adjacent letters, and these letters are each pronounced in their default normal state (iẓhār). There is no assimilation in these pairs of letters.

Examples include the highlighted pairs of adjacent letters in the following words:

اَلْحَـــمْدُ [the meem followed by dāl]

اَلْقُـــرْآنُ [the rā followed by hamzah]

تُكَـــلِّمُونَ [the tā followed by kāf]

Let us summarize all of these rules in one table:

<table>
<tr><th>Type</th><th>Configuration</th><th colspan="5">Default Rule</th></tr>
<tr><td rowspan="2">Mithlayn letters</td><td>Ṣaghīr</td><td colspan="5">Idghām in all cases</td></tr>
<tr><td>Kabīr</td><td colspan="2">Iẓhār</td><td colspan="3">Exception: Idghām in 6 verses</td></tr>
<tr><td rowspan="6">Mutaqāribayn letters</td><td rowspan="5">Ṣaghīr</td><td rowspan="5">No uniform rule, but:</td><td rowspan="4">Idghām:</td><td>ل</td><td>→</td><td>ر</td></tr>
<tr><td>ل</td><td>→</td><td>الحُرُوف الشَّمسِيَّة</td></tr>
<tr><td>ق</td><td>→</td><td>ك</td></tr>
<tr><td>ن</td><td>→</td><td>يرملون</td></tr>
<tr><td>Iẓhār:</td><td colspan="3">The remaining examples</td></tr>
<tr><td>Kabīr</td><td colspan="5">Iẓhār</td></tr>
<tr><td rowspan="10">Mutajānisayn letters</td><td rowspan="9">Ṣaghīr</td><td rowspan="9">No uniform rule, but:</td><td rowspan="5">Idghām:</td><td>د</td><td>→</td><td>ت</td></tr>
<tr><td>ت</td><td>→</td><td>د</td></tr>
<tr><td>ت</td><td>→</td><td>ط</td></tr>
<tr><td>ذ</td><td>→</td><td>ظ</td></tr>
<tr><td>ط</td><td>→</td><td>ت</td></tr>
<tr><td rowspan="2">Both allowed:</td><td>ث</td><td>→</td><td>ذ</td></tr>
<tr><td>ب</td><td>→</td><td>م</td></tr>
<tr><td>Iẓhār:</td><td colspan="3">All remaining examples</td></tr>
<tr><td>Kabīr</td><td colspan="5">Iẓhār</td></tr>
<tr><td>Mutabā‘idayn letters</td><td colspan="6">No cases of assimilation (Iẓhār in all cases)</td></tr>
</table>

FIGURE 9 — RULES OF ASSIMILATION

Chapter NINE: THE RULES OF ELONGATION [MADD]

أَحكَامُ المَدِّ

IN THIS CHAPTER

What is the madd?
Why is this topic last?
To what letters do these rules apply?
What are the types of madd?
What are the various durations of elongation?

The final section of the Tuḥfah text deals with the topic of madd, which has to do with the length and duration of certain vowel sounds. This topic is considered an advanced one among the rules of Tajweed, and hence is usually discussed last. Violations of madd principles are among the most common mistakes among students of the Qur'ān. But it is really the madd, among a few other topics, which really distinguishes those who truly know Tajweed.

The Meaning of Madd

The root word *madda* literally means to increase, elongate, lengthen, extend or prolong. It is used in its literal meanings in the following verses of the Qur'ān:

إِذْ تَقُولُ لِلْمُؤْمِنِينَ أَلَن يَكْفِيَكُمْ أَن يُمِدَّكُمْ رَبُّكُم بِثَلَاثَةِ آلَافٍ مِّنَ الْمَلَائِكَةِ مُنزَلِينَ

بَلَىٰ ۚ إِن تَصْبِرُوا وَتَتَّقُوا وَيَأْتُوكُم مِّن فَوْرِهِمْ هَٰذَا يُمْدِدْكُمْ رَبُّكُم بِخَمْسَةِ آلَافٍ مِّنَ الْمَلَائِكَةِ

مُسَوِّمِينَ

And when You did say to the believers: Is it not sufficient for you that your Lord should increase/support you with three thousand angels sent down? Nay, but if you persevere, and keep from evil, and (the enemy) attack you suddenly, your Lord will increase/help you with five thousand angels sweeping on.

[The Qur'ān 3:124-125]

فَقُلْتُ اسْتَغْفِرُوا رَبَّكُمْ إِنَّهُ كَانَ غَفَّارًا

يُرْسِلِ السَّمَاءَ عَلَيْكُم مِّدْرَارًا

وَيُمْدِدْكُم بِأَمْوَالٍ وَبَنِينَ وَيَجْعَل لَّكُمْ جَنَّاتٍ وَيَجْعَل لَّكُمْ أَنْهَارًا

And I have said: Seek pardon of your Lord. Lo! He was ever-Forgiving. He will let loose the sky for you in plenteous rain, and will increase you with wealth and sons, and will assign unto you Gardens and will assign unto you rivers.

[The Qur'ān 71:10-12]

In Tajweed terminology, the madd refers to the elongation of certain vowel sounds in specific circumstances. It is perhaps the only Tajweed term found explicitly in the Sunnah. Imām al-Bukhārī in his *Ṣaḥīḥ* entitled a chapter, *The madd of recitation* [Madd al-Qirā'ah] and includes in it the following narration:

> Qatādah narrates that he asked Anas b. Mālik about the recitation of the Prophet, and Anas replied:

كَانَ يَمُدُّ مَدًّا

He would stretch the words when reciting.[86]

Another tradition that is indicative of the importance of madd involves the Companion Ibn Mas'ūd who was once teaching a man who recited the following portion of a verse:

إِنَّمَا الصَّدَقَاتُ لِلْفُقَرَاءِ وَالْمَسَاكِينِ

[The Qur'ān 9:60]

This man recited the word *fuqarā'* without elongating the ending vowel, to which Ibn Mas'ūd responded, "That is not how the Prophet taught me." When the person inquired how the Prophet taught him, Ibn Mas'ūd recited the verse in the following way:

فَمَدَّهَا فِي الفُقَرَاءِ

He articulated the madd in *fuqarā.*[87]

Ibn Mas'ūd basically elongated the ending vowel of the word *fuqarā'* as such—*fuqaraaaa.* The leading scholars of the Qur'ān, including Ibn al-Jazarī and al-Suyūṭī, affirm that this text proves that the principle of madd—and the science of Tajweed in general—is a continuous practice (sunnah) originating with the Prophet himself and transmitted to us in a tawātur manner.[88]

In Tajweed terminology, the madd is basically the elongation of the vowel sound of the three madd letters. There are two types of madd: Basic and Derived.

---

[86] Ḥadīth of Anas b. Mālik related by al-Bukhārī 4657, al-Nasā'ī 1004, Abū Dāwūd 1253, Ibn Mājah 1343 and Aḥmad 11753, 11835, 11891, 12532, 12577, 13562.

[87] Ḥadīth of Mūsā b Yazīd al-Kindī related by al-Ṭabarānī in *al-Mu'jam al-Kabīr* and authenticated by al-Haythamī in *Majma' al-Zawāid*, al-Suyūṭī in *al-Itqān* and by Ibn al-Jazarī in *al-Nashr*.

[88] Tawātur transmission is multiplicitous narration by such large and overwhelming numbers as to make errors impossible.

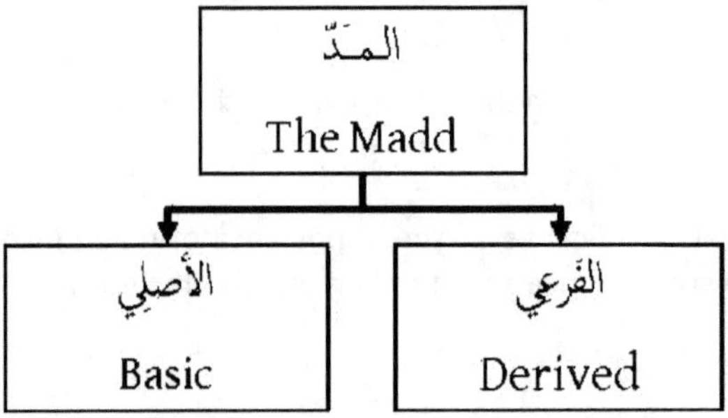

The Basic Madd

All of the madd rules are built upon the three basic madd letters, which were previously mentioned in the chapter on makhraj and are as follows:

1. The unvowelled alif (ا) preceded by the vowel fatḥah:

قَـالَ

2. The unvowelled yā (ي) preceded by the vowel kasrah:

قِـيلَ

3. The unvowelled wāw (و) preceded by the vowel ḍammah:

يَقُـولَ

These three madd letters are remembered by the mnemonic واي and demonstrated in the word نُوحِيهَا .

The above three cases are referred to as madd letters because some elongation is intrinsically and naturally a part of their articulation. This madd is called the Basic Madd [*Madd Aṣlī*] or Natural Madd [*Madd Ṭabī'ī*] and has a duration of exactly two ḥarakahs. It is never prolonged beyond that, unless there are additional circumstances that warrant that (see the section on Derived Madd), nor is it shortened less than two durations. This limitation of the duration of this basic madd to two ḥarakahs is sometimes referred to as *Qaṣr* [literally "shortening"] in order to distinguish it from the more lengthy durations of the other types of madd.

This madd is named Basic or Natural Madd because this madd is a necessary feature of these three madd letters. In fact, if the duration is not lengthened to at least two ḥarakahs, the letters change as do the meanings of the words they are contained in. It is not possible to maintain these letters or these meanings without this basic madd.

For instance the word [إِنَّا], articulated as *innaa* with two ḥarakahs on the ending vowel, is an emphatic pronoun combination that means *Indeed we . . .* If we shorten the duration of the ending vowel to one ḥarakah, with the word being articulated as *inna,* then it becomes a different word—namely [إِنَّ] meaning *Indeed.* Therefore the meaning would completely change.

Also the word [أَخَذْنَا] with two ḥarakahs at the end means *we took,* but were the duration to be shortened to one ḥarakah, it would mean *the women took* [أَخَذْنَ]. Both forms of these words occur in the Qur'ān, and it is quite clear that mixing them leads to major changes in the meanings of the verses.

Madd Līn

In addition to these three basic madd letters, there is a modified form of these letters, known as *madd līn* letters, which are as follows:

1. The unvowelled wāw (و) preceded by the vowel fatḥah:

يَــوْمَ

2. The unvowelled yā (ي) preceded by the vowel fatḥah:

بَــيْنَ

The duration of the Madd Līn, which is a modified type of madd, is actually slightly less than two ḥarakahs, because it is somewhat difficult or cumbersome to prolong the sound beyond that. But for practical purposes, it can be considered to be part of the Basic Madd with a duration of two ḥarakahs.

The Basic Madd is the most common type of madd in the Qur'ān, with nearly every verse of the Qur'ān containing examples of it. Consider, for instance, the following beginning verse of Sūrah al-Baqarah:

﴿ ذَٰلِكَ ٱلْكِتَٰبُ لَا رَيْبَ ۛ فِيهِ ۛ هُدًى لِّلْمُتَّقِينَ ﴿٢﴾ ﴾

This is the book, no doubt about it; in it is guidance for the God-fearing.
[The Qur'ān 2:2]

This verse contains five examples of Basic Madd, which are highlighted as follows:

↓ ↓ ↓ ↓ ↓ ↓

﴿ ذَٰلِكَ ٱلْكِتَٰبُ لَا رَيْبَ ۛ فِيهِ ۛ هُدًى لِّلْمُتَّقِينَ ﴿٢﴾ ﴾

articulated as: *Dhaalikal kitaabu laa rayba feehi hudan lil muttaqeen.*

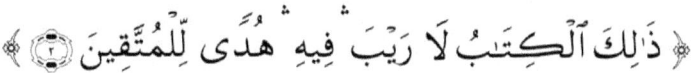

Other Types That Follow the Basic Madd Rule

In addition, there are a number of additional types of madd that follow the pattern of the Basic Madd.

1. Five Disjointed Letters

The first of these are five disjointed letters that begin some of the Qur'ānic chapters, which in their articulation follow the pattern of the Basic Madd and have a duration of two ḥarakahs. These letters are as follows:

حيّ طُهر

Each of these letters is articulated as follows:

ح → حَا

ي → يَا

ط → طَا

هـ → هَا

ر → رَا

Therefore, when reciting any of these disjointed letters, they must be articulated with a basic madd of two durations, even if the letters occur in combination with other disjointed letters with longer durations.

An example is the opening of Sūrah Ṭāhā:

طه

[The Qur'ān 20:1]

articulated as: *Ṭaa haa*

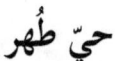

2. Madd 'Iwaḍ [The Substitute Madd]

مَد عِوَض

When you stop on a word that ends with tanwīn in the fatḥah configuration (double fatḥah ـً), the tanwīn is dropped according to the rules of reading with the resulting articulation being that of a fatḥah vowel of two durations. Consider the following examples:

	Normally articulated as:	During stop, articulated as:
شَكُورًا	*shakūran*	*shakūraa*
هُدًا	*hudan*	*hudaa*
مَاءً	*maa'an*	*maa'aa*
بِنَاءً	*binaa'an*	*binaa'aa*

Again, this only occurs when you stop on these words, but if you continue reciting beyond them they are articulated with their normal tanwīn. Also note that this rule does NOT apply in the case of words ending with the feminine gender element known as the *tā marbūta* or *hā al-ta'nīth* [ة], as in the following examples:

	Normally articulated as:	During stop, articulated as:
رَحمَةً	*raḥmatan*	*raḥmah*
نِعمَةً	*ni'matan*	*ni'mah*

In these cases, when stopping on the word this ending tā is converted to an unvowelled hā.

3. Madd al-Ṣilah al-Ṣughrā [The Lesser Connecting Madd]

مَدّ الصِّلَة الصُّغرَى

The case of the attached third-person masculine pronoun [*hā al-ḍamīr*] also follows the Basic Madd at times. This pronoun represents the third person and is normally attached to nouns to indicate possession. It occurs in the form of the letter hā and carries either a ḍammah or kasrah vowel. Examples are as follows:

كِتَابَهُ	*His book . . .*
عِبَادِهِ	*His servants . . .*
إِنَّهُ	*Indeed he . . .*

The basic rule is as follows: if this pronoun is vowelled and positioned between two vowelled letters, its duration is lengthened to a basic madd (i.e. two ḥarakahs). In most printed copies of the Qur'ān, this is indicated by a small wāw or yā written after the pronoun. Consider the following examples:

﴿ مَثَلُهُمْ كَمَثَلِ ٱلَّذِى ٱسْتَوْقَدَ نَارًا فَلَمَّآ أَضَآءَتْ مَا حَوْلَهُۥ ذَهَبَ ٱللَّهُ بِنُورِهِمْ وَتَرَكَهُمْ فِى ظُلُمَٰتٍ لَّا يُبْصِرُونَ ﴾

Their parable is that of people who kindle a fire: but as soon as it has illumined all around them, Allah takes away their light and leaves them in utter darkness, wherein they cannot see.
[The Qur'ān 2:17]

Our word of interest is:

حَولَهُ

This word ends with the masculine pronoun which has a single ḍammah vowel on it (normally articulated as *ḥawlahu*). However, since this pronoun is preceded by a vowelled letter (in the same word) and followed by a vowelled letter (in the next word), its duration is extended to two ḥarakahs (and thus articulated as *ḥawlahuu*). This is called the Madd al-Ṣilah al-Ṣughrā and is indicated by the small wāw symbol following it in the verse.

This rule is also applied in the case of the feminine pronoun *hādhihī*:

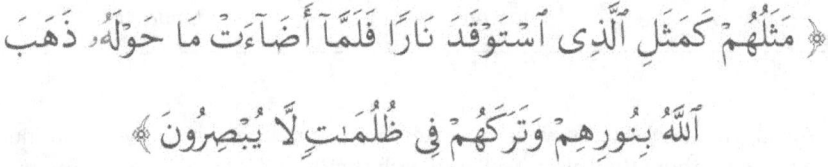

هَـٰذِهِۦ

As in the following verse:

﴿ هَـٰذِهِۦ نَاقَةُ ٱللَّهِ لَكُمْ ءَايَةً ﴾

This she-camel belonging to God shall be a token for you.
[The Qur'ān 7:73]

Note that this rule does not apply to the word [فِيهِ] and those that resemble it since the pronoun in this case is preceded by an unvowelled yā. The rule states that the pronoun must be surrounded by *vowelled* letters on both sides.

Exceptions

It should also be noted that at times there are significant exceptions to these and other rules of Tajweed not on the basis of any other rule or principle but only because it was transmitted to us in that manner. The important point to be understood is that Qur'ānic recitation is a transmitted science from the Prophet and its stated rules and principles are tools developed by later scholars in order to facilitate its study and implementation. As such, there are exceptions in many verses which are memorized and taught as they were taught to us. In the issue of the Madd al-Ṣilah al-Ṣughrā, there are two exceptions in the following two verses:

﴿ وَإِن تَشْكُرُواْ يَرْضَهُ لَكُمْ ﴾

If you are grateful, He is pleased with you.
[The Qur'ān 39:7]

﴿ يُضَٰعَفْ لَهُ ٱلْعَذَابُ يَوْمَ ٱلْقِيَٰمَةِ وَيَخْلُدْ فِيهِۦ مُهَانًا ﴾

The doom will be doubled for him on the Day of Resurrection, and he will abide therein disdained forever.
[The Qur'ān 25:69]

In the first verse, the highlighted pronoun is articulated with one ḥarakah rather than two though it is surrounded by two vowelled letters. In the second verse, the highlighted pronoun is articulated with two ḥarakahs (and indicated as such by the yā symbol following it) rather than one although it doesn't fit the rule and is preceded by an unvowelled yā. There is no simple rule governing this, and these exceptions should simply be memorized as such.

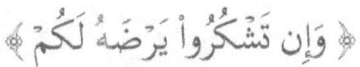

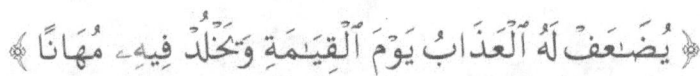

The Secondary or Derived Madd

In certain situations, this natural madd of the above letters is prolonged and extended to longer durations. These cases of madd are referred to as the Derived or Secondary Madd [*Madd Farʿī*], and they occur basically when one of these basic madd letters is combined with an additional cause of madd. There are two additional causes of madd—hamzah and sukūn.

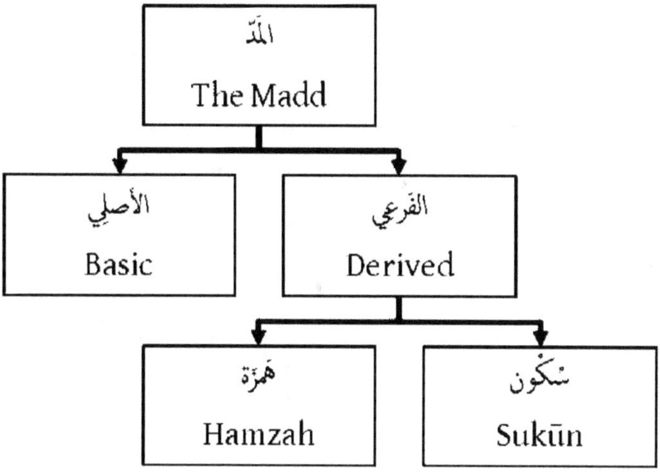

The Sukūn

Let us begin with the case of the sukūn. On occasion, the madd letters are followed immediately by an unvowelled letter. Obviously, the sukūn can only occur after a madd letter and not before it since the madd letters by definition are preceded by a vowel. This sukūn is of two types: actual and presented.

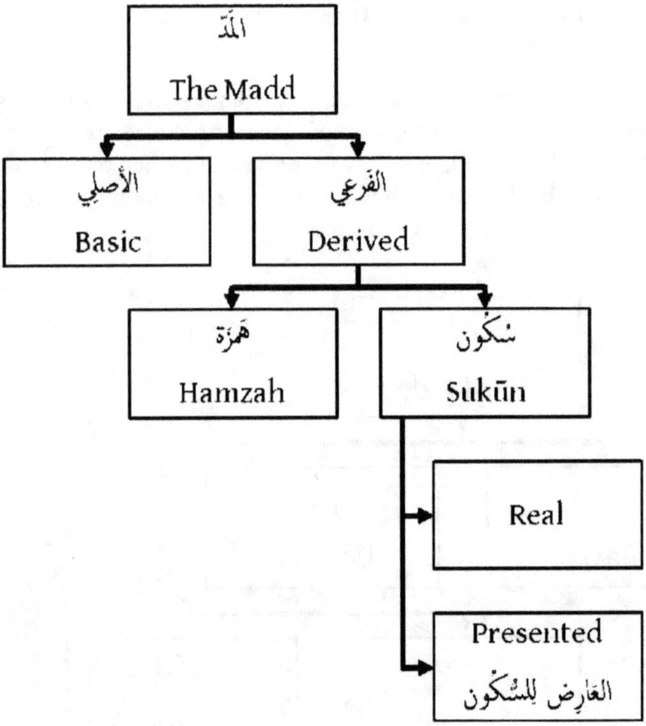

Madd Lāzim

An actual sukūn after a madd letter forces the duration of the madd to extend to the maximal length—six ḥarakahs. This type of madd is called Madd Lāzim [Binding Madd], due to its ruling which is mandatory lengthening. It is sufficient for correct recitation to know this Madd up to this level alone, for the further divisions below are for purposes of classification and instruction alone and do not change the duration of the madd.

For example, the following word begins with hamzah followed by the madd alif (which normally has two durations) followed by sukūn (which forces it to have six durations):

ءَآلْئَٰنَ

articulated as: *aaaaaal'aana* rather than *aal'aana*

Note that after the unvowelled lām is another hamzah followed by a madd alif (which has two durations) which is turn followed by a vowelled nūn. Since there is no sukūn following this second madd letter, it remains on its original two durations. So this word has two madd letters, the first of six durations and the second of two durations.[89]

The Madd Lāzim can occur in a word (in which case it is also called Madd Kalimī) or in the disjointed letters that begin some chapters of the Qur'ān (this case is called Madd Ḥarfī).

Madd Lāzim Kalimī

The case of the Madd Lāzim occurring within a word is further divided into two types: if the madd letter is followed by a simple sukūn it is called Light [Mukhaffaf], whereas if it is followed by a shaddah (a stressed letter, which is essentially an unvowelled letter merged into a vowelled one) it is called Heavy [Muthaqqal]. The only Qur'ānic word that represents the former type (Mukhaffaf) is the same word we just examined:

ءَآلْـَٔنَ

This word occurs in the following two verses of Sūrah Yūnus:

﴿ ءَآلْـَٔنَ وَقَدْ كُنتُم بِهِۦ تَسْتَعْجِلُونَ ﴾

Pronounced: . . . *aaaaaal'āna wa qad kuntum bihī . . .*
What! Now (you believe), when (until now) you have been hastening it on (through disbelief)?
[The Qur'ān 10:51]

﴿ ءَآلْـَٔنَ وَقَدْ عَصَيْتَ قَبْلُ وَكُنتَ مِنَ ٱلْمُفْسِدِينَ ﴾

Pronounced: . . . *aaaaaalāna wa qad 'aṣayta qablu . . .*
What! Now! When hitherto you have rebelled and been of the wrong-doers?
[The Qur'ān 10:91]

This word is a case of a madd letter followed by an actual sukūn, in this word on the letter lām. Therefore it is an example of Madd Lāzim Kalimī Mukhaffaf—

[89] There are in fact alternate ways of articulating this particular word in other modes of Qur'ānic readings, including even some narrations of the Ḥafṣ reading, in which the first madd is not lengthened to six durations but is pronounced as two separate hamzahs with the second hamzah in a modified form known as tas'hīl.

Lāzim because it is followed by an actual sukūn rather than a presented one; *Kalimī* because it is exemplified within a word and not a letter; and *Mukhaffaf* because it is followed by a sukūn rather than a shaddah. In fact, the first description alone (Lāzim) is sufficient to know its articulation and duration—six ḥarakahs. The other descriptions are merely for purposes of categorization and teaching.

The Madd Lāzim Kalimī Muthaqqal is that which is followed by a shaddah within a word, as in the following examples:

الحَآقَّةُ

الطَّآمَّةُ

الصَّآخَّةُ

There are numerous such examples throughout the Qur'ān.

Madd Lāzim Ḥarfī

The other case of Madd Lāzim occurs in the case of the disjointed letters and is called Madd Lāzim Ḥarfī. In essence you must write out the way the letter is articulated to illustrate this. Basically this occurs in the eight letters of the following mnemonic:

كم عسل نقص

Each of these letters when pronounced has a madd letter in the middle, which is clearly seen when each letter is written out as it is articulated:

س → سِينْ

ن → نُونْ

ق → قَافْ

ص → صَادْ

ل → لَامْ

كَافْ → ك

مِيمْ → م

This middle madd letter in each of these letters ends with sukūn (i.e. is followed by an unvowelled letter)—which is a cause for madd—and is thus articulated with a duration of six ḥarakahs.

To determine if each case is an example of Mukhaffaf or Muthaqqal, you must write out the letters in succession. If the letters as spelled out end with sukūn it is considered Mukhaffaf, while if it ends with shaddah it is considered Muthaqqal. Again, the distinction is largely academic as the duration is the same in both. An example of Mukhaffaf would be middle lām in the following:

الر

pronounced:

أَلِفْ لَامْ رَا

An example of Madd Ḥarfī Muthaqqal is in the lām in the following disjointed letters:

الم

pronounced:

أَلِفْ لَامْ مِيمْ

↓

أَلِفْ لَآمِّيمْ

In the case of the letter ʻayn, the middle letter is an example of Madd Līn, which is a modified form of the madd rather than the basic madd.

عَيْنْ → ع

Because of this, there are various ways to articulate this madd among the Qur'ānic scholars, ranging from two to four to six ḥarakahs. The majority of reciters do so with six ḥarakahs as an example of Madd Lāzim Ḥarfī.

The remaining examples of disjointed letters in the Qur'ān are pronounced with two ḥarakahs as examples of the Basic Madd since they are not followed by any cause of madd (hamzah or sukūn):

حيّ طهر

[ح] → حَا

[ي] → يَا

[ط] → طَا

[هـ] → هَا

[ر] → رَا

Permissible Madd

[Madd Jāiz or Madd 'Āriḍ li'l-Sukūn]

مَدّ عَارِض لِلسُّكُون

The next example is the case of a madd letter followed by a presented or incidental sukūn rather than a real one. This basically happens when you are stopping on a word. In other words, though the word ends with a vowelled letter, when you end your recitation on that word, the ending vowel is dropped and the last letter is articulated with a sukūn. Consider the following word:

العَالَمِينَ

al-'ālamīna

When stopping on this word, it is articulated as such:

الْعَالَمِينْ

al-'ālamīn

Since this ending is an effective sukūn, which is a cause of madd, this allows the preceding madd letter to be articulated with a longer duration. However, since it is not an actual sukūn, this madd is not mandatory. Therefore it is called Madd Jā'iz [Permissible Madd], and its duration can be either two or four or six ḥarakahs, all of them being permissible.

Therefore, the following verse can be recited in several ways when stopping on it, as follows:

الْحَمْدُ لِلَّهِ رَبِّ الْعَالَمِـــــــينَ

All praise is due to Allah, Lord of the worlds.
[The Qur'ān 1:1]

May be pronounced:
al-ḥamdu lillahi rabbil 'ālameen (2 ḥarakahs).
al-ḥamdu lillahi rabbil 'ālameeeen (4 ḥarakahs).
al-ḥamdu lillahi rabbil 'ālameeeeeen (6 ḥarakahs).

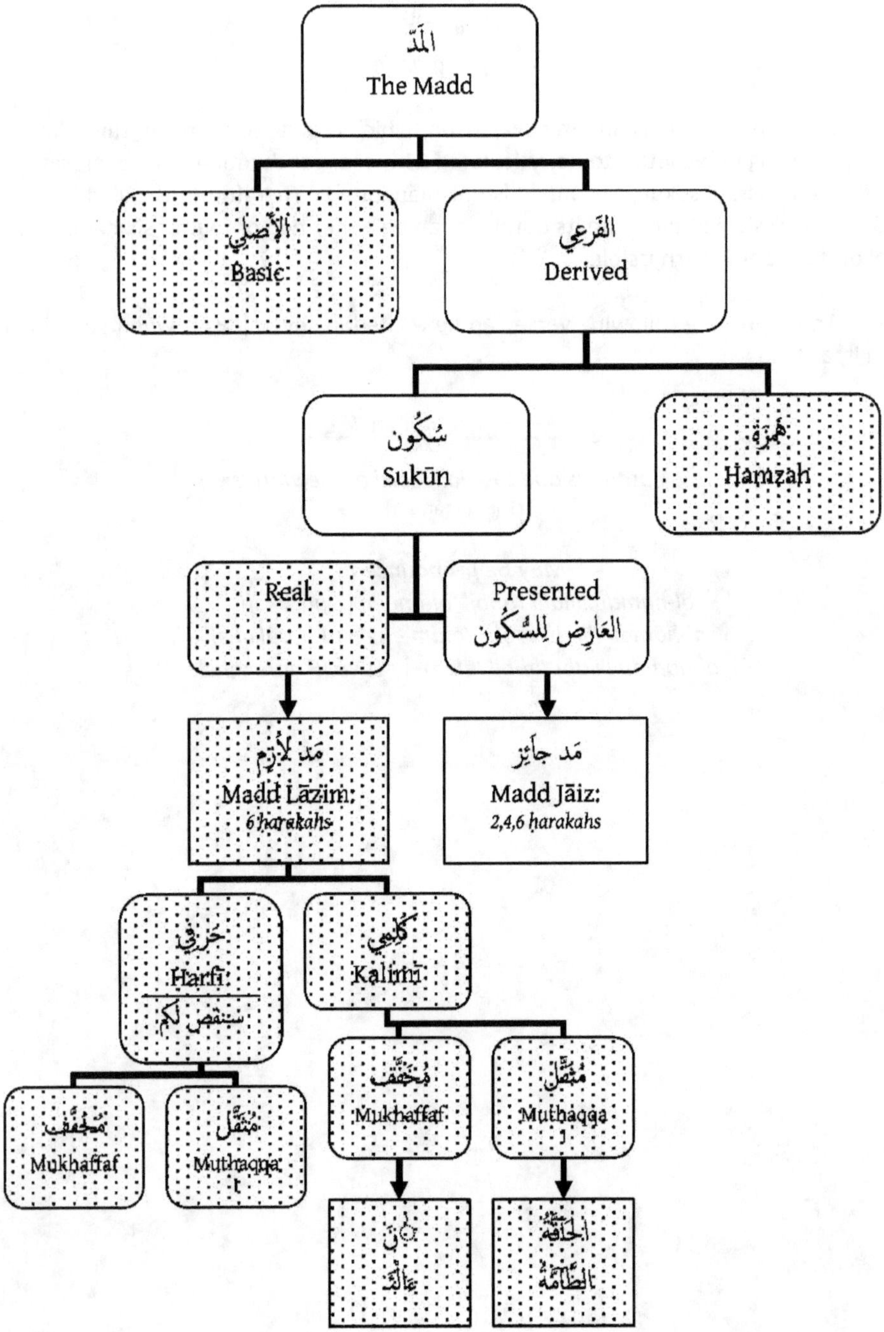

المَدّ
The Madd
الأَصلي
Basic
الفَرعي
Derived
سُكُون
Sukūn
هَمزَة
Ḥamzah
Real
Presented
العَارِض لِلسُّكُون
مَد لأزم
Madd Lāzim:
6 ḥarakahs
مَد جائز
Madd Jāiz:
2,4,6 ḥarakahs
حَرفِي
Harfī:
سنقص لكم
كَلِمِي
Kalimī
مُخَفَّف
Mukhaffaf
مُثَقَّل
Muthaqqa
l
مُخَفَّف
Mukhaffaf
مُثَقَّل
Muthaqqa
l

The Hamzah

The next cause of madd is the hamzah, which can occur before the madd or after it, and can occur within a word or in different words when it follows the madd letter.

Madd Badal

When the hamzah precedes the madd letter, it is referred to as Madd Badal [Substitute Madd], as in the following cases:

ءَا	pronounced:	*ā (aa)*
إِي	pronounced:	*ī (ii)*
أُو	pronounced:	*ū (oo)*

The reason it is called Badal has to do with its linguistic origins. These three cases were originally two hamzah letters, the first vowelled and the second unvowelled, and the second hamzah became converted to a madd letter:

[أَأْ] → ءَا

[إِأْ] → إِي

[أُؤْ] → أُو

These cases of Madd Badal have a duration of two ḥarakahs, and care should be taken not to extend them beyond that. The ruling of this madd is thus that of permissibility, and they are also considered to be from the Madd Jā'iz (according to the Ḥafṣ rendition, though in some other modes of recitation it is lengthened). Examples include the highlighted words in the following verses:

﴿ إِنَّ ٱللَّهَ ٱصۡطَفَىٰٓ ءَادَمَ وَنُوحًا وَءَالَ إِبۡرَٰهِيمَ وَءَالَ عِمۡرَٰنَ عَلَى ٱلۡعَٰلَمِينَ ﴾

BEHOLD, God raised Adam, and Noah, and the House of Abraham, and the House of 'Imrān above all mankind.

[The Qur'ān 3:33]

This verse has two words that are examples of Madd Badal, one of them repeated twice:

ءَادَمَ

ءَالَ

Other Qur'ānic words that contain examples of Madd Badal include:

أُوذُوا

إِيمَانًا

ءَامَنَ

أَنبِئُونِي

مَئَابٍ

المنشئات

Madd Muttaṣil [Attached Madd]

If the hamzah occurs after the madd letter in the same word, it is called Madd Muttaṣil and its ruling its obligatory extension to four or five ḥarakahs (also called Madd Wājib or Madd Wājib Muttaṣil). Examples include the following highlighted words in this verse:

﴿ وَءَاتُواْ ٱلنِّسَآءَ صَدُقَٰتِهِنَّ نِحۡلَةٗۚ فَإِن طِبۡنَ لَكُمۡ عَن شَيۡءٖ مِّنۡهُ نَفۡسٗا فَكُلُوهُ هَنِيٓـٔٗا مَّرِيٓـٔٗا ﴾

And give unto women their marriage portions (dowry) in the spirit of a gift; but if they, of their own accord, give up unto you aught thereof, then enjoy it with pleasure and good cheer.
[The Qur'ān 4:4]

This above verse contains three cases of Madd Muttaṣil, in the following words:

ٱلنِّسَآءَ pronounced: *nisaaaa'a*

هَنِيٓـٔٗا pronounced: *haneeee'an*

مَرِيٓـٔٗا pronounced: *mareeee'an*

The duration of four ḥarakahs is sometimes called *tawassuṭ* [توسّط] while the five ḥarakah duration is called *fuwaiq al-tawassuṭ* [فويق التوسّط].

Madd Munfaṣil [Separated Madd]

If the hamzah follows a madd letter but in a different word, then its ruling is that of permissible madd [Madd Jāiz]. In other words, the madd is optional, and so it can be limited to its default of two ḥarakahs, or extended to four or five ḥarakahs.

It must be noted that consistency be maintained in one's recitation. If one chooses to shorten this type of madd, then it must be done so for all such cases in the recitation. However, if one stops and starts another session of recitation, then the other option can be selected (i.e. lengthening) and should be maintained for that session.

Examples of Madd Munfaṣil include the highlighted words in the verses below:

﴿ لَآ أَعۡبُدُ مَا تَعۡبُدُونَ ۝٢ ﴾

﴿ وَلَآ أَنتُمۡ عَٰبِدُونَ مَآ أَعۡبُدُ ۝٣ ﴾

﴿ وَلَآ أَنَا۠ عَابِدٞ مَّا عَبَدتُّمۡ ۝٤ ﴾

﴿ وَلَآ أَنتُمۡ عَٰبِدُونَ مَآ أَعۡبُدُ ۝٥ ﴾

I do not worship that which you worship, nor do you worship that which I worship. And I will not worship that which you have worshipped, nor will you worship that which I worship.
[The Qur'ān 109:2-5]

In each verse above, the word *lā* [لَا] is followed by a hamzah in the next word. Therefore, this is a case of an optional Madd Jāiz Munfaṣil, which may be shortened to two ḥarakahs or lengthened to four or five.

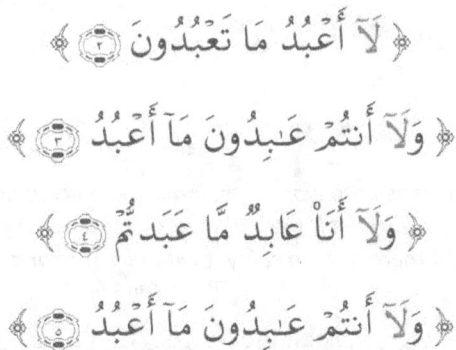

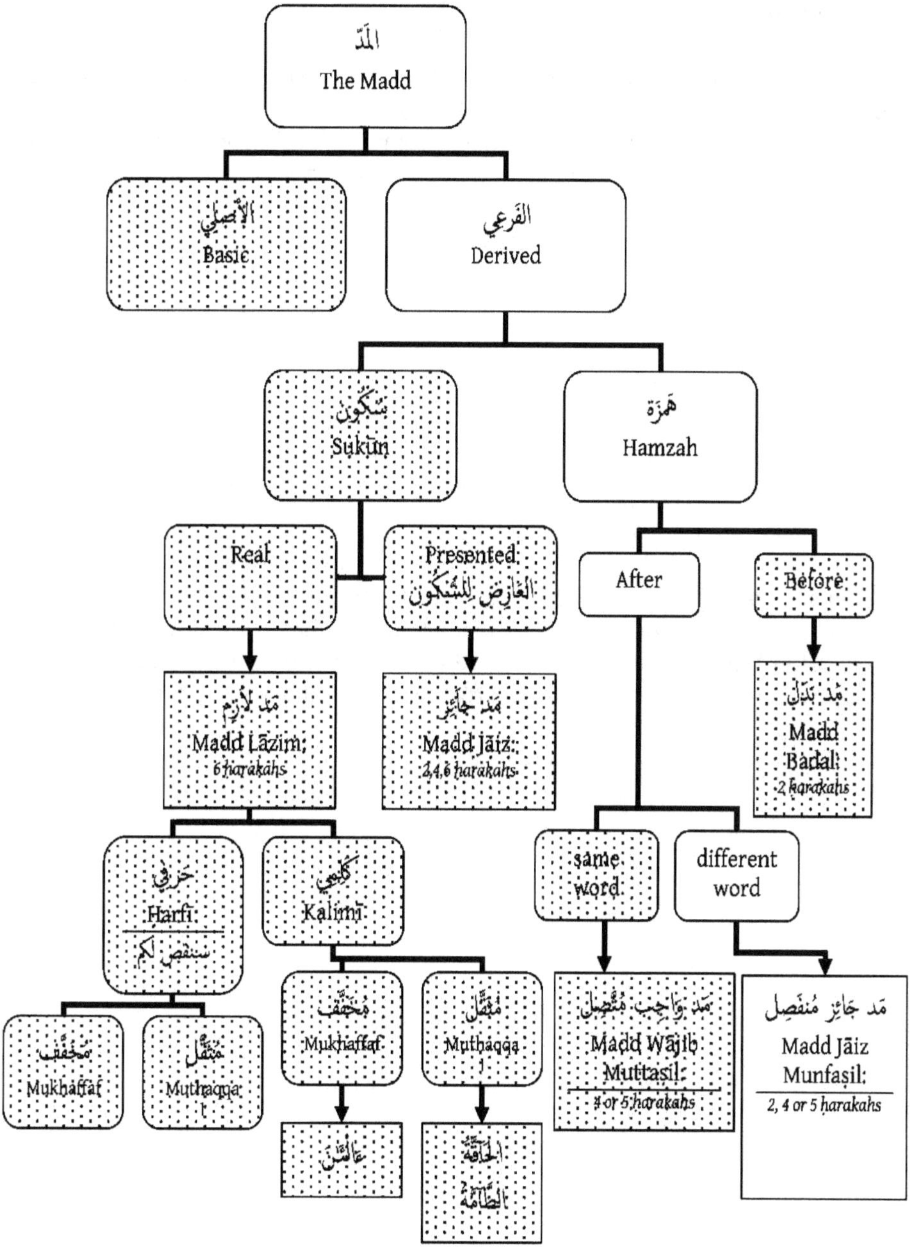
المَدّ
The Madd
الأَصلِي
Basic
الفَرعِي
Derived
سُكُون
Sukūn
هَمزَة
Hamzah
Real
Presented
العَارِض لِلسُّكُون
After
Before
مَد لَازِم
Madd Lāzim:
6 ḥarakahs
مَد جَائِز
Madd Jāiz:
2,4,6 ḥarakahs
مَد بَدَل
Madd Badal:
2 ḥarakahs
حَرفِي
Harfi
كَلِمِي
Kalimi
same word
different word
مُخَفَّف
Mukhaffaf
مُثَقَّل
Muthaqqal
مَد وَاجِب مُتَّصِل
Madd Wājib Muttaṣil:
4 or 5 ḥarakahs
مَد جَائِز مُنفَصِل
Madd Jāiz Munfaṣil:
2, 4 or 5 ḥarakahs
الحَاقَّة
الطَّامَّة

Caution

These rules obviously require some basic knowledge of Arabic as to where one word ends and the next begins, which is usually obvious in most cases and in most printed copies of the Qur'ān but not always. Sometimes two words are written in a combined form that appears to be one word but are actually two separate words, as in the following Qur'ānic words:

يَٰٓإِبۡرَٰهِيمُ	←	يَا + إِبرَاهِيمُ
يَٰٓأَيُّهَا	←	يَا + أَيُّهَا
هَٰٓؤُلَآءِ	←	هَا + أُلَاءِ

In each of these cases above, it would appear that these are cases of Madd Muttaṣil since the hamzah follows the madd letter in what appears to be the same word, but in fact these are cases of Madd Munfaṣil because they are actually two words. Therefore, the madd may be shortened to two ḥarakahs or extended beyond that.

Madd al-Ṣilah al-Kubrā [The Greater Connecting Madd]

مَدّ الصِّلَة الكُبرى

We covered the case of the third person masculine pronoun which is written with a hā and follows the natural madd rule if it is vowelled and surrounded by two vowelled letters [Madd al-Ṣilah al-Ṣughrā or Lesser Connecting Madd]. If this pronoun in this state of Natural Madd is followed by a hamzah, then it becomes an example of Madd Jāiz Munfaṣil and can either be shortened to two durations or extended to four or five. It is referred to as Greater Connecting Madd to distinguish it from the Lesser one. Examples include the following verses:

﴿ أَيَحْسَبُ أَن لَّمْ يَرَهُۥٓ أَحَدٌ ﴾

[The Qur'ān 90:7]

May be articulated as:

. . . *lam yarahuu aḥad* [2 ḥarakahs]
. . . *lam yarahuuu aḥad* [4 ḥarakahs]
. . . *lam yarahuuuu aḥad* [5 ḥarakahs]

﴿ قَالَ فَأْتِ بِهِۦٓ إِن كُنتَ مِنَ ٱلصَّٰدِقِينَ ﴾

[The Qur'ān 26:31]

May be articulated as:

. . . *fa'ti bihii inkunta . . .* [2 ḥarakahs]
. . . *fa'ti bihiii inkunta. . .* [4 ḥarakahs]
. . . *fa'ti bihiiiii inkunta . . .* [5 ḥarakahs]

Combination of Madds

It must be noted that sometimes two types of madd can be combined in one word, as more than one cause of madd may exist. This occurs, for instance, when you stop on a word with Madd Muttaṣil (a madd followed by hamzah in the same word), as in the following word:

وَإِذَا قِيلَ لَهُمْ آمِنُوا كَمَا آمَنَ النَّاسُ قَالُوا أَنُؤْمِنُ كَمَا آمَنَ السُّفَهَاءُ

When it is said to them, 'Believe as the people believe,' they say,
'Shall we believe as the fools believe?'

[The Qur'ān 2:13]

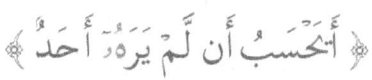

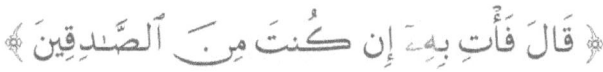

The last word in the verse is an example of Madd Wājib Muttaṣil, which is articulated with four or five ḥarakahs. In addition, when you stop on this word in recitation it also becomes an example of Madd Jāiz (Madd 'Āriḍ li'l-Sukūn) due to the presented sukūn created by the stop at its end. This Madd Jāiz is articulated with two or four or six ḥarakahs. However when you combine the two types in this particular example, the result is that you may articulate the word in stopping with four or five or six ḥarakahs, and not two. The reason for this is that the basic state of the word is the Madd Muttaṣil which must be articulated with a minimum of four, and cannot be reduced.

Therefore, when more than one reason for madd is combined in a word, you must look at all the reasons together and take the strongest one. The order of strength of the various types of Madd is as follows, from strongest to weakest:

1. Madd Lāzim → 6 ḥarakahs

2. Madd Muttaṣil → 4 or 5 ḥarakahs

3. Madd 'Āriḍ → 2 or 4 or 6 ḥarakahs

4. Madd Munfaṣil → 2 or 4 or 5 ḥarakahs

5. Madd Badal → 2 ḥarakahs

Consider the following example:

وَلَا آمِّينَ الْبَيْتَ الْحَرَامَ

The highlighted word above begins with hamzah followed by the madd letter, which is an example of Madd Badal, whose duration is expected to be two ḥarakahs:

ءَامِّينَ

However, when you continue further examining the word, this madd letter is followed by a shaddah, which is a type of sukūn and makes the Madd Lāzim whose duration must be six ḥarakahs. Since this cause of madd is stronger than the previous one, we implement the stronger cause and articulate this madd with six ḥarakahs.

We end with a summary of the rules of madd in one chart:

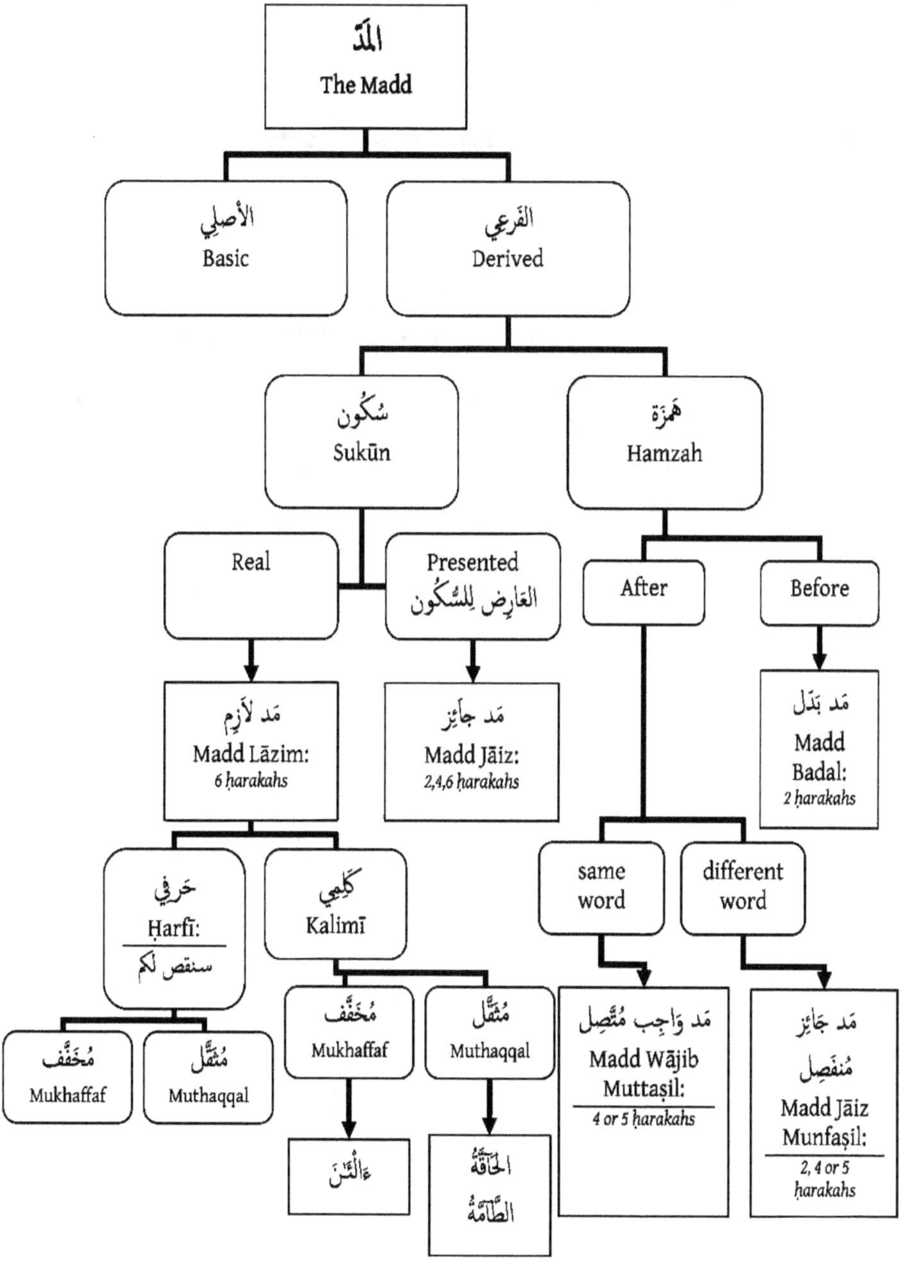

FIGURE 10—RULES OF MADD

APPENDIX ONE: MISTAKES IN TAJWEED

اللَّحنُ فِي التَّجوِيد

IN THIS CHAPTER

What are the various types of mistakes?

What is the ruling on mistakes in Tajweed?

What are the types of reciters?

The recitation of the speech of Allah is quite obviously a matter that is extremely weighty and delicate at the same time. It is also known that mistakes are inevitable in the process of learning. So what about mistakes in Tajweed, and exactly how serious are they?

Scholars generally divide these mistakes into major and minor ones. Major mistakes (often referred to as *laḥn jaliyy*) are those mistakes that lead to changes in meanings or word structures in the Qur'ān. They are considered major since they change the meanings and words of the Qur'ān. These types of mistakes are generally discernible to scholars of Tajweed as well as many laypersons. Examples of major mistakes include:

Addition of words or other elements in the recitation
Deletion or omission of entire words
The changing of one letter into another
The changing of a vowel to another

Major mistakes are deemed forbidden by the general agreement of scholars, especially if done deliberately or out of wanton disregard.

Minor mistakes (*laḥn khafiyy*), on the other hand, occur when more minute rules of Tajweed are violated. These types of mistakes are really discernible only to experts or those who are well-versed in Tajweed. Minor mistakes include violations in matters such as the ghunnah nasalization, the exact lengthening and duration of the madd and other similar elements. The general view is that minor mistakes are discouraged but not actually forbidden (*makrūh*), although some scholars have held the view that minor mistakes in recitation are also forbidden.

It should be noted that the Companions of the Prophet and early Muslims took this matter quite seriously and were intolerant of all types of mistakes relating to Qur'ānic recitation. This was due to their extreme reverence for the Holy Book. Ubayy b. Ka'b used to say, *Teach the mistakes in the Qur'ān just as you teach the Qur'ān itself*. In the previously mentioned narration, Mūsā b. Yazīd al-Kindī once observed Ibn Mas'ūd correcting a student of his who was reciting verse 60 of Sūrah al-Tawbah and did not sufficiently lengthen the last vowel of the word *fuqarā'*. Ibn Mas'ūd said to his student, *This is not how the Messenger of Allah taught me*.[90] Though the meaning of the word was not changed in any way and this would thus be considered a minor mistake, he did not tolerate it because of the nature of Tajweed as a transmitted practice tracing back to the Prophet and the sensitivity of the Qur'ān being the Divine speech of Allah.

---

[90] Ḥadīth of Mūsā b Yazīd al-Kindī related by al-Ṭabarānī in *al-Mu'jam al-Kabīr* and authenticated by al-Haythamī in *Majma' al-Zawāid*, al-Suyūṭī in *al-Itqān* and by Ibn al-Jazarī in *al-Nashr*.

The Blessed Prophet, on the other hand, had a brighter and more upbeat perspective on this issue. His mission, after all, was to inspire optimism and hope rather than despair. And so he shifted the focus away from the mistakes of Tajweed, and instead highlighted the persons involved in the recitation:

الَّذِي يَقْرَأُ الْقُرْآنَ وَ هُوَ مَاهِرٌ بِهِ مَعَ السَّفَرَةِ الْكِرَامِ الْبَرَرَةِ ، وَ الَّذِي يَقْرَأُهُ وَ هُوَ عَلَيْهِ شَاقٌّ لَهُ أَجْرَانِ

The one who recites the Qur'ān with skill and expertise will be with pure and noble scribes, while the one who struggles with it has a double reward.[91]

Based upon this Prophetic classification, scholars have divided people with respect to Tajweed into three basic types:

1. **The proper reciters**
2. **Those who make mistakes that are excused**
3. **Those who make mistakes that are blameworthy**

The proper reciters (al-māhir) are those who recite correctly, with due consideration of all the rules of Tajweed. These are the experts, and their great reward is the noble company of the finest angels.

As for those whose mistakes are excused, they are the ones who are actively struggling to learn, those with physical handicaps of the tongue that preclude their ability to articulate certain elements correctly, or those with neither the opportunity nor the means to learn the skills of Tajweed as much as they would like to do so. This is all implied in the Prophetic description *the one who struggles with it*. What is truly inspiring is that according to the Prophet, not only are the mistakes of these people excused, but they deserve a double reward! In other words, with the right intentions, even mistakes can be rewarded.

Finally, those whose mistakes are blameworthy are the ones who refuse to avail themselves of the opportunity to learn Tajweed, do not consider it important to do so, or consider themselves to be experts while they are not.

Common Tajweed Mistakes

The most common Tajweed mistakes involve mispronouncing certain Arabic letters. This is the domain of makhārij (points of articulation) and attributes, as discussed in previous chapters. These mistakes vary from person-to-person and across geographical regions.

---

[91] Ḥadīth of 'Āisha related in slightly varying wordings in al-Bukhārī 4556, Muslim 1329, al-Tirmidhī 2829, Abū Dāwūd 1242, Ibn Mājah 3769, Aḥmad 23080, 23493, 23526, 23644, 24197, 24413, 24835, 25093, and al-Dārimī 3234. The wording above is that of Aḥmad 23080.

For those accustomed to the North American vernacular of speaking, the letters r and l are always sounded in a heavy manner, whereas in Tajweed they are variably heavy or light. Therefore American reciters typically have trouble with the lighter articulation of these letters.

For South Asians from India, Pakistan and related countries, the distinction between the following letters are generally blurred to the point that they erroneously sound exactly the same:

- **Hamzah [أ] and ʿayn [ع]**
- **Sīn [س], ṣād [ص], and thā [ث]**
- **Zay [ز], dhal [ذ], ẓā [ظ], and ḍād [ض]**
- **Hā [هـ] and ḥā [ح]**
- **Wāw [و], which is the English w sound, often is sounded like the English v, which has no Arabic equivalent**

These common mistakes are manifested in the English spellings of various common names, which are spelled differently depending upon which region you are from. And so Usman is written in place of Uthman, Ramzan in place of Ramaḍān, Abū Zarr in place of Abū Dharr, Khizr in place of Khiḍr, etc.

Native Arabic speakers make their own set of mistakes, stemming from reciting the Qurʾān similar to their customary Arabic speech, but these mistakes generally involve rules such as iqlāb, ikhfā and idghām rather than makhārij.

Common mistakes universal to all groups of people are the inappropriate prolongation or shortening of the madd vowels, which are sometimes stretched excessively for artificial melody and sound, or shortened entirely without any prolongation at all.

In the end, Tajweed should be viewed as a skill set with a spectrum of competency, such that there are grades of proficiency, rather than a simple "right or wrong" approach. The Qurʾān itself and the Prophet provided ample incentive for reciting correctly and seeking greater competence and skill in the noble act of Qurʾānic recitation. And that applies to us all.

Appendix TWO: THE VIRTUE OF TAJWEED

An Anthology of Forty Ḥadīth on the Virtue of Qur'ānic Recitation

فَضلُ التَّجوِيد

Reciting the Noble Qur'ān as it was meant to be recited (i.e. with Tajweed) is full of immense and unparalleled merit and virtue. This distinction can be viewed from many aspects and is garnered from numerous texts of the Qur'ān itself as well as the Prophetic traditions. A comprehensive survey of these traditions reveals an extraordinary journey that spans the breadth of human existence.

The Divine Connection

Any survey on the merits of Qur'ānic recitation must necessarily begin by duly noting that the distinction of the science of Tajweed has to do with its relationship to Allah the Exalted and Majestic Himself. Undoubtedly, the single greatest merit of Tajweed lies in the fact that the Qur'ān is the noble speech of Allah. As such, Tajweed is perhaps the only religious practice (sunnah) we perform which is traced back not just to the human Messenger of Allah but to the Creator Himself. The Qur'ān, by the definition agreed upon by the consensus of orthodox Muslim scholars, is the literal speech of Allah revealed to humanity through the archangel Jibrīl. In a sense, when we recite the Qur'ān we are articulating the speech of our Creator. The merit of Allah's speech needs no further comment beyond the words of the very Prophet who was chosen to deliver that speech to us:

فَضْلُ كَلاَمِ اللهِ عَلَى سَائِرِ الكَلاَمِ كَفَضْلِ اللهِ عَلَى خَلْقِهِ

The virtue of Allah's speech over all other speech is like the virtue of Allah over all of His creation.[92]

Therefore, Tajweed—the proper recitation of the Qur'ān—is the only act of worship we are called upon to perform which is traced not just to the Prophet but to Allah Himself. The traditional study of Tajweed in this manner is a continuous chain that goes back, not to certain spiritual personalities as in the chains of taṣawwuf, nor to certain Muslim authors as in the chains of Islamic books and texts, nor even to the Prophet Muḥammad himself as in the chains of ḥadīth transmission, but rather, it is a chain that directly links one to the Creator of the Heavens and the Earth! Can there be a greater honor and virtue than that?

This virtue is best illustrated by examining the traditional isnād, or chain of transmitters, possessed by individuals who have learned the Qur'ān in the

[92] Ḥadīth of Abū Sa'īd al-Khudrī recorded by al-Tirmidhī in his *Sunan* 2850, al-Dārimī 3222, al-Bazzār, al-Mundhirī in *al-Targhīb*, al-Dhahabī in *Mizān al-I'tidāl*, Ibn al-Mulaqqin in *Tuhfah al-Muhtāj*, Ibn Mufliḥ in *Ādāb al-Shar'iyyah* and al-Tabrīzī in *al-Mishkāt al-Maṣābīḥ*; Ibn Ḥajr authenticated it as *hasan* in *Hidāyah al-Ruwāt* as well as Abū Isḥāq al-Huwaynī in his footnotes to Ibn Kathīr's *Kitāb Faḍā'il al-Qur'ān* (see Zarabozo's *How to Approach and Understand the Quran*), but according to al-Shawkāni and al-Albāni it is weak (see *Ḍa'īf al-Jāmi'* and *Ḍa'īf al-Targhīb*).

traditional manner, from teachers who have learned it from their teachers, going back generations to the Prophet himself. The final links in such chains usually read in the manner of the following: . . . *from Abū 'Abdu'l-Raḥmān al-Sulamī who recited [the Qur'ān] to 'Abdullah Ibn Mas'ūd who recited it to the Prophet, who in turn received the Noble Qur'ān from the angel Jibrīl and recited it to him, who in turn received it from Allah the Exalted and Majestic.*

It is this very virtue that made the Messenger of Allah come out one day to his Companions and proudly proclaim, as narrated by Abū Shurayḥ al-Khuzā'ī:

أَبْشِرُوا أَبْشِرُوا أَلَيْس تَشْهَدُونَ أَنْ لَا إِلَهَ إِلاَّ اللهُ وَأَنِّي رَسُولَ الله

Rejoice! Rejoice! Do you not testify that there is none worthy of worship save Allah and that I am His Messenger?

When the Companions responded, *Of course we do,* the Prophet proceeded to tell them:

فَإِنَّ هَذَا الْقُرْآنَ سَبَبٌ طَرَفُهُ بِيَدِ اللهِ وَطَرَفُهُ بِأَيْدِيكُمْ فَتَمَسَّكُوا بِهِ فَإِنَّكُمْ لَنْ تَضِلُّوا وَلَنْ تَهْلِكُوا بَعْدَهُ أَبَدًا

Verily this Qur'ān- one part of it is in the hands of Allah and the other part in your hands. Therefore hold on to it, and you will never go astray, nor be destroyed after that.[93]

On another occasion, he delivered the same momentous news by saying:

كِتَابُ اللَّهِ هُوَ حَبْلُ اللهِ الْمَمْدُودُ مِنَ السَّمَاءِ إِلَى الأَرْضِ

The Book of Allah is the Rope of Allah extending from the heavens to the earth.[94]

---

[93] Ḥadīth reported by Abū Shurayḥ al-Khuzā'ī as well as Jubayr b. Muṭ'im and recorded by Ibn Ḥibbān in his *Ṣaḥīḥ*, Ibn Abī Shaybah, al-Ṭabarānī in *al-Mu'jam al-Ṣaghīr* and *al-Mu'jam al-Kabīr*, al-Mundhirī in *Targhīb,* al-Bazzār in his *Musnad*, 'Abd b. Ḥumayd in his *Musnad,* al-Hindī in *Kanz al-'Ummāl* and al-Bayhaqī in *Shu'b al-Īmān*, and authenticated by al-Haythamī in *Majma' al-Zawāid,* al-Safārīnī al-Ḥanbalī in *Lāwaiḥ al-Anwār al-Sunniyah,* al-Wādi'ī in *al-Ṣaḥīḥ al-Musnad*, and by al-Albānī in *Saḥīḥ al-Targhīb* and *al-Silsilah al-Aḥādīth al-Ṣaḥīḥah.*

[94] Ḥadīth of Abū Sa'īd al-Khudrī found in early works of tafseer such as al-Ṭabarī, and which, iaccording to Aḥmad Shākir has a weak chain but sound meaning, but was authenticated by al-Albānī in *al-Silsilah al-Ṣaḥīḥah* and *Ṣaḥīḥ al-Jāmi'.*

The Prophet was teaching humanity a grand lesson and proclaiming the greatest news. Let there be no mistake about it—the Qur'ān is our Divine link, a direct connection between us and our Creator!

Allah Himself affirms this fact by referring to the Qur'ān as *His rope* to human beings and makes it a means of unifying the believers:

وَاعْتَصِمُوا بِحَبْلِ اللَّهِ جَمِيعًا وَلَا تَفَرَّقُوا

And hold fast to the rope of Allah and be not divided.
[The Qur'ān, 3:103]

According to many early Qur'ānic commentators, including 'Alī, Ibn Mas'ūd, Qatādah, al-Suddī and al-Ḍaḥḥāk, the *rope of Allah* mentioned in this verse refers to the Noble Qur'ān.[95]

Such is the sublime nature of the Glorious Qur'ān. Those who grasp this rope—this Divine connection—become associated with Allah in a very unique way. The Companion Anas b. Mālik relates that the Prophet also said in this same regard:

إِنَّ لِلَّهِ عَزَّ وَ جَلَّ أَهْلِينَ مِنَ النَّاسِ

Verily there are certain people among human beings that belong to Allah!

قِيلَ : مَنْ هُمْ يا رَسُولَ اللهِ

It was asked, *Who are they, Messenger of Allah?*

قَالَ أَهْلُ القُرآنِ هُمْ أَهْلُ اللهِ وَ خَاصَّتُهُ

He replied: *It is none other than the people of the Qur'ān who are Allah's people and His elite.*[96]

Allah refers to this elite group with an honorary title: *Ahl Allah*—Allah's People! They are none other than the companions of the Qur'ān, who are—according to the exposition and commentaries of most Muslim scholars—those who busy themselves with the Qur'ān, including memorizing it, reciting it constantly and applying its teachings.[97]

---

[95] Refer to *Tafsīr al-Ṭabarī*, *Tafsīr Ibn Kathīr*, Ibn al-Jawzī's *Zād al-Masīr fī 'Ilm al-Tafsīr*, and al-Suyūṭī's *al-Durr al-Manthūr fi'l-Tafsīr bi'l-Ma'thūr* among others.

[96] Ḥadīth of Anas b. Mālik recorded by Aḥmad 11831, 11844, 13053, al-Dārimī 3192, Ibn Mājah 211, as well as by al-Hākim, al-Nasā'ī in *Sunan al-Kubrā,* and al-Mundhirī and authenticated by Abdul Qādir al-Arna'ūṭ, Zubayr 'Alī Za'ī and al-Albānī.

[97] See, for example, the commentary on Sunan Ibn Mājah by al-Sindī.

This magnificent feature of the Qur'ān alone is sufficient to establish the true magnitude of its value and worth to human beings. This should suffice as motivation for believers to singularly devote themselves to this wonderful Book. But there is much more.

The Elite Prophetic School

The Prophet was responsible for not only communicating the Divine message and informing people but also for training and nurturing a generation of believers around the Qur'ān. That he did par excellence, and its echoes are still felt in the world today.

The Prophet had an elite school of believers to whom he devoted special attention—the school of Ṣuffah in Madīnah. One of his first acts upon migrating to the newly founded Islamic nation, he constructed a portion of the masjid to house the indigent among his Companions and the students. Those who lived there received exclusive attention. They were his elite students.

PHOTO 4: A reproduction of the original Mosque of the Prophet, indicating the Ṣuffa school, courtesy of the Center of Islamic Culture Exhibit in Madinah.

In return, this school provided the soldiers and the martyrs for every battle of the Prophet. This school was responsible for preserving the details of the Islamic principles and teachings for posterity. Warrior-students by day, worshippers by night, the graduates of this school of higher learning became Islam's leading teachers and thinkers in the coming era. These included luminaries such as Bilāl the mu'adhdhin, Abū Hurayrah the most prolific narrator of ḥadīth, 'Abdullah ibn

Mas'ūd the repository of fiqh and learning, Suhayb al-Rūmī, Ḥudhayfah b. al-Yamān, Abu Dharr al-Ghifārī, Salmān al-Fārisī, Khabbāb b. al-Arat, Ka'b b. Mālik, Sālim the *mawlā* (client) of Abū Ḥudhayfah, and many others.

Their training centered around the Qur'ān, as one of these very students, 'Uqbah b. 'Āmir al-Juhanī, testifies: *One day the Messenger of Allah came out to us in Ṣuffah and said:*

أَيُّكُمْ يُحِبُّ أَنْ يَغْدُوَ كُلَّ يَوْمٍ إِلَى بُطْحَانَ أَوْ إِلَى الْعَقِيقِ فَيَأْتِي مِنْهُ بِنَاقَتَيْنِ كَوْمَاوَيْنِ،
.فِي غَيْرِ إِثْمٍ وَلاَ قَطْعِ رَحِمٍ؟» فَقُلْنَا: يَا رَسُولَ اللهِ نُحِبُّ ذٰلِكَ
قَالَ: «أَفَلاَ يَغْدُو أَحَدُكُمْ إِلَى الْمَسْجِدِ فَيَعْلَمُ أَوْ يَقْرَأُ آيَتَيْنِ مِنْ
كِتَابِ اللهِ عَزَّ وَجَلَّ خَيْرٌ لَهُ مِنْ نَاقَتَيْنِ. وَثَلاَثٌ خَيْرٌ لَهُ مِنْ ثَلاَثٍ. وَأَرْبَعٌ
خَيْرٌ لَهُ مِنْ أَرْبَعٍ. وَمِنْ أَعْدَادِهِنَّ مِنَ الإِبِلِ

Which one of you would like to go out in the morning everyday to Buṭḥān or al-'Aqīq (two places in Madīnah) and bring back two large she-camels without that involving any sin nor severing of family ties? We said, "Messenger of Allah we would like that very much." He replied: *For one of you to go to the masjid in the morning and learn or recite two verses from the Book of Allah is better that two she-camels, and three are better than three, and four better than four, and so on.*[98]

Another elite student of the Ṣuffah school—Abū Hurayrah, relates this same type of training from the Prophet:

أَيُحِبُّ أَحَدُكُمْ إِذَا رَجَعَ إِلَى أَهْلِهِ أَنْ يَجِدَ فِيهِ ثَلاَثَ خَلِفَاتٍ عِظَامٍ سِمَانٍ؟
قُلْنَا : نَعَمْ. قَالَ: «فَثَلاَثُ آيَاتٍ يَقْرَأُ بِهِنَّ أَحَدُكُمْ فِي صَلاَتِهِ. خَيْرٌ لَهُ مِنْ
ثَلاَثِ خَلِفَاتٍ عِظَامٍ سِمَانٍ

Would any of you like to go back to his family and find among them three large, fat, pregnant she-camels? We said, *Yes.* He said, *Three verses that one of you recites in his prayer are better for him than three large, fat, pregnant she-camels.*[99]

---

[98] Related by Muslim 1823, Aḥmad 17079, Ibn Ḥibbān, Ibn Abī Shaybah in his *Muṣannaf,* al-Mundhirī in *al-Targhīb,* al-Hindī in *Kanz al-'Ummāl,* al-Ṭabarānī, and al-Bayhaqī.

[99] Related by Muslim 1822, Aḥmad 9059, Ibn Mājah 3865, al-Bayhaqī, and al-Hindī in *Kanz al-'Ummāl.*

It should be noted that camels were the most prized possession and the most precious wealth of the Arabs, and the most valuable among them were those that were pregnant. As such, this training provided a crucial and timely lesson—that the recitation of the Qur'ān and its teaching was more valuable than the best material wealth in the world.

The Abiding Virtue of Reciting the Qur'ān

This amazing Book has virtues and merits that continue to assist and benefit human beings in every stage and journey of their lives—from birth to death, resurrection and beyond. The real companions of the Qur'ān find its ceaseless treasures and endless wonders throughout the duration of their fleeting earthly lives, then continuing into the solitary desolate realm of the graves, before finally culminating with full glorious manifestation in the amazing world of the Hereafter after resurrection.

And so it behooves the one who desires ultimate success to make this single Book the centerpiece of his or her life. The path to eternal bliss is exceedingly simple and conversely, the road to eternal ruin equally so. It is all about this one Book. The Prophet Muḥammad stated this reality as such:

الْقُرْآنُ شَافِعٌ مُشَفَّعٌ وَ مَاحِلٌ مُصَدَّقٌ ، مَنْ جَعَلَهُ أَمَامَهُ قَادَهُ إِلَى الْجَنَّةِ ، وَ
مَنْ جَعَلَهُ خَلْفَهُ قَادَهُ إِلَى النَّارِ

The Qur'ān is an accepted intercessor for you or a disputant whose claim is upheld. Whoever places it before him, it will lead him to Paradise, and whoever places it behind him, it will take him to the Fire.[100]

The simple formula for eternal success is this—*Place this Book before you and let it lead you to Paradise*.

How exactly can it do that? Let us survey its position and its effects on the various journeys of our existence, focusing on its recitation and reading. We begin with the Qur'ān in our present lives.

Firstly, the proper recitation of Allah's Book has immense intrinsic reward, which is magnified at the level of the individual letters of the words. The Prophet stated:

---

[100] Ḥadīth of Jābir recorded by Ibn Ḥibbān, al-Bayhaqī in *Shu'b al-Īmān*, Ibn Abī Shaybah in his *Muṣannaf* and al-Ṭabarānī, and authenticated by al-Albānī.

تَعَلَّمُوا هَذَا القُرْآنَ فَإِنَّكُمْ تُؤْجَرُونَ بِتِلاَوَتِهِ بِكُلِّ حَرْفٍ عَشْرَ حَسَنَاتٍ ، أَمَا إِنِّي لاَ أَقُولُ بِ (الم) وَلَكِنْ بِأَلِفٍ وَ لاَمٍ وَ مِيمٍ ، بِكُلِّ حَرْفٍ عَشْرُ حَسَنَاتٍ

Learn this Qur'ān, for you will indeed be rewarded for its recitation, with ten rewards for each letter. And I am not saying that *Alif Lām Meem* is one letter, but rather, *alif* is one letter, *lām* is another letter, and *meem* is another letter, with each letter rewarded ten times.[101]

To further add to this virtue, this tremendous reward is recorded by the choicest of angelic scribes and magnified for those who struggle to recite properly, a moving incentive to learn the art of proper Tajweed. The Prophet stated:

الَّذِي يَقْرَأُ القُرْآنَ وَ هُوَ مَاهِرٌ بِهِ مَعَ السَّفَرَةِ الكِرَامِ البَرَرَةِ ، وَ الَّذِي يَقْرَأُهُ وَ هُوَ عَلَيْهِ شَاقٌّ لَهُ أَجْرَانِ

The one who recites the Qur'ān with skill and expertise will be with pure and noble scribes, while the one who struggles with it has a double reward.[102]

Al-Qāḍī 'Iyād and other scholars have offered various possible explanations for the meaning of being with the pure and noble scribes, including the fact that it is these angels that record the reward of recitation, or the fact the reciters of the Qur'ān will be in the company of these pure angels in the Hereafter, or that these reciters are similar in characteristics to these angels in their noble deed of reciting and memorizing the Qur'ān as devotion to Allah. Irrespective of the correct view, the virtue is quite obvious. Scholars also point out that expertise here refers to reciting it flawlessly (which involves proper articulation as well as memorization) while the one who struggles with it is the one who struggles with its rules of recitation as well as his memory. In fact, the wording of this ḥadīth in Ṣaḥīḥ al-Bukhārī is quite explicit in this regard and uses the additional words: *the one who recites the Qur'ān and memorizes it* [حَافِظٌ لَهُ] in place of *the one who recites the Qur'ān with skill and expertise.*[103]

[101] Ḥadīth of 'Abdullah b. Mas'ūd recorded in al-Dārimī 3174, al-Dāruquṭnī, al-Khaṭīb in *al-Tārīkh*, al-Daylamī and others, and authenticated by al-Albānī in *al-Silsilah al-Ṣaḥīḥah.* The text is from al-Dārimī.

[102] Ḥadīth of 'Āisha related in slightly varying wordings in al-Bukhārī 4556, Muslim 1329, al-Tirmidhī 2829, Abū Dāwūd 1242, Ibn Mājah 3769, Aḥmad 23080, 23493, 23526, 23644, 24197, 24413, 24835, 25093, and al-Dārimī 3234. The wording above is that of Aḥmad 23080.

[103] al-Bukhārī 4556.

The Prophet would strongly advise the miswāk for his Companions prior to prayer in order to freshen the breath and obtain the company and closeness of the angels:

إنَّ العَبْدَ إذا قَامَ يُصَلِّي أَتَاهُ المَلَكُ فقامَ خَلْفَهُ يَسْتَمِعُ القُرآنَ ويَدْنُو، فَلا يَزَالُ يَسْتَمِعُ ويَدْنُو حَتَّى يَضَعُ فاهُ عَلَى فِيْهِ، فَلاَ يَقْرَأُ آيَةً إلا كَانَتْ فِي جَوْفِ المَلَكِ

Indeed when the servant stands to pray, an angel comes to pray behind him, listening to the Qur'ān and drawing ever closer to him, until its mouth is over the mouth of the servant and every verse that is recited enters the angel.[104]

The intrinsic reward of recitation is so immense that it can overshadow greater and more-time consuming acts of worship, as the Prophet alluded to in these words:

مَنْ قرأَ بمائةِ آيةٍ في ليلةٍ كُتِبَ لهُ قُنُوتُ لَيلَةٍ

Whoever recites a hundred verses in a night will be written as if he spent the entire night in worship.[105]

The spiritual ranks of those who recite the Qur'ān are many, as the Prophet confirmed:

مَنْ قَامَ بِعَشْرِ آيَاتٍ لَمْ يُكتَب مِنَ الغَافِلِينَ، وَمَن قَامَ بِمَائَةِ آيةٍ كُتِبَ مِنَ القَانِتِينَ، وَمَن قامَ بِأَلفِ آيةٍ كُتِبَ مِنَ المقَنْطِرِينَ

Whoever stands with ten verses (reciting them in the night prayer) will not be written among the negligent, and whoever stands with one hundred verses will be written among the

[104] Ḥadīth of 'Alī related by al-Bayhaqī in *al-Sunan al-Kubrā,* al-Bazzār in his *Musnad,* Ibn Mājah, 'Abd al-Razzāq al-Ṣan'ānī in his *Muṣannaf* and authenticated by al-Haythamī in *Majma' al-Zawā'id,* al-Mundhirī in *al-Targhīb wa'l-Tarhīb* and al-Albānī in *al-Silsilah al-Ṣaḥīḥah.*

[105] Ḥadīth of Tamīm al-Dārī related by Aḥmad in his *Musnad,* al-Dārimī, al-Nasā'ī in *al-Sunan al-Kubrā,* and authenticated by Ibn Ḥajar and al-Albānī.

devoted and whoever stands with one thousand verses[106] *will be written among the outstanding.*[107]

Beyond the accumulation of rewards and the angelic company, the recitation of the Qur'ān in this world produces other benefits, including creating a state of tranquility and serenity. This lesson was demonstrated in the lifetime of the Prophet during an incident that occurred involving one of the Companions that was narrated by al-Barā' b. 'Āzib:

كَانَ رَجُلٌ يَقْرَأُ سُوْرَةَ الكَهْفِ وَ عِنْدَهُ فَرَسٌ مَرْبُوْطٌ بِشَطَنَيْنِ فَتَغَشَّتْهُ سَحَابَةٌ فَجَعَلَتْ تَدُوْرُ وَ تَدْنُوْ وَ جَعَلَ فَرَسُهُ يَنْفِرُ مِنْهَا ، فَلَمَّا أَصْبَحَ أَتَى النَّبِيَّ صَلَّ اللهُ عَلَيهِ وَ سَلَّمَ فَذَكَرَ ذَلِكَ لَهُ فَقَالَ تِلْكَ السَّكِيْنَةُ تَنَزَّلَتْ لِلْقُرْآنِ

A man was once reciting Sūrah al-Kahf, close to a horse tied to a lengthy rope. Suddenly a cloud covered the animal, which began to move back and forth restlessly. The next day, this man mentioned what happened to the Prophet who remarked, "That was the tranquility that descended for the Qur'ān."[108]

The word *sakīnah* literally refers to a state of serenity and tranquility, and scholars discussed at length its exact meaning in these and other traditions. Al-Ṭabarī narrated from 'Ali that it is a flowing wind. It is narrated from Wahb ibn Munabbih that is a special spirit [*rūḥ*] from Allah, and from al-Ḍaḥḥāk (and favored by al-Ṭabarī) that it is mercy and tranquility of the heart. Yet others have opined that it is calmness, stillness, and dignity. Imām al-Nawawī summarized these views by writing that it is something from the creation of Allah that contains tranquility and mercy and is accompanied by angels.

The Prophet further outlined four heavenly effects of group Qur'ānic recitation in the masājid:

---

[106] It has been noted by Ibn Ḥajar that Sūrah al-Mulk to the end of the Qur'ān is 1000 verses, as quoted by al-Mundhirī in *al-Targhīb.*

[107] Ḥadīth of 'Abdullah b. 'Amr b. al-'Āṣ related by Abū Dāwūd, Ibn Khuzaymah in his *Ṣaḥīḥ*, Ibn Ḥibbān in his *Ṣaḥīḥ*, and Abū Dāwūd al-Ṭayālīsī in his *Musnad,* and authenticated by Ibn Ḥajar in *Natā'ij al-Afkār* and al-Albānī in his various works.

[108] This incident is narrated on the authority of al-Barā' b. 'Āzib in various similar versions in al-Bukhārī 3345, 4462, 4625, Muslim 1325, 1326, al-Tirmidhī 2810, Aḥmad 17744, 17776, 17851, 17893. The wording used above is that of Muslim 1325.

وَ مَا اجْتَمَعَ قَوْمٌ فِيْ بَيْتٍ مِنْ بُيُوْتِ اللهِ يَتْلُوْنَ كِتَابَ اللهِ وَ يَتَدَارَسُوْنَهُ بَيْنَهُمْ
إِلاَّ نَزَلَتْ عَلَيْهِمُ السَّكِيْنَةُ وَ غَشِيَتْهُمُ الرَّحْمَةُ وَ حَفَّتْهُمُ المِلاَئِكَةُ وَ ذَكَرَهُمُ اللهُ
فِي مَنْ عِنْدَهُ

When any group of people gather to recite and study the Book of Allah among themselves, tranquility descends upon them, mercy covers them, the angels surround them and Allah mentions them to those around Him (in His Divine Company).[109]

This narration highlights the tremendous excellence of gathering together and meeting for the purposes of Qur'ānic recitation and study. According to many scholars, this virtue is not limited to houses of worship but also applies to those who gather in schools, homes and other places for this same purpose.[110]

Beyond producing this tranquility, Qur'ānic recitation is a powerful means of removing anxiety, sorrows and worries. In fact it is instrumental in producing a sound and healthy mental state.

Abdullah b. Mas'ūd relates that the Prophet said once, *No individual is afflicted with any type of anxiety or sorrow, and he makes the following supplication [see below], except that Allah removes from him that anxiety or sorrow and replaces it with some way out for that person.* It was then asked, *Should we not teach this supplication then, O Messenger of Allah?* He replied, *Of course, everyone who hears it should teach it to others.*

مَا أَصَابَ أَحَدًا قَطُّ هَمٌّ وَ لاَ حَزَنٌ فَقَالَ

اللَّهُمَّ إِنِّيْ عَبْدُكَ وَابْنُ عَبْدِكَ وَابْنُ أَمَتِكَ نَاصِيَتِيْ بِيَدِكَ مَاضٍ فِيَّ حُكْمُكَ عَدْلٌ فِيَّ قَضَاؤُكَ أَسْأَلُكَ بِكُلِّ اسْمٍ هُوَ لَكَ سَمَّيْتَ بِهِ نَفْسَكَ أَوْ عَلَّمْتَهُ أَحَدًا مِنْ خَلْقِكَ أَوْ أَنْزَلْتَهُ فِيْ كِتَابِكَ أَوِ اسْتَأْثَرْتَ بِهِ فِيْ عِلْمِ الغَيْبِ عِنْدَكَ أَنْ تَجْعَلَ القُرْآنَ رَبِيْعَ قَلْبِيْ وِ نُوْرَ صَدْرِي وَ جِلاَءَ حُزْنِي وَ ذَهَابَ هَمِّي

إِلاَّ أَذْهَبَ اللهُ هَمَّهُ وَ حُزْنَهُ وَ أَبْدَلَهُ مَكَانَهُ فَرَجًا ، فَقِيْلَ يَا رَسُوْلَ اللهِ أَلاَ
نَتَعَلَّمُهَا ؟ فَقَالَ بَلَى يَنْبَغِيْ لِمَنْ سَمِعَهَا أَنْ يَتَعَلَّمَهَا

---

[109] Narrated as a portion of a larger ḥadīth on the authority of Abū Hurayrah in Muslim 4867, al-Tirmidhī 2869, Abū Dāwūd 1243, Ibn Mājah 221 and Aḥmad 7118.

[110] See al-Nawawī's commentary on *Ṣaḥīḥ Muslim*, al-'Adhīmabādī's commentary on *Sunan Abī Dāwūd* and al-Sindī's commentary on *Sunan Ibn Mājah*.

The Supplication:

'O Allah, I am Your servant, son of Your servant, son of Your maidservant, my forelock is in Your hand, Your command over me is forever executed and Your decree over me is just. I ask You by every name belonging to You which You name Yourself with, or revealed in Your Book, or You taught to any of Your creation, or You have preserved in the knowledge of the unseen with You, that You make the Qur'ān the life of my heart and the light of my breast, and a departure for my sorrow and a release for my anxiety.'[111]

This beautiful Prophetic supplication teaches us what our proper orientation should be towards this Noble Book. The Qur'an should really be the spring of our hearts, the light of our chests and the eraser of our worries and concerns. Our hearts should be moved and revived when reading it. When the Companions heard the stunning power of this magnificent and eloquent supplication, it amazed them to the point that they were forced to ask the Prophet T, in near disbelief, if they could inform others. The Prophet responded that it was in fact their duty to do so.

And finally, the recitation of the Qur'ān blesses its reciters with the greatest of spiritual blessings: the love of Allah. This is one of the true treasures in this world, experienced by the fortunate few. As the Prophet said:

مَنْ سَرَّهُ أَنْ يُحِبَّ اللهَ وَ رَسُوْلَهُ فَلْيَقْرَأْ فِي الْمُصْحَفِ

Whoever is pleased to love Allah and his Messenger should recite from the muṣḥaf (the Qur'ān).[112]

Beyond these purely spiritual and religious blessings, the recitation and memorization of the Qur'ān is also a source for worldly honor and respect, though it must be noted that this does not qualify as a legitimate incentive and should never be sought for its sake. Abu Mūsa al-'Ash'arī reported that the Prophet said:

إِنَّ مِنْ إِجْلاَلِ اللهِ إِكْرَامَ ذِي الشَّيْبَةِ المسْلِمِ وَ حَامِلِ القُرْآنِ
غَيْرِ الغَالِي فِيْهِ وَ الجَافِيْ عَنْهُ وَ إِكْرَامَ ذِي السُّلْطَانِ المقْسِطِ

[111] Ḥadīth of 'Abdullah b. Mas'ūd related by Aḥmad 3528 and authenticated by al-Albānī in *al-Silsilah al-Ṣaḥīḥah*.

[112] Related by Abū Na'īm in *Ḥilyah al-Awliyā'* and al-Hindī in *Kanz al-'Ummāl* among others and authenticated by al-Albānī in *Ṣaḥīḥ al-Jāmi'* and *al-Silsilah al-Ṣaḥīḥah*.

Part of showing glory to Allah is to show respect to a gray-haired Muslim, a carrier of the Qur'an who does not exceed its bounds nor ignores it, and a just ruler.[113]

This Prophetic tradition clearly mandates respect and veneration to the carriers of the Qur'ān in this world. According to Mullah 'Alī al-Qārī, the carrier of the Qur'ān here refers to the reciter of the Qur'ān, the one who memorizes it and the one who interprets it (correctly). The one who exceeds its bounds is the one who violates its rules of recitation, points of articulation as well as its implementation, while the one who ignores it is the one who turns away from its recitation and ignores its rules of Tajweed and does not implement it.[114] This great virtue is that all believers are called upon to respect and honor the people of the Qur'ān just as they would honor Allah Himself!

These companions of the Qur'ān are also to be given preference in many other worldly matters, including leadership in prayer and battles. The Prophet used to instruct his Companions as follows:

فَإِذَا حَضَرَتِ الصَّلَاةُ فَلْيُؤَذِّنْ أَحَدُكُمْ وَلْيَؤُمَّكُمْ أَكْثَرُكُمْ قُرْآنًا

When the time for prayer comes, let one of you give the adhān and let the one with the most Qur'ān lead the others.[115]

In the era of the Prophet as well as that of his Companions, those who memorized the Qur'ān—especially its longest chapter al-Baqarah—were clearly given respect and public prominence, and often given leadership positions. The Prophet in difficult times of battle would call out to rally the troops and motivate the ranks—*Yā Aṣḥābal Baqarah! (O Companions of Sūrah al-Baqarah!)* This tradition continued beyond the Prophetic era into that of the Rightly-Guided Caliphate. Abu Bakr faced one of the gravest situations facing the Muslim nation in the devastating aftermath of the death of the Prophet. It was a time of widespread despair coupled with mass confusion and outright pockets of rebellion that threatened to finish the Muslim nation and all that the Prophet had struggled to build. Abu Bakr chose to confront the rebellion head on, and the Muslims eventually clashed with the largest of the rebel forces under the leadership of the false prophet and eloquent orator Musaylimah the Liar. The Battle of Yamāmah witnessed 11,000 faithful believers confronting 50,000 soldiers of Musaylimah. Those Muslim forces included many reciters and memorizers of the Qur'ān, including more than 500 in a single battalion.

---

[113] Ḥadīth of Abū Mūsa al-Ash'arī related by Abū Dāwūd 4203, al-Mundhirī in *al-Targhīb* and al-Bayhaqī in *Shu'b al-Īmān,* and authenticated by al-Nawawī in *al-Tibyān*, Ibn Mufliḥ in *al-Ādāb al-Shar'iyyah*, Ibn Ḥajar in *Hidāyah al-Ruwāt,* 'Abd al-Haqq al-Ishbīlī in *al-Aḥkām al-Ṣughrā,* and by al-Albānī in *Ṣaḥīḥ al-Targhīb.*

[114] See the commentary on Sunan Abī Dāwūd *'Awn al Ma'būd* by al-'Adhīmabādī'.

[115] A portion of a lengthy ḥadīth narrated by 'Amr b. Salamah and related in al-Bukhārī 3963, Nasā'ī 632, Abū Dāwūd 495, 496, and Aḥmad 15337, 19443, 19444, 19764.

Among the rallying cries heard in that battle was *Yā Aṣḥābal-Baqarah!* echoing from the days of the Prophet. The Muslims scored a decisive victory but not without major casualties, including more than 53 huffādh. In fact, it was this loss that eventually prompted the Muslims to compile the Qur'ān in written form in an attempt to preserve the Divine Revelation for subsequent generations.

The Qur'ān makes leaders and elevates its companions. The second Caliph 'Umar b. al-Khaṭṭāb once appointed a person named Nāfi' b. 'Abd al-Ḥārith as the governor of Makkah during his reign. One day he came across Nāfi' in one of his journeys, in a region known as 'Usfān, and questioned him as to whom he had left in charge of Makkah. Nāfi' replied, *Ibn Abzā*. 'Umar did not know him and asked who he was. Nāfi' replied that he was one of his former slaves. 'Umar then remarked, *You left a former slave in charge of Makkah?* Nāfi' justified his decision by saying, *He is knowledgeable in the Qur'ān and also knowledgeable in legal rulings*. 'Umar approved his judgment and reasoning and added, *And indeed your Prophet himself has stated*:

إِنَّ اللهَ يَرْفَعُ بِهَذَا الكِتَابِ أَقْوَامًا وَ يَضَعُ بِهِ آخَرِيْنَ

Verily Allah elevates some people by means of this Book and debases others through it.[116]

[116] Ḥadīth of 'Umar b. al-Khaṭṭāb recorded by Muslim 1353, Ibn Mājah 214, Aḥmad 226, al-Dārimī 3231 and al-Dāruquṭnī, and authenticated by al-Albānī in *Ṣaḥīḥ al-Jāmi'* and *Ṣaḥīḥ Ibn Mājah*.

PHOTO 5: Courtyard of the Qarawiyeen University in Fez, Morocco, the world's first university.

The memorization of the Qur'ān was also accepted in the Prophet's time as a substitute for dowry (*mahr*) in the case of indigent individuals who could not afford to get married. Sahl b. Sa'd narrates that a woman came once to the Prophet and offered herself to him in marriage. He declined, replying that he had no need for additional wives. Another man came forward and asked the Prophet to marry her to him. The Prophet asked him whether he had anything to give her as dowry. He replied that he did not. The Prophet instructed him to go and search for something to give her. The man left and came back empty-handed, unable to find anything. The Prophet instructed him to go back and find something even as simple as an iron ring. The man searched in vain and came back with nothing, saying, *I have nothing but this lower garment (izār).* The Prophet remarked that if he gave that to her in dowry and continued to wear it, it would not really be hers, while if he took it off to give it to her, he would have nothing to wear! The Prophet then asked him if he had memorized any portion of the Qur'ān, and he informed the Prophet which chapters he had memorized. The Prophet approved of his memorization and said:

إِذْهَبْ فَقَدْ مُلِّكْتَهَا بِمَا مَعَكَ مِنَ الْقُرْآنِ

Go, for you are married to her with what you memorized from the Qur'ān.[117]

The honor of the Qur'ān, or more specifically, its memorization and understanding, is that it equals—rather, surpasses—material wealth and possessions in value and worth. In some cases it can even be substituted for material objects. Imām al-Nawawī notes in his commentary on *Ṣaḥīḥ Muslim* that this narration proves that the teaching of the Qur'ān is a valid dowry in marriage, and also the permissibility of receiving wages for the teaching of the Qur'ān.

A further worldly virtue of the Qur'ān is that it is the people of the Qur'ān who deserve the rank and title of scholars in this world. The Prophet stated:

مَنْ أَخَذَ السَّبْعَ الأُوَلَ مِنَ الْقُرْآنِ فَهُوَ حَبْرٌ

Whoever memorizes the first seven chapters of the Qur'ān then he is a scholar.[118]

Because of these numerous virtues, the recitation and memorization of the Qur'ān has been made a legitimate source of competition among believers and even merits a lawful form of jealousy, as the Prophet instructed:

لاَ حَسَدَ إِلاَّ فِي اثْنَتَيْنِ : رَجُلٌ عَلَّمَهُ اللهُ الْقُرْآنَ فَهُوَ يَتْلُوهُ آنَاءَ اللَّيْلِ وَ آنَاءَ النَّهَارِ فَسَمِعَهُ جَارٌ لَهُ فَقَالَ لَيْتَنِي أُوتِيتُ مِثْلَ مَا أُوتِيَ فُلاَنٌ فَعَمِلْتُ مِثْلَ مَا يَعْمَلُ ، وَ رَجُلٌ آتَاهُ اللهُ مَالاً فَهُوَ يُهْلِكُهُ فِي الحَقِّ فَقَالَ رَجُلٌ لَيْتَنِي أُوتِيتُ مِثْلَ مَا أُوتِيَ فُلاَنٌ فَعَمِلْتُ مِثْلَ مَا يَعْمَلُ

There is no envy save in two cases: a person whom Allah taught the Qur'ān and he recites it all night and day, while his neighbor hears him and remarks, "Would that I had what this person has and do what he does"; and a person whom Allah had given abundant wealth and he expends it for the truth and another

[117] Ḥadīth of Sahl b. Sa'd al-Sā'idī recorded by al-Bukhārī 4752, Muslim 2554, al-Tirmidhī 1032, al-Nasā'ī 3228, 3306, Ibn Mājah 1879, Abū Dāwūd 1806, Aḥmad 21733, 21783, al-Muwaṭṭa' of Imām Mālik 968, and al-Dārimī 2104.

[118] Ḥadīth of 'Āisha recorded by Aḥmad 23305, 23390 and authenticated by al-Albānī in *al-Silsilah al-Ṣaḥīḥah.*

person remarks, “Would that I had what he has and I would do what he does.”[119]

These are all individual benefits, but the blessings of the recitation of the Qur’ān are not confined to such, but rather extend their reach to bless and benefit others. The Prophet drew a fitting series of analogies to illustrate this very point when he said:

مَثَلُ المؤْمِنِ الَّذِي يَقْرَأُ القُرْآنَ مَثَلُ الأُتْرُجَّةِ رِيحُهَا طَيِّبٌ وَ طَعْمُهَا طَيِّبٌ ،
وَ مَثَلُ المؤْمِنِ الَّذِي لاَ يَقْرَأُ القُرْآنَ مَثَلُ التَّمْرَةِ لاَ رِيْحَ لَهَا وَ طَعْمُهَا حُلْوٌ ،
وَ مَثَلُ المنَافِقِ الَّذِي يَقْرَأُ القُرْآنَ مَثَلُ الرَّيْحَانَةِ رِيْحُهَا طَيِّبٌ وَ طَعْمُهَا مُرٌّ ،
وَ مَثَلُ المنَافِقِ الَّذِي لاَ يَقْرَأُ القُرْآنَ كَمَثَلِ الحَنْظَلَةِ لَيْسَ لَهَا رِيْحٌ وَ طَعْمُهَا مُرٌّ

The likeness of a believer who recites the Qur’ān is like that of a citron: its scent is fragrant and its taste delicious. The likeness of a believer who does not recite the Qur’ān is like that of a date: it has no fragrance and its taste is delicious. The likeness of a hypocrite who recites the Qur’ān (i.e. without faith) is like that of a water lily: its scent is fragrant and its taste bitter. And the likeness of a hypocrite who does not recite the Qur’ān is like that of a bitter colocynth: it has no fragrance and its taste is bitter.[120]

These Prophetic words in their unique style and manner demonstrate the fact that the recitation of the Qur’ān [*qirā’ah*] benefits others, even if the reciter is devoid of faith itself!

[119] Ḥadīth of Abū Hurayrah recorded by al-Bukhārī 4638, Aḥmad 9824. and with similar wordings from ‘Abdullah b. ‘Umar in al-Bukhārī 4637, Muslim 1350, 1351, al-Tirmidhī 1859, Ibn Mājah 4199, Aḥmad 4322, 4688, 5361, 5891, 6115.

[120] Ḥadīth of Abū Mūsa al-Ash‘arī recorded by al-Bukhārī 5007, Muslim 1328, al-Tirmidhī 2791, al-Nasā’ī 4952, and Abū Dawūd 4191, Ibn Mājah 210, Aḥmad 18728, 18789, 18833, al-Dārimī 3229. The wording above is that of Muslim.

PHOTO 6: Entrance to a date garden in Madinah, taken by the author October 2014.

More tangible than that are the effects of the Qur'ān in the realm of ethics and morality. One of the greatest assets of a sound and healthy society is an advanced system of ethics. In fact, noble conduct and character is also one of the major purposes and higher objectives of the religion of Islam. The Prophet articulated his very mission in terms of ethics when he said, *Indeed I have been sent for the perfection of sound character.*[121] And it is nothing other than the Noble Qur'ān that leads to this goal. In fact, the greatest model of refined ethics and morality was the Messenger of Allah as the Qur'ān itself testified:

وَإِنَّكَ لَعَلَىٰ خُلُقٍ عَظِيمٍ

And you are indeed on an exalted standard of character.
[The Qur'ān, Sūrah al-Qalam 68:4]

Sa'd b. Hishām al-Anṣārī a native of Madīnah who later died in India, asked 'Āishah about the character of the Prophet and she replied in the following way:

كَانَ خُلُقُهُ الْقُرْآنَ

[121] Ḥadīth of Abū Hurayra recorded by Aḥmad 8595, Ibn 'Abd al-Barr in *al-Tamheed,* al-Bukhārī in *al-Adab al-Mufrad* and others with the Arabic text: [إِنَّمَا بُعِثْتُ لأُتَمِّمَ صَالِحَ الأَخْلاَقِ] and authenticated by al-Haythamī in *Majma' al-Zawāid,* al-Zarqānī in *Mukhtaṣar al-Maqāṣid,* al-Safārīnī al-Ḥanbalī in *Sharḥ Kitāb al-Shihāb,* al-Wādi'ī in *Ṣaḥīḥ al-Musnad,* and by al-Albānī in *Ṣaḥīḥ al-Adab al-Mufrad* and *Ṣaḥīḥ al-Jāmi'.*

His character was the Qur'ān.[122]

The full extent of the effects of this remarkable Book is amazing and extends throughout the lives of those who recite and live this Book. It doesn't leave its companions for a moment, devotion for devotion and loyalty for loyalty. It endears itself to those who endeared themselves to it. To summarize the status of the recitation of this Noble Qur'ān in the life of a believer, the Prophet stated the following to those who came to him seeking advice:

عَلَيْكَ بِتِلاَوَةِ الْقُرْآنِ فَإِنَّهُ نُورٌ لَكَ فِي الأَرْضِ وَ ذُخْرٌ لَكَ فِي السَّمَاءِ

Enjoined upon you is the recitation of the Qur'ān, for verily it is illumination for you in the earth and a treasure hoarded for you in the heavens.[123]

وَ عَلَيْكَ بِذِكْرِ اللهِ وَ تِلاَوَةِ الْقُرْآنِ فَإِنَّهُ رَوحُكَ فِي السَّمَاءِ وَ ذِكْرُكَ فِي الأَرْضِ

And enjoined upon you is the remembrance of Allah and the recitation of the Qur'ān, for verily it is your refreshment in the heavens and your remembrance in the earth.[124]

Beyond Death

The life of the companion of the Qur'ān is remarkable and inspiring indeed. But every life must come to an inevitable end, and every soul must taste the pangs of death. And with death, nearly all things come to an abrupt end. The doors of repentance are shut as are the records of our deeds. We are buried deep within the same, pure earth we originated from. Our relatives eventually leave us in that desolate place that day, many never to return again. We leave behind our lives and legacies and memories, for better or for worse. Our judgment begins.

But there is still hope. Something still remains open for these companions. The wonder of the Qur'ān is that its benefit doesn't end with death but continues beyond it.

---

122 Ḥadīth of 'Āishah recorded in Aḥmad 23460, 24139 and by al-Bukhārī in *al-Adab al-Mufrad* and authenticated by al-Albānī in *Ṣaḥīḥ al-Adab al-Mufrad* and *Ṣaḥīḥ al-Jāmi'*.

123 Ḥadīth of Abū Dharr al-Ghifārī related by al-Mundhirī in *al-Targhīb,* Ibn Ḥibbān and al-Ḥākim as a portion of a larger ḥadīth, and authenticated by al-Albānī in *Ṣaḥīḥ al-Targhīb*. It is also found in a number of other, longer versions that have weaker chains.

124 Related by Abū Sa'īd al-Khudrī in Aḥmad 11349 as a portion of a larger ḥadīth that has been authenticated by al-Haythamī in *Majma' al-Zawāid* and by al-Albānī in *al-Silsilah al-Aḥādīth al-Ṣaḥīḥah*.

Firstly, at the time of death, preference is given to the people of the Qur'ān in matters of burial. In the devastating aftermath of the Battle of Uḥud, the Prophet instructed his Companions to dig deeply and bury the martyrs in groups of twos or threes, with precedence to be given to those who had memorized more of the Qur'ān:

احْفِرُوْا وَ أَعْمِقُوْا وَأَحْسِنُوْا وَ ادْفِنُوْا الإِثْنَيْنِ وَ الثَّلاَثَةَ فِي قَبْرٍ وَاحِدٍ ،
قَالُوْا فَمَنْ نُقَدِّمُ يَا رَسُولَ اللهِ ؟ قَالَ قَدِّمُوْا أَكْثَرَهُمْ قُرْآنًا

Dig deeply and well, and bury the dead by twos or threes in a single grave. The Companions asked, *Who should we start with Messenger of Allah?* He replied, *Those with the most Qur'ān.*[125]

There were many casualties in the battle of Uḥud and many demoralized, exhausted survivors, some of them severely wounded. These survivors faced the grim task of burying the numerous dead. The sheer exhaustion of battle and the difficult task of digging so many graves in the earth prompted the Companions to turn to the Prophet for instruction. He in turn instructed them to bury the dead in groups, two to three to a grave. The Qur'ānic reciters and memorizers were to be given precedence. 'Abd al-Raḥmān al-Mubārakpūrī (died 1353H) in his commentary to the Sunan of al-Tirmidhī mentions that this preference consisted of burying these individuals of the Qur'ān before others, with greater care and closer to the *laḥd*—which is the edge of the grave facing the qiblah. In that way, these individuals would be in closer proximity to the Ka'bah than others.

---

[125] Ḥadīth of Hishām b. 'Āmir al-Anṣārī recorded by al-Nasā'ī 1983, al-Tirmidhī 1635, Abū Dāwūd 2800 and authenticated by Ibn Ḥazm in *al-Muḥallā,* 'Abd al-Haqq al-Ishbīlī in *al-Aḥkām al-Ṣughrā* and by al-Albānī in *Irwā' al-Ghalīl.* The wording is that of al-Nasā'ī.

PHOTO 7: The Mountain of Uhud with the burial ground of the martyrs, from June 2013.

With respect to the role of the Qur'ān beyond death, the Companion al-Barā b. Āzib narrates from the Prophet those remarkable details and how the Qur'ān provides protection in those critical moments:

> We once attended the funeral of a man from the Anṣār, and after we finished burying him in his grave, the Messenger of Allah sat down while his Companions sat around him, silent and motionless as if birds were perched on their heads. The Prophet had a wooden stick in his hand with which he was tracing the ground, and then he raised his head and said to us two or three times:
>
> اسْتَعِيذُوا بِاللهِ مِنْ عَذَابِ الْقَبْرِ
>
> *Seek refuge in Allah from the punishment of the grave!*
> *Seek refuge in Allah from the punishment of the grave!*
>
> The he began to provide us the details of what happens beyond death:
>
> *Verily the Believer-servant when he approaches the end of his life and heralds the Hereafter, an angel descends to him from the heavens, with a face as bright as the sun, holding a shroud from the shrouds of Paradise and some fragrance from Paradise, until it settles near him at a distance as far as the eye can see. Then the*

angel of death comes and sits at his head, and says, "Pure soul, come out to the forgiveness of your Lord and His good pleasure!" Then the soul flows out of the body as effortlessly as drops of water flow from the spout of a container. The angel of death grasps the soul and immediately places it in the shroud and perfume. From the shrouded body emanates the sweetest fragrance on earth, and the angel begins to ascend the heavens with the body, and every group of angels that encounters the body asks, "Who is this pure soul?"And they are told the name of the person, from the best names that were ascribed to him in the world. Then they reach the limits of the earth's skies, and further gates are opened for them, and they are escorted through the heavens, one level after another, until they reach the seventh heaven. Then Allah orders, "Write the book of my servant in the 'Illiyyūn registers and then bring him back to the earth, for indeed from it I created them and in it I return them and from it I will bring them forth once again!" Then his soul is returned to his body, and then two angels come and sit next to him and begin to ask him a series of questions.

They first ask, "Who is your Lord?"

The person will respond, "My Lord is Allah."

They then ask, "What is your religion?"

He will respond, "My religion is Islām."

They then ask, "Who is this man who was sent among you?"

He will reply, "He is the Messenger of Allah."

Then they will ask the final question:

وَمَا عِلْمُكَ

And what is your knowledge?

He will respond:

قَرَأْتُ كِتَابَ اللَّهِ فَآمَنْتُ بِهِ وَصَدَّقْتُ

I read the Book of Allah, believed in it and affirmed it.

Then a caller will proclaim, "My servant has spoken the truth, so prepare his abode in Paradise and clothe him from Paradise and open a gate of Paradise for him." Then some of its refreshment and fragrance will reach him, and his grave will be expanded as far as the eye can see. Then a person will come to him with a beautiful face and beautiful clothes and sweet fragrance and say, "Rejoice with what pleases you. This is the day you were promised!" The person will ask, "Who are you, for your face is one that brings nothing but good?" He will respond, "I am your good deeds." Then the person will say, "Lord establish the Hour so I can return to my people and property."[126]

Therefore it is clear that the Qur'ān—believing in it and reciting it—is at the heart of these defining moments, the questioning in the grave that will determine our fate forever.

Equally important is the fact that the Prophet wanted to inspire us with the news that when all things close for human beings with their demise, three things still remain for the believers—three ways to continue amassing reward and benefit:

إِذَا مَاتَ الإِنْسَانُ انْقَطَعَ عَنْهُ عَمَلُهُ إِلاَّ مِنْ ثَلاَثَةٍ :
إِلاَّ مِنْ صَدَقَةٍ جَارِيَةٍ أَوْ عِلْمٍ يُنْتَفَعُ بِهِ أَوْ وَلَدٍ صَالِحٍ يَدْعُوا لَهُ

When the human being dies, his deeds come to a close save for three: recurring charity or knowledge that continues to benefit or a righteous child that prays for him.[127]

In another authentic narration, the Prophet stated the following in more explicit terms:

إِنَّ مِمَّا يَلْحَقُ المؤْمِنَ مِنْ عَلَمِهِ وَ حَسَنَاتِهِ بَعْدَ مَوتِهِ : عِلْمًا عَلَّمَهُ وَ نَشَرَهُ ،
وَ وَلَدًا صَالِحًا تَرَكَهُ ، وَ مُصْحَفًا وَرَّثَهُ ، أَو مَسْجِدًا بَنَاهُ ، أَو بَيْتًا لِابْنِ السَّبِيلِ بَنَاهُ ،
أَو نَهْرًا أَجْرَاهُ ، أَو صَدَقَةً أَخْرَجَهَا مِنْ مَالِهِ فِي صِحَّتِهِ وَ حَيَاتِهِ يَلْحَقُهُ مِنْ بَعْدِ مَوتِهِ

Verily from the deeds that meet a believer after his death are: knowledge that he taught and spread, a righteous child he leaves behind, a copy of the Qur'ān (muṣḥaf) that he leaves as a legacy, a masjid that he builds, a house that he builds for travelers, a canal that he digs, and charity that he

---

[126] Related by Abu Dāwūd 4127 and Aḥmad 17803 on the authority of al-Barā' b. Āzib and authenticated by al-Ṭabarī, al-Qurṭubī, Ibn Mandah in *al-Īmān*, Ibn Taymiyyah in *Majmū' al-Fatāwā*, al-Mundhirī in *al-Targhīb wal-Tarhīb*, Aḥmad Shākir in *'Umdah al-Tafsīr* and al-Albānī in his various works.

[127] Ḥadīth of Abū Hurayrah related in Muslim 3084, al-Tirmidhī 1297, al-Nasā'ī 3591, Abū Dāwūd 2494, Aḥmad 8489 and al-Dārimī 558. The wording is from Muslim.

spent from his wealth during his lifetime when he was in good health. These deeds will reach him after his death.[128]

Al-Sindī writes that this latter ḥadīth is essentially an explanation of the previous one, which mentions three basic categories which are inclusive of all other deeds. Among these deeds that continue to benefit one beyond death is beneficial knowledge, and without doubt, the greatest knowledge is the knowledge of the Qur'ān—its recitation, reading, reflection, memorization, explanation, etc. Those who learned and taught the Qur'ān to others will continue to accrue its reward so long as that knowledge continues to be taught and practiced!

In addition to that, the Qur'ān in a very direct way aids its companions in the grave by warding off the punishment of the grave, as the Prophet stated:

يُؤْتَى الرَّجُلُ فِي قَبْرِهِ فَإِذَا أَتَى مِنْ قِبَلِ رَأْسِهِ دَفَعَتْهُ تِلَاوَةُ الْقُرْآنِ وَ إِذَا أَتَى مِنْ قِبَلِ يَدَيْهِ دَفَعَتْهُ الصَّدَقَةُ ، وَ إِذَا أَتَى مِنْ قِبَلِ رِجْلَيْهِ دَفَعَهُ مَشْيُهُ إِلَى الْمَسْجِدِ

A man enters his grave and from the direction of his head comes his recitation of the Qur'ān to protect him, while from the region of his hands, his charity comes to his aid, and from his feet his walking to the masjid defends him.[129]

PHOTO 8: Graves from the Baqee Cemetery in Madinah.

---

[128] Narrated by Abū Hurayrah and recorded by Ibn Mājah 238, al-Bayhaqī in *Shu'b al-Īmān,* and al-Mundhirī in *al-Targhīb*, and authenticated by Ibn Khuzaymah, Ibn al-Mulaqqin in *al-Badr al-Munīr*, al-'Ajlūnī in *Kashf al-Khafā'*, and by al-Albānī as hassan in *Ṣaḥīḥ al-Targhīb* , *Ṣaḥīḥ al-Jāmi'*, *Ṣaḥīḥ Ibn Mājah, Aḥkām al-Janā'iz*, and his checking of *al-Mishkāt al-Maṣābīḥ*. According to Zubayr 'Alī Za'ī, however, its chain is weak.

[129] Ḥadīth of Abū Hurayah recorded by al-Ṭabarānī in *al-Mu'jam al-Awsaṭ* and authenticated by al-Haythamī in *Majma' al-Zawāid* and by al-Albānī as ḥasan in *Ṣaḥīḥ al-Targhīb*.

Beyond Resurrection

Finally, the full glory of the honor and protection accorded by the Qur'ān to its people is manifested in the realm of existence beyond the final resurrection of human beings, in the amazing world of the Hereafter. Like a faithful guide, the Qur'ān continues to protect and shield its reciters until they reach their final resting place.

All beings must face the inevitable Judgment in the court of the King of all Kings. That is the single most important moment in every human being's existence. How one fairs in this trial will determine his fate for all eternity. It is at this crucial juncture that the Qur'ān manifests its role as an active intercessor for those who recited and applied it. Abu Umāmah Al-Bāhilī reports that the Prophet said:

اقْرَءُوا القُرْآنَ فَإِنَّهُ يَأْتِي يَوْمَ القِيَامَةِ شَفِيْعًا لِأَصْحَابِهِ ،
اقْرَءُوا الزَّهْرَاوَيْنِ البَقَرَةَ وَ سُورَةَ آلِ عِمْرَانَ فَإِنَّهُمَا تَأْتِيَانِ يومَ القِيَامَةِ
كَأَنَّهُمَا غَمَامَتَانِ أَوْ كَأَنَّهُمَا غَيَايَتَانِ أَوْ كَأَنَّهُمَا فِرْقَانِ مِنْ طَيْرٍ صَوَافَّ تُحَاجَّانِ عَنْ أَصْحَابِهِمَا ،
اقْرَءُوا سُورَةَ البَقَرَةِ فَإِنَّ أَخْذَهَا بَرَكَةٌ وَ تَرَكَهَا حَسْرَةٌ وَ لاَ تَسْتَطِيْعُهَا البَطَلَةُ

> "Recite the Qur'ān, for verily it will become on the Day of Judgment interceding for its companions. Recite the two bright ones—al-Baqarah and Āl 'Imrān—for they will both come on the Day of Judgment as if they were two clouds, or as if they were two shadows, or two flocks of birds in ranks, pleading on behalf of their companions. Read Sūrah al-Baqarah, for verily holding on to it is a blessing, and forsaking it a regret, and magicians cannot withstand it.[130]

Al-Nawwās bin Sam'ān reports that he heard the Messenger of Allah on another occasion saying:

يُؤْتَى بِالقُرْآنِ يومَ القِيَامَةِ وَ أَهْلِهِ الَّذِينَ كَانُوا يَعْمَلُونَ بِهِ ، تَقْدُمُهُ سُورَةُ البَقَرَةِ
وَ آلِ عِمْرَانَ ، وَ ضَرَبَ لَهُمَا رَسُولُ اللهِ صلى الله عليه و سلم ثَلاَثَةَ أَمْثَالٍ مَا
نَسِيتُهُنَّ بَعْدُ ، قَالَ : كَأَنَّهُمَا غَمَامَتَانِ أَو ظُلَّتَانِ سَوْدَاوَانِ بَينَهُمَا شَرْقٌ ، أَو
كَأَنَّهُمَا فِرْقَانِ مِنْ طَيرٍ صَوَافَّ تُحَاجَّانِ عَنْ صَاحِبِهِمَا

---

[130] Related by Muslim 1337 and Aḥmad 21126, 21136, 21169, 21186.

"The Qur'ān and its people—those who applied and practiced it—will be brought on the Day of Resurrection, led by the chapters al-Baqarah and Āl Imrān," and the Messenger of Allah likened them to three things, which we did not forget afterwards. He said, "As if they are two clouds, or two black canopies with light between them, or as two flocks of birds in ranks, pleading in behalf of those who applied them.[131]

In these ḥadīth narrations and others, the Prophet is informing us that the Qur'ān will be miraculously personified and given a shape and form in a way that enables it to speak. And what will it say? It will argue, advocate, and intercede on behalf of those who cared for it in this world. The Noble Qur'ān becomes their most forceful advocate!

In this matter, the Qur'ān as a whole intercedes for its companions, as well as some of its individual chapters. In fact, it is clear that some chapters of the Qur'ān have precedence over others. The first two major sūrahs—al-Baqarah and Āl Imrān—are the foremost and have a leading role in this advocacy and intercession. In addition, there are other chapters that come to our aid, as the Prophet informed us:

إِنَّ سُورَةً مِنَ القُرْآنِ ثَلاَثُونَ آيَةً شَفَعَتْ لِرَجُلٍ حَتَّى غُفِرَ لَهُ ، وَ هِيَ سُورَةُ تَبَارَكَ الَّذِي بِيَدِهِ الملكُ

And verily there is a chapter of the Qur'ān of thirty verses that continues to intercede for a person until he is forgiven, and that chapter is *Tabārakalladhī biyadihil mulk* (Sūrah al-Mulk).[132]

In addition to this advocacy and intercession, the Qur'ān will further honor its companions in more amazing ways. The Prophet stated:

يَجِيْءُ القُرْآنُ يومَ القِيَامَةِ فَيَقُولُ : يَا رَبِّ حَلِّهِ فَيُلْبَسُ تَاجَ الكَرَامَةِ ، ثُمَّ يَقُولُ : يَا رَبِّ زِدْهُ ، فَيُلْبَسُ حُلَّةُ الكَرَامَةِ ، ثُمَّ يَقُولُ : يَا رَبِّ ارْضَ عَنْهُ ، فَيَرْضَى عَنْهُ فَيُقَالُ لَهُ : اقْرَأْ وَ ارْقَ وَ تُزَادُ بِكُلِّ آيَةٍ حَسَنَةً

The Qur'ān will come on the Day of Judgment and say about the companion of the Qur'ān, "Lord decorate him." And he will be

[131] Ḥadīth of al-Nawwās bin Sam'ān al-Kilābī in Muslim 1338 and al-Tirmidhī 2808.

[132] Ḥadīth of Abū Hurayrah recorded by al-Tirmidhī 2816, Abū Dāwūd 1192, Ibn Mājah 3776, al-Mundhirī in *al-Targhīb*, and authenticated by Ibn Taymiyyah in *Majmū' al-Fatāwā*, al-Shawkānī in *Nayl al-Awṭār*, Aḥmad Shākir, al-Albānī in *Ṣaḥīḥ al-Jāmi'* and *Ṣaḥīḥ al-Targhīb*.

donned with a crown of nobility. The Qur'ān will then insist, "Lord, give him more!" He will then be adorned with a robe of nobility. Then it will insist, "Lord be pleased with him!" And He will become pleased with him. And it will then be said to him, "Recite and rise, and be increased in reward for each single verse."[133]

A crown of honor and a cloak of honor! Followed by more:

يَجِيءُ الْقُرْآنُ يَوْمَ الْقِيَامَةِ كَالرَّجُلِ الشَّاحِبِ فَيَقُولُ لِصَاحِبِهِ: هَلْ تَعْرِفُنِي ؟ أَنَا الَّذِي كُنْتُ أُسْهِرُ لَيْلَكَ، وَأُظْمِىءُ هَوَاجِرَكَ، وَإِنَّ كُلَّ تَاجِرٍ مِنْ وَرَاءِ تِجَارَتِهِ، وَأَنَا لَكَ الْيَوْمَ مِنْ وَرَاءِ كُلِّ تَاجِرٍ، فَيُعْطَى الْمُلْكَ بِيَمِينِهِ وَالْخُلْدَ بِشِمَالِهِ، وَيُوضَعُ عَلَى رَأْسِهِ تَاجُ الْوَقَارِ،

وَيُكْسَى وَالِدَاهُ حُلَّتَيْنِ لاَ تَقُومُ لَهُمَا الدُّنْيَا وَمَا فِيهَا، فَيَقُولاَنِ: يَا رَب أَنَّى لَنَا هٰذَا ؟ فَيُقَالُ لَهُمَا: بِتَعْلِيمِ وَلَدِكُمَا الْقُرْآنَ

The Qur'ān will come on the Day of Judgment like a discolored man, and say to its companion, "Do you recognize me? I am the one that kept you up at night, and made you thirsty in the day, and just as every merchant yearns for profit through his trade, today you are rewarded for your trade." Then he will be given the Kingdom in his right hand and immortality in his left, and donned with a crown of dignity on his head. And his parents will be adorned with crowns as well, unlike anything in this world. They will say, "O Lord why is this ours?" It will be said, "Due to your teaching your child the Qur'ān."[134]

The kingdom in his right hand and immortality in his left, topped by a crown of dignity on his head!

The ultimate result of the advocacy of the Qur'ān for its companions is protection from the Fire of Hell. That is the supreme triumph, and the Prophet forthrightly made the claim that should be the ultimate motivation for believers:

---

[133] Ḥadīth of Abū Hurayrah related by al-Tirmidhī 2839, Ibn Khuzaymah, al-Ḥākim, and al-Mundhirī in *al-Targheeb*, and authenticated by 'Abd al-Ḥaqq al-Ishbīlī in *al-Aḥkām al-Ṣughrā*, Zubayr 'Alī Za'ī and al-Albānī in *Ṣaḥīḥ al-Targheeb, Ṣaḥīḥ al-Jāmi'* and *Ṣaḥīḥ al-Tirmidhī*.

[134] Ḥadīth of Abū Hurayrah related by al-Ṭabarānī in *al-Mu'jam al-Awsaṭ,* al-Suyūṭī and others and authenticated by al-Albānī in *al-Silsilah al-Ṣaḥīḥah*. This narration has also been related from Buraydah al-Aslamī in a longer version with slightly variant wording by Aḥmad 21872, al-Dārimī 3257, Ibn Mājah, al-Bayhaqī in *Shu'b al-Īmān,* Ibn Abī Shaybah in his Muṣannaf, Abd al-Razzāq, al-Baghawī in *Sharḥ al-Sunnah,* and authenticated by Ibn Kathīr in his tafsīr as meeting the conditions of Muslim, by al-Haythamī in *Majma' al-Zawāid*, by Ibn Ḥajar as ḥasan in *al-Maṭālib al-'Āliyah*, and by al-Suyūṭī in *al-Budūr al-Sāfirah*.

لَو كَانَ الْقُرْآنُ فِي إِهَابٍ مَا مَسَّتْهُ النَّارُ

If the Qur'ān is gathered in a skin (i.e. a human being), the fire will never touch it.[135]

He also stated the same in more explicit terms:

اِقْرَءُوا الْقُرْآنَ وَلاَ تَغُرَّنَّكُمْ هٰذِهِ الْمَصَاحِفُ الْمُعَلَّقَةُ، إِنَّ اللّٰهَ تَعَالَىٰ لاَ يُعَذِّبُ قَلْباً وَعَىٰ الْقُرْآنَ الْحَكِيمَ

Recite the Qur'ān and do not let these hanging muṣḥafs delude you, for verily Allah does not punish a heart that carries the Wise Qur'ān.[136]

It is the faithful companions of the Qur'ān that will endure in those difficult times until finally, with the direct and indirect assistance of the very Book that they used to recite, these fortunate souls will enter their final destinations—blissful Paradise. But, wonder of wonders! Even then, the Qur'ān is not finished! It will assist its companions and bring them into higher levels and ranks within Paradise itself. The Prophet informed us that Qur'ānic recitation is a direct cause of raising one's ranks in Paradise:

يُقَالُ لِصَاحِبِ القُرآنِ : اقْرَأْ وَارْتَقِ وَ رَتِّلْ كَمَا كُنْتَ تُرَتِّلُ فِي الدُّنْيَا ، فَإِنَّ مَنْزِلَكَ عِنْدَ آخِرِ آيَةٍ تَقْرَأُهَا

"It will be said to the reciter of the Qur'ān (when he enters Paradise), "Recite and ascend! Recite measuredly just as you used to do so in the world, and your final station will be at the final verse you recite!"[137]

---

[135] Ḥadīth of 'Uqbah b. 'Āmir recorded by Aḥmad 16725, 16768, 16779, al-Dārimī 3176, and authenticated by Ibn Ḥajar as ḥasan in *Hidāyah al-Ruwāt*, and by al-Albānī as ḥasan in his checking of *al-Mishkāt al-Maṣābīḥ, al-Silsilah al-Ṣaḥīḥah* and *Ṣaḥīḥ al-Jāmi'*.

[136] Ḥadīth of Abu Umāmah al-Bāhilī related by al-Hindī in *Kanz al-'Ummāl*, Ibn Baṭṭah al-'Ukburī in *al-Ibānah al-Kubrā*, al-Bukhārī in *Khalq Af'āl al-'Ibād;* according to Ibn Ḥajar its chain is authentic, while al-Albānī deemed it weak.

[137] Ḥadīth of 'Abdullah b. 'Amr b. al-'Āṣ related by Aḥmad 6508, al-Tirmidhī 2838, and Abū Dāwūd 1252, as well as by Ibn Hibbān, al-Ḥākim, and authenticated by Ibn Ḥajar in *Hidāyah al-Ruwāt,* Abdul Qādir al-Arna'ūṭ and al-Albānī in his checking of *Mishkāt al-Maṣābīḥ*.

Glorious ascension in glorious Paradise, the companions of the Qur'ān embark on their final flight, the grand conclusion of their long list of honors for their companionship with this Book. Al-Mundhirī relates in *al-Targhīb* that there is a report from the early generations that the number of degrees in Paradise are equivalent to the number of verses of the Qur'an, and the reciters/memorizers will be rewarded accordingly. This reward is for those who memorized these verses, recited them with proper Tajweed and acted upon them.[138]

Matchless merit! Immeasurable honor, unbounded glory! Does there remain, following that, any excuse for believers not to pursue the Noble Qur'ān in order to become its devoted companions and faithful servants, to make it the pivot and centerpiece of their lives?

This enlightened perspective on the amazing Qur'ān informed the Companions' minds and drove their actions. It was this that made the great Caliph 'Uthmān b. 'Affān make this profound observation:

لَو طَهُرَتْ قُلُوبُنَا مَا شُبِعَتْ مِن كَلامِ اللهِ عَزَّ وَجَلّ

If our hearts were truly purified, they would never be fully satisfied with the words of Allah!

It was this that made even the great general Khālid b. Walīd make these remarks, with great regret, on his deathbed having lived his remarkable life:

لَقَد مَنَعَنِي كَثِيرًا مِن القِرَاءَةِ الجِهَادُ فى سَبِيلِ اللهِ

I regret that fighting in Allah's cause has prevented me from reciting the Qur'ān much![139]

Because of these virtues and others, the study and teaching of Tajweed clearly ranks among the noblest acts of worship. For this reason, the Prophet made it quite clear as to who are, without qualifications, the absolute best people on the face of this earth:

خَيرُكُمْ مَنْ تَعَلَّمَ القرْآنَ وَ عَلَّمَهُ

"The best of you are those who learn the Qur'ān and teach it to others."[140]

---

[138] See al-Sindī's commentary on Sunan Abī Dāwūd, *'Awn al-Ma'būd.*

[139] Related by Abū Ya'lā and authenticated by al-Haythamī in *Majma' al-Zawā'id* and Ibn Ḥajr in *al-Maṭālib al-'Āliyyah.*

[140] Ḥadīth of 'Uthmān b. 'Affān related through various chains and slightly different wordings in al-Bukhārī 4639, 4640, Abū Dāwūd 1240, al-Tirmidhī 2832, 2833, al-Dārimī 3204, Ibn Mājah 207, 208, Aḥmad 382, 389, 469, and authenticated by al-Albānī in *Ṣaḥīḥ al-Jāmi'.*

Appendix THREE: THE BROKEN CHAINS OF TUḤFAT AL-AṬFĀL

A Closer Look at the Transmission of the Text

The poem *Tuḥfat al-Aṭfāl* has been memorized, taught and kept alive by countless individuals since its authorship more than two centuries ago, making it the single most utilized resource for learning Tajweed to this day. Since that time, it has continued to be transmitted in the traditional manner, in the line of great classical works of Islamic learning, complete with formal authorization (*ijāzah*) and chains of transmission (*isnād*) tracing the line of one's teachers back to the author. These documents exist across the Muslim world in various shapes and forms, handwritten, transcribed and sometimes even oral; at times free-standing and sometimes as part of larger written works.

Despite its great popularity as a traditional text, however, the chain of transmission of *Tuḥfat al-Aṭfāl* to the author remains problematic for a variety of reasons. We simply don't know a whole lot about the author. Although he left behind a small number of surviving works, it is not entirely clear when he passed away. Traditionally, the year of death has always provided a convenient method of identifying and classifying Muslim scholars. We do know from the record that he was born around 1160H, corresponding to the year 1747 of the Gregorian calendar, and from the *Tuḥfat al-Aṭfāl* text itself (verse 59) that it was written in 1198H/1783-4 CE. Some early writings indicate that he was teaching as late as the year 1227H. Beyond that, there exists no clear documented record of students who transmitted from al-Jamzūrī by way of Ijāzah—neither the Qur'ān nor any of his own texts including the *Tuḥfah*. As far as we know today, there is no surviving isnād of the Qur'ān that extends through him, nor an isnād of any other text—apart from the *Tuḥfah*—that reaches him. This is more perplexing keeping in mind that al-Jamzūrī was a conventional scholar who spent his life teaching the Qur'ān and its related sciences in the traditional manner, which was always based upon chains of transmission.

Moreover, the current isnāds of the text contain some seemingly contradictory details which raise further concerns for discerning scholars of transmission. Many of these chains go back to al-Jamzūrī through individuals about whom questions have been raised, while others simply go to an intermediary some generations below al-Jamzūrī and close with the general expression *"and through his chain to the author."*[141]

[141] In Arabic the term is usually as follows: [بسنده إلى الجمزوري].

For these reasons and others, most Qur'ānic scholars have considered the circulating chains of *Tuḥfat al-Aṭfāl* today to be disconnected (in ḥadīth terminology, *munqaṭi'*) and thus, not very strong from the perspective of transmission. Every teacher I personally received this text from, for instance, confirmed this same impression to me, including Shaykh Saad Ḥassanin and Shaykh Tawfīq 'Alī Nuḥās. There have also been efforts on the part of various researchers to uncover the exact nature of this transmission and prove its continuity, but nothing has been produced to date that has been irrefutably convincing to everyone.

Nevertheless, most scholars have still allowed—and even participated in—the transmission of this text by way of isnād, for the purposes of maintaining the continuity of this living tradition and the dissemination of this vital knowledge. Since this is neither the Qur'ān nor a Prophetic ḥadīth, some degree of laxity has been allowed in the entire matter. An incomplete chain is better than no chain at all. And so the text had remained alive today.

It must be noted, also, that because of the decentralized nature of Islamic learning and transmission, isnād studies lend themselves to constant revision based upon historical research, ongoing discovery of Islamic manuscripts and examination of personal isnāds of individuals throughout the Muslim world. I have no doubt that we are bound to hear more on this matter from Qur'ānic scholars in the hopefully not so distant future.

To make sense of the state of current and future research on this issue, a brief historical survey is in order. There are a number of characters in the story of al-Jamzūrī who are key to understanding this entire matter.[142]

The Teacher

The most important figure is the teacher of al-Jamzūrī himself: Shaykh Nūr al-Dīn al-Mīhī (d. 1204H/1789CE). His full name was Nūr al-Dīn 'Alī b. 'Umar b. Aḥmad b. 'Umar b. Nājī b. Funaysh al-'Awnī al-Manūfī al-Shāfi'ī al-Mīhī, although in some sources his name is incorrectly given as 'Alī b. 'Alī b. Aḥmad b. 'Umar. Also the name Funaysh (فنيش) incorrectly appears as Qays (قيس) in some documents, which upon examination is obviously an error of mistranscription of the Arabic script.

In the very opening passage of the text (verse 4), al-Jamzūrī praises his teacher and, as a gesture of humility, attributes to him the source of the material of his own text. The praise is immense to the extent of inviting criticism from commentators

[142] For this section, I have relied on the various texts, manuscripts and isnāds at my disposal, as well as the thorough research of Shaykh Muṣṭafā Sha'ban (available at http://www.ahlalhdeeth.com/vb/showthread.php?t=284430), who was gracious enough to receive my correspondence and respond to some of my inquiries.

for being excessive, an indication of the great esteem and respect the student had for the teacher.

سَمَّيتُهُ بِتُحفَةِ الأطْفَالِ
عَنْ شَيخِنَا المِيهِيِّ ذِى الكَمَالِ

I have resolved to title it *the Children's Bequest,*
relating from our shaykh al-Meehī, masterful, adept.

Born in 1139H, Shaykh Nūr al-Dīn al-Mīhī was a well-known Azharī scholar of his time who does feature prominently in Qur'ānic isnāds today. He happened to be blind and was known for his tremendous humility and piety in addition to his learning. The ascription al-Mīhī indicates his origin from the village of Almay (الماي) in the Manūfiyyah district of Egypt, not far from the hometown of al-Jamzūrī. A graduate of the renowned al-Azhar University, he spent his life teaching in various institutions across the region, eventually settling in the city of Ṭanṭā until he passed away in 1204H. There are some isnāds, including that of the renowned reciter Maḥmūd Khalīl al-Ḥuṣarī, that indicate his date of death as 1229H, having lived a lifespan of ninety years.[143]

Some Qur'ānic scholars are of the opinion that the chain of *Tuḥfat al-Aṭfāl* is contiguous to the teacher of al-Jamzūrī, which is by no means problematic given the fact that the author himself attributes the material to the teacher, an indication that he invariably must have read or presented it to the teacher.

The Teacher's Sons

What complicates matters further is the fact that the teacher had at least two sons who were associated with al-Jamzūrī and his text in some way. Much less is known about the first son, Muḥammad al-Mīhī al-Aḥmadī, than his father Nūr al-Dīn or his father's student al-Jamzūrī. The son authored an extant commentary on the *Tuḥfah* entitled *Fatḥ al-Malik al-Muta'āl bi Sharḥ Tuḥfat al-Aṭfāl,* which clearly indicates that he was an associate of al-Jamzūrī. In this commentary, Muḥammad al-Mīhī lavishly praises the author by referring to him as "the righteous brother, the successful expert, one who was surrounded by divine help, our master Mawlānā Sulaymān al-Affendī."[144] His use of the term *brother* (*al-akh*) suggests that their relationship was that of peers and colleagues rather than that of teacher-student.

---

[143] See, for instance, http://www.ahlalhdeeth.com/vb/showthread.php?t=251572.

[144] Pg. 16, Muḥammad al-Meehī al-Aḥmadī, *Fatḥ al-Malik al-Muta'āl fī Sharḥ Tuḥfah al-Aṭfāl.* Maktabah Awlād al-Shaykh a l-Turāth, Egypt. 1418. The Arabic text is as follows: [الأخ الصالح و المتقن الفالح المحفوف بعناية المعيد المبدي مولانا الشيخ سليمان الأفندي].

Because they share the same last name/ascription (al-Mīhī), many sources tend to obscure the teacher and son. It is not clear when the son passed away, but his date of death is sometimes given as 1204H (the same as that of his father), which is an obvious error based upon this same confusion.

Shaykh al-Jamzūrī himself wrote a commentary on his own poem, which he entitled *Fatḥ al-Aqfāl bi Sharḥ Tuḥfat al-Aṭfāl,* in which he admits that he borrowed mostly from a similar commentary written by this son of his teacher Muḥammad al-Mīhī.[145] Both have abundant praise for each other in their respective works.

Although this son is relevant to our narrative, I have not personally come across any chains of the *Tuḥfah* that mention him by name in any of their links.

Many isnāds, including some of my own, include the name of a second son to the teacher—named Muṣṭafā b. ʿAlī al-Mīhī—as receiving the text from al-Jamzūrī. He is generally described the son of Shaykh ʿAlī al-Mīhī and brother to the commentator on the *Tuḥfah* (i.e. the first son Muḥammad al-Mīhī). Little else is known about him, including when he died. Since his brother was clearly a colleague and his father a teacher of al-Jamzūrī, his receiving the text from al-Jamzūrī is not at all implausible. His name also features prominently in some Qur'ānic isnāds.

A Third al-Mīhī ?

Other chains go back to an individual listed as Aḥmad al-Mīhī from al-Jamzūrī, but there is no clear record of any such family member. Is he a mistaken reference to the teacher or one of his sons? Most probably it's a reference to the teacher since his full name does include Aḥmad at some point (ʿAlī b. ʿUmar b. Aḥmad), although that could plausibly apply to either son as well.

al-Hūrīnī: The Only True Student ?

The most intriguing person for many researchers is Naṣr al-Hūrīnī (d. 1291H/1874CE), another Egyptian Azharī scholar whose full name was Abu'l-Wafā' Naṣr b. al-Shaykh Naṣr Yūnus al-Wafā'ī al-Hūrīnī. A specialist in linguistics and Arabic grammar, he was sent by the Egyptian government to France to serve as an imam for a period of time, where he learned French and served the Muslim community. He authored a number of works, including *al-Maṭāliʿ al-Naṣriyyah* (المطالع النصرية) on the principles of Arabic writing and a critical edition as well as commentary of al-Fayrūzābādī's renowned dictionary.

---

[145] pg. 18, Sulaymān al-Jamzūrī, *Fatḥ al-Aqfāl bi Sharḥ Tuḥfat al-Aṭfāl.*The College of Qur'ānic Studies, Babylon University, Iraq. 2010. The Arabic text is as follows: [و جعلت أصله شرح ولد شيخنا الشيخ محمد الميهي نظر الله إلينا و إليه ، واعتمدت فيما تركته من هذا الشرح عليه لأني اقتصرتُ فيه على مجرد سرد الأحكام مريداً بذلك بلوغ المرام...].

In his *al-Maṭāliʿ al-Naṣriyyah*, he refers to al-Jamzūrī as *"our shaykh"* and references a fine grammatical point to what he saw in al-Jamzūrī's notes to his own commentary and poem during al-Hūrīnī's visit to the Aḥmadī Mosque around 1227H, a point which was personally confirmed by al-Jamzūrī in his lessons.[146] This establishes that al-Jamzūrī was teaching as late as 1227H, some thirty years after he authored *Tuḥfat al-Aṭfāl*, and that al-Hūrīnī was attending his teaching circles on *Tuḥfat al-Aṭfāl*. It is thus fairly certain that al-Hūrīnī studied this text from the author, if not in its entirety, then at least partially. There are some chains of the *Tuḥfah* today that extend to al-Jamzūrī through al-Hūrīnī, and for this reason many scholars consider these chains to be stronger and more connected.

An Intermediary

Many chains, perhaps the majority of them, stop at an individual named Muḥammad b. Aḥmad al-Mutawallī and end with the words *"and with his well-known chain to al-Jamzūrī."*

Born in 1248H/1832CE in Cairo, his full name was Muḥammad b. Aḥmad b. al-Ḥasan b. Sulaymān. After memorizing the Qurʾān, he completed his studies at al-Azhar and specialized in the Qurʾānic readings, quickly surpassing his peers and colleagues and earning the titles Ibn al-Jazarī al-Ṣaghīr ("the smaller Ibn al-Jazarī") and the "Seal of the Experts."

He left behind almost fifty works on the Qurʾānic readings and other fields, many of them considered references. He is considered a node in the transmission of the Qurʾān such that most of the Qurʾānic chains of the region go through him. There are only 25 links between him and the Prophet. He died in 1313H/1895CE at the age of 65. He was blind and known for his tremendous humility and refined character.

Because Muḥammad al-Mutawallī was a prominent and towering figure in the Qurʾānic sciences and the Readings, his Qurʾānic chains are widespread and well-known. However, his link to al-Jamzūrī is less clear. Having been born some twenty years after al-Jamzūrī was last known to be alive, he obviously could not have been a direct student. Who, and how many, were the intermediaries between him and al-Jamzūrī? We simply do not know at present, but as more manuscripts, isnāds and historical research comes to light, we may perhaps one day come to know.

Conclusions

The isnād is a distinctive and laudable trait of Muslim scholarship, as observed by Muḥammad b. Ḥātim: "Allah did indeed honor this nation and gave it preeminence with the isnād, which was not part of any other nation in human

[146] Pg. 140, Naṣr al-Hūrīnī, *al-Maṭāliʿ al-Naṣriyyah*. Resalah Publishers: Beirut, Lebanon. 1422/2001.

history."[147] It serves to provide a medium of connection to our great authors and teachers, and promotes a spirit of continuity and balance in our scholarship across diverse regions and time periods. For some, it is a key part of the divine plan to assure the preservation of this religion. Because of this, the isnād was always a part of our scholarly heritage, affirmed by the broad consensus of Muslim scholars from our earliest times. At the same time, the isnād has also always been subjected to historical scrutiny and verification by a portion of scholars—usually the ḥadīth specialists—who adopted this task in order to ensure the integrity of the Islamic tradition.

And so it is not at all surprising that *Tuḥfat al-Aṭfāl* has been transmitted in this traditional fashion, and it is also not unusual that many have raised very specific objections to the nature of that transmission. In the final analysis, the chains of *Tuḥfat al-Aṭfāl* appear to connect to the author through a number of individuals:

1. Naṣr al-Hūrīnī from al-Jamzūrī
2. Muṣṭafā al-Mīhī from al-Jamzūrī
3. Muṣṭafā al-Mīhī from his father ʿAlī al-Mīhī from al-Jamzūrī
4. Aḥmad al-Mīhī from al-Jamzūrī
5. Muḥammad al-Mutawallī through his chain to al-Jamzūrī (an intermediary, thus making the chain broken)

Some scholars have considered Naṣr al-Hūrīnī to be the only confirmed student of al-Jamzūrī based upon historical evidence, while others have maintained that the connection through al-Jamzūrī's teacher or his sons to be equally plausible as well.

In the end, it should be noted that the isnād is primarily a spiritual-academic connection to a text, author or discipline. The comprehension and application of the text is independent of the isnād, although it may certainly be enhanced by it. Indeed most Islamic books and subjects continue to be learned, understood and taught without recourse to the isnād. So why the isnād then? It essentially enhances the learning experience by providing an organic connection to the sources of knowledge and fostering a sense of connectedness to tradition.

For this purpose, in my humble view, all of the chains above are both plausible and acceptable. The foundational era of Islamic scholarship is long gone, as is the task of compiling the Qurʾān and documenting the Prophetic Sunnah. Though the general task of scrutinizing narrations and evidences in order to authenticate them will always continue, *Tuḥfat al-Aṭfāl* and similar texts deserve a level of laxity above

---

[147] Pg. 84, ḥadīth no.71, al-Khaṭīb al-Baghdādī, *Sharaf Aṣḥāb al-Ḥadīth.* Maktabah Ibn Taymiyyah. Cairo, Egypt. 1996. The chain of the narration to Muḥammad b. Ḥātim is authenticated by ʿAmr ʿAbd al-Munʿim Salīm, and its Arabic text is as follows: [إن الله قد أكرم هذه الأمة وشرفها وفضلها بالإسناد ، وليس لأحد من الأمم كلها قديمها وحديثها إسناد].

that accorded to the primary sources of the Qur'ān and Sunnah. A majority of our great Imāms even allowed the limited use of Prophetic narrations whose links were found to be weak, so what about texts such as *Tuḥfat al-Aṭfāl?* The traditional transmission of this particular text has continued to inspire and inform generations of individuals for over two hundred years in their sacred task of reciting Allah's Book in the proper manner, and there is no reason that should stop today.

BIBLIOGRAPHY

TAJWEED WORKS

Kareema Carol **Czerepinski**, *Tajweed Rules of the Qur'an.* Dar al-Khair Islamic Books Publisher, Jeddah. 2000. Volumes 1-3.

Dr. Syed Kalimullah **Husaini**, *Easy Tajweed.* Dawah Center, Bombay. 1974.

Kāmil Muḥammad **al-Masīrī**, *Al-Jāmi' Fī Tajweed al-Qur'ān al-Karīm.* Dar al-Eman, Alexandria. 2002.

Muḥammad al-Meehī **al-Aḥmadī**, *Fatḥ al-Malik al-Muta'āl fī Sharḥ Tuḥfah al-Aṭfāl.* Maktabah Awlād al-Shaykh a l-Turāth. 1418.

Alī Muḥammad **al-Ḍabbā'**, *Sharḥ Tuḥfah al-Aṭfāl wa'l-Ghilmān fī Tajwīd al-Qur'ān.* Unpublished.

Ibn 'Abd al-Wahhāb **al-Sālimī**, *al-Tuḥfah al-'Anbariyyah fī Sharḥ Tuḥfah al-Aṭfāl.* Unpublished.

Fāiz 'Abd al-Qādir Shaykh **al-Zawr**, *al-Sharḥ al-Mukhtaṣar li Manẓūmah Tuḥfah al-Aṭfāl wa al-Ghilmān.* Unpublished.

Burba'ṭāsh **Muḥammad**, *al-Bayān fī Sharḥ Tuḥfah al-Aṭfāl fī Tajwīd al-Qur'ān.* The Qur'ānic Madrasah, Masjid al-Īmām 'Abd al-Ḥamīd bin Bādīs, Algeria. 2006.

Shaykh Muḥammad Makkī Naṣr **al-Jarīsī**, *Nihāyah al-Qawl al-Mufīd fī 'Ilm Tajwīd al-Qur'ān al-Majīd,* Dār al-Kutub al-'Ilmiyyah, 2003

Muḥammad al-Ṣādiq **Qamḥāwī**, *al-Burhān fī Tajwīd al-Qur'ān.* Maktabah Ibn Taymiyyah, Cairo. 1992.

Shaykh Abū Khālid Aḥmad **al-'Utaybī**, *Sharḥ Matn Ṭuḥfah al-Aṭfāl,* from www.imanway.com.

Wā'il b. 'Alī b. Aḥmad **al-Disūqī**, *Ḥāshiyah al-Disūqīyyah 'alā Ṭuḥfah al-Aṭfāl.* 1430H.

Maḥmūd Khalīl **al-Ḥuṣarī**, *Aḥkām Qirā'ah al-Qur'ān al-Karīm.* Dār al-Bashā'ir al-Islāmiyyah. 1417H.

TAFSEER AND QUR'ĀN WORKS

Abdurraḥmān b. Nāṣir **al-Sa'dī**, *Taysīr al-Karīm al-Raḥmān Fī Tafsīr Kalām al-Mannān*. Dar al-Mughni, Riyadh. 2001.

Abul-Fidā' Isma'īl b. 'Umar **Ibn Kathīr**, *Tafsīr al-Qur'ān al-'Adhīm*. Dar Ibn Hazm, Beirut. 2000.

Syed Abul A'lā **Maudūdi**, *The Meaning of the Qur'an*. Islamic Publications Ltd., Lahore. 1990.

Jamaal al-Din M. **Zarabozo**, *How to Approach and Understand the Quran*. Al-Basheer Company for Publications and Translations. 1999.

ḤADĪTH WORKS

Abū Zakariyyā Yaḥya b. Sharaf **Al-Nawawī**, *Riyāḍ al-Ṣālihīn*. Darussalam, Riyadh. 1998.

Shams al-Haqq **al-'Adhīmābādī**, *'Awn al-Ma 'būd Sharḥ Sunan Abī Dāwūd*. Dārul-Kutub al-'Ilmiyyah, Beirut. 1415H.

Mullā 'Alī **al-Qārī**, *Mirqāt al-Mafātīḥ*. Dar al-Fikr. 1994.

'Alī b. Abī Bakr b. Sulaymān **al-Haythamī**, *Majma' al-Zawā'id*. Dar al-Fikr.

Abū Muḥammad Zaki al-Dīn **Al-Mundhirī**, *al-Targhīb wa'l-Tarhīb*. Dar al-Kutub al-'Ilmiyyah. 2003.

al-Khaṭīb al-Baghdādī, *Sharaf Aṣḥāb al-Ḥadīth*. Maktabah Ibn Taymiyyah. Cairo, Egypt. 1996.

SEERAH WORKS

Dr. 'Alī Muhammad **al-Sallaabee**, *The Noble Life of the Prophet*. Darussalam, Riyadh. 2005.

OTHER WORKS

Aḥmad **Ibn Qudāmah** al-Maqdisī. *Mukhtasar Minhāj al-Qāsideen*. Maktabah Dar al-Bayan, Damascus. 1999.

Muḥammad b. Ṣāliḥ **al-Munajjid**, IslamQA.com.

The American Heritage® Dictionary of the English Language, Fourth Edition. Houghton Mifflin Company, 2004. 16 Jan. 2007.

Sulaymān b. Nāṣir b. 'Abdullah **al-'Ulwān**, *al-Ijābah al-Mukhtaṣirah fī al-Tanbīh 'alā Ḥifẓ al-Mutūn al-Mukhtaṣirah* [*A Concise Response in Encouraging Memorization of Summarized Texts*]. Al-Buraydah, Saudia Arabia. 1994.

Shaykh Aḥmad **Ḥuṭaybah**, *al-Jāmi' al-Aḥkām al-Ṣiyām wa A'māl Shahr Ramaḍān.* Third edition. Taken from www.hotaybah.com.

Naṣr **al-Hūrīnī**, *al-Maṭāli' al-Naṣriyyah.* Resalah Publishers: Beirut, Lebanon. 1422/2001.

www.ingramcontent.com/pod-product-compliance
Lightning Source LLC
LaVergne TN
LVHW051516070426
835507LV00023B/3149